The Creoles of Sierra Leone

Responses to Colonialism, 1870–1945

THE CREOLES OF SIERRA LEONE

Responses to Colonialism, 1870–1945

LEO SPITZER

The University of Wisconsin Press

Published 1974
The University of Wisconsin Press
Box 1379, Madison, Wisconsin 53701

The University of Wisconsin Press, Ltd.
70 Great Russell Street, London

First printing

Printed in the United States of America

For LC CIP information see the colophon

ISBN 0-299-06590-1

Publication of this book was made possible in part
by a grant from the Andrew W. Mellon Foundation.

In memory of my father

Contents

Illustrations

Acknowledgments

This book could not have been written without the help of many friends.

Professor Philip D. Curtin, an inspiring scholar and wise critic, was my mentor throughout. It was under his direction that I carried out the research in Africa and Great Britain which has served as the basis for this book. My debt to him is immense.

Professors Philip S. Benjamin of Temple University, J. Garry Clifford of the University of Connecticut, and Harry N. Scheiber of the University of California, San Diego, read parts of this book at various stages of its development. Their criticisms were useful and welcome. I am particularly grateful to Professors Charles T. Wood and Jonathan Mirsky of Dartmouth College and Allen Howard of Livingston College for their intelligent and close reading of an earlier version of this study. Professor LaRay Denzer of the University of Illinois, Chicago Circle, helped critically and factually with the chapter dealing with Wallace-Johnson and the West African Youth League. I have taken their commentary very seriously and adopted many of their suggestions. All, of course, are entirely absolved from any errors which might remain.

I shared many hours of fruitful debate and intellectual interchange with Allen Howard, John Cartwright, Fred Hayward, and Henry Rogers—contemporaries doing research in Sierra Leone on topics which, while unrelated to my own, expanded my total understanding of this area of Africa. Each aided me materially, with factual information, and psychologically, with kindness and toleration. Likewise, David Dalby of the School of Oriental and African Studies often challenged my preconceptions about Africa and Africans and, along with Eldred Jones, professor of English at Fourah Bay College, did most to introduce me to Krio and the study of the Creoles' attitudes toward their language.

Dr. Davidson Nicol, then principal of the University College of Sierra Leone, generously allowed my wife and me to reside at Fourah Bay College during our initial stay in Freetown in 1965-1966. His successor, the Reverend Harry Sawyerr, was equally hospitable during my subsequent visits to Sierra Leone in 1969 and 1970. He, Dr. Nicol, Mr. and Mrs. Jonathan Hyde, Thomas Decker, and Professor Arthur Porter supplied me with invaluable information about Creole life and customs. For this I am extremely thankful. No one, however, led me to understand Creole ways more intimately than M. A. Deen and Victor Williams of Circular Road, Freetown. They and their families generously "adopted" my wife and me and, over numerous delicious meals of foo-foo and palava sauce, taught us to love their culture and to empathize with Creole history and aspirations.

I owe special gratitude to Professor Christopher Fyfe, who, with his vast knowledge of Sierra Leone's history, helped me find a number of valuable sources and aided me with advice and criticism, and to Dr. E. W. Blyden III, who stimulated my ideas about Creole political actions in the 1930s. D. H. Simpson, librarian of the Royal Commonwealth Society in London, and Michael Joliffe, librarian of the Fourah Bay College Library in Freetown until 1969, went far beyond their duty in their personal efforts to help me. Michael Crowder, then director of the Institute of African Studies at Fourah Bay College, gave me the benefit of his advice and counsel on numerous occasions. The institute encouraged an atmosphere of free interchange and discussion among students, faculty, and visiting researchers which made my first experience in Sierra Leone an unforgettable one, both intellectually and culturally.

This study would not have been possible without a generous fellowship from the Foreign Area Fellowship Program in New York. The FAFP not only financed much of my graduate training at the University of Wisconsin but also eighteen months of research in Sierra Leone and Great Britain and six months in Madison to begin writing up my dissertation. Never once did I feel the slightest constraint on my research activities and methods. The FAFP, of course, is in no way responsible for the presentation or conclusions in this study.

I am also grateful to Dartmouth College for supporting my research at the Public Records Office in England during the summer of 1970 and for the defrayment of manuscript typing and duplicating costs.

Above all, I offer my special appreciation to my wife Manon, who shared professionally and emotionally in the creation of this book. Its completion would have been impossible without her.

L. S.

Hanover, New Hampshire
March 1974

The Creoles of Sierra Leone

Responses to Colonialism, 1870–1945

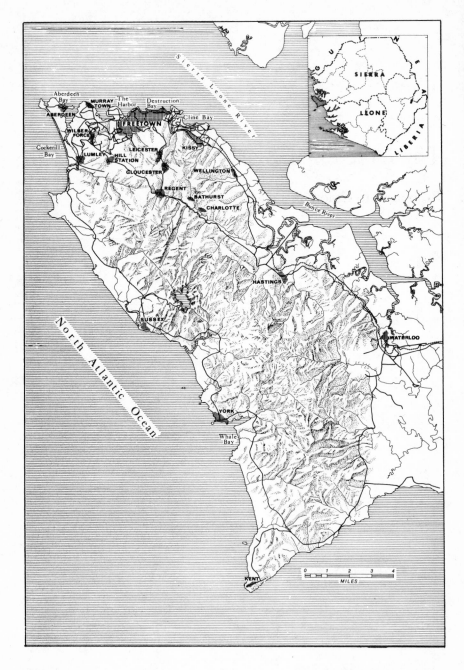

Figure 1. Map of the Sierra Leone peninsula. (Adapted from D.O.S. Map 419 by Lloyd Hickman.)

Introduction

This book examines the responses of the Sierra Leone Creoles to their colonial experience in the years between 1870 and 1945, their growing awareness of the inequities of colonialism, and their progression toward liberation. My primary focus is on the development and expression of Creole ideas about themselves, their British mentors and colonial masters, and other Africans. Because Creole intellectual responses became increasingly integral with political ones, particularly in the period following World War I, I have sought to deal with these as well.

The history of the Creoles is an especially rich source for this kind of study. Although born in Sierra Leone, Creoles descended from immigrants to this land: liberated slaves who were racially and, often, culturally akin to the indigenous inhabitants, but who had also been exposed to Western culture through European education and Christianity. The Creoles, even more than their forefathers, were taught to prize Europeanization[1] and the status that it conferred in the colonial order. But toward the end of the nineteenth century, during the heightened racism which characterized the age, they were increasingly rejected by the British and began to undergo a crisis of cultural self-confidence. Many Creoles began to look within their own society, to analyze its character and values, even questioning the major premise on which

1. "Europeanization" is defined here, and throughout this work, as the conscious or unconscious assimilation of cultural traits and values which, in the broadest sense, can be identified as "European." In the case of the ancestors of the Creoles, these would include elements derived from North America and the British West Indies, New World modifications of European culture.

their culture rested—the acceptance of European models as African standards.

While this study predominantly reflects the ideas, sentiments, and perplexities of better-educated, wealthier Creoles—those who were most intimately aware of and affected by changing British attitudes and colonial policies—it is also reflective of a broader spectrum of Creole society. Before arriving in Sierra Leone to undertake fieldwork for the first time in 1965, I had expected that Creole intellectual responses would divide along class lines— that is, along lines roughly corresponding to a person's literacy in English and degree of Western education. I had believed that literate Creoles would express their ideas in writing—in newspapers, books, essays—and that the non- or less-literate would express them orally in their proverbs, songs, and poems. I had also believed that these divisions would be more or less exclusive. But, in fact, I was mistaken. Communication between members of Creole society was too great for their intellectual reactions to divide sharply along these lines. This was particularly true in Freetown, where even the best educated and well-to-do Creoles were occasionally brought together in social, family, or day-to-day business circumstances with people of a lower "class"—less educated or even illiterate—but who nonetheless shared in the historical and cultural experiences which led to the formation of Creole society. It was common, as Martin Kilson pointed out in his discussion of the "asymmetrical structure" of the Creole upper class, for one member of a family to rise to the top of the social ladder while the rest continued as farmers or manual laborers. This did not mean that these persons would then detach themselves from their kin and, with others who were similarly endowed, form a self-sufficient, selfish group, out of step in outlook and deed with the rest of society. On the contrary, in Kilson's words, "the members of the upper level [were] impelled by force of traditional obligations, to assist their poorer kin, and usually in ways that mitigate[d] a great widening of the social distance between the upper and middle categories and the poorer sections."[2]

To distinguish the nature of Creole responses to the colonial experience after 1870 I begin this study with a glance backwards to the origins of the Sierra Leone experiment and its ideals. Chapter 1 presents the historical setting against which subsequent Creole reactions of an intellectual and political nature can be understood. To appreciate the peculiar homogeneity of Creole society, the distinct blend of European and African influences which had become characteristic by 1870, I also briefly examine the practices, values, and style of life which, European criticism notwithstanding, made Creole culture dynamic and unique. Discussion of Creole intellectual

2. Martin L. Kilson, *Political Change in a West African State: A Study of the Modernization Process in Sierra Leone* (Cambridge, Mass., 1966), pp. 87-88.

reactions to colonialism is taken up in chapter 2 and continues through the next two chapters, which make up Part II of the book. With the exception of the discussion of Creole attitudes toward Krio included in chapter 4, these chapters are largely restricted to the years between 1870 and World War I. The analysis of Creole political reactions to colonialsim up to 1945 is contained in chapters 5 and 6 of Part III.

Since the Colony and Protectorate of Sierra Leone did not become the politically independent nation of Sierra Leone until 1961, the choice of 1945 as the closing date for a study of Creole responses to colonialism requires some explanation.

By 1945 the direction and shape of the political and social developments which would lead to independence for Sierra Leone could already be discerned. Two milestones stand out: the increasing economic and political integration of the colony with the protectorate, starting in the mid-1920s but accelerated in the decade of the 1930s, and the formation of the West African Youth League. The former created a single unitary colonial entity perceived by the outside world as Sierra Leone; the latter was the first extensive attempt by Creoles to reach out beyond the confines of their own ethnic group and self-interest and to form an alliance with up-countrymen based on racial unity and the perception of imperialism as exploitative of *all* peoples of African descent in Sierra Leone, not just Creoles.

Strictly speaking, therefore, it would not be particularly germane to carry an analysis which concentrates exclusively on *Creole* ideas and actions past 1945. The old Sierra Leone colony, based on the geographical entity of the peninsula, had by this date been politically and economically overshadowed by the protectorate. The Creoles, a minority of the population in the larger Sierra Leone unit, were in the process of becoming reconciled to this new reality. Despite British success in halting the growth of the Youth League movement, the seeds for national cooperation remained alive. Many Creoles were to play an important and active role in the multi-ethnic Sierra Leone nationalist movement which emerged in the post-1945 period. Although the richness of their contribution to Sierra Leone independence should not be denied or underestimated, to single it out for special analysis here is unwarranted.

Part I: A Special Relationship

Chapter ONE
The Era of Good Feelings

"Au di bata de bit—na so de dans de go."
(As the drum is beaten so the dance must go.)
Creole Proverb

From Liberated Settlers to Creoles

In 1787 about four hundred "Black-Poor" from Great Britain went as settlers to the peninsula of Sierra Leone. Freemen in England, thanks to Lord Mansfield's judgment that slavery was illegal on English soil, many of them had been unemployed and indigent—a black African *lumpen-proletariat* surviving mainly by begging. In a nation grown conscious of the evil effects of slavery, they had become a social blemish of sufficient dimensions to attract the attention of a group of philanthropists, including Granville Sharp, who successfully pressured the British government to permit their transportation to Sierra Leone.

The so-called "Sierra Leone Experiment" was a sad one. The rainy season, lack of adequate shelter, disease, and hostilities with African peoples who had "sold" Sierra Leone peninsula to the Black-Poor Committee, took a heavy toll among the settlers once they landed in West Africa. Disheartened, the surviving immigrants quickly dispersed when an indignant indigenous subchief burned down their settlement.

But it was not long afterwards that the Sierra Leone Company was chartered, listing the famed humanitarians William Wilberforce, Thomas

9

Clarkson, Granville Sharp, and Henry Thornton among its directors. The company aimed to substitute legitimate commerce between Africa and Great Britain for the slave trade and was empowered to take over all lands in Sierra Leone which had been acquired by purchase or grant from indigenous chiefs.

Two groups of black settlers came under the aegis of company rule. The first, the "Nova Scotians," was composed of ex-slaves from the United States who had fought for the British during the American War for Independence and had been relocated in Nova Scotia after the termination of hostilities. In Nova Scotia they had found the climate unsuitable and the land grants promised them largely unattainable—situations which prompted Thomas Peters, one of their leaders, to travel to England, where the directors of the Sierra Leone Company agreed to convey willing members of his group from America to West Africa. In this way, over 1,100 Nova Scotians, sailing in sixteen vessels, arrived in Sierra Leone in 1792. Upon hearing of the new settlement, surviving Black-Poor were attracted by renewed prospects of security and returned from their dispersion to be gradually absorbed into the community. They were all joined in 1800 by more than five hundred Maroons[1]—slaves who had revolted against their masters in Jamaica, run off to live an independent existence in the hills for a number of years, and finally been defeated and forcibly removed to Nova Scotia by the British. But there they, too, brooded over the cold climate and broken promises of land grants until the Sierra Leone Company, in return for British government support of their West African scheme, consented to transport and settle them in Freetown.

The Sierra Leone Company was unable to survive financially. Burdened with debts and increasing expenses, the company transferred Sierra Leone to the Crown of Great Britain in January 1808. With Britain's abolition of the slave trade, a vice-admiralty court and, later, a court of mixed commission were established in Freetown—both empowered to try slavers and to dispose of slave ships captured by British naval squadrons off West Africa. Sierra Leone became a point of liberation for slaves "recaptured" by the patrol. And as the colony grew in population, missionaries were imported to educate and Christianize the new arrivals.

The "Recaptives" or "Liberated Africans," as these freed slaves were called, made up the fourth and largest group of settlers in Sierra Leone. Unlike the Black-Poor, Nova Scotians, or Maroons—many of whom had come to Sierra Leone already detribalized and partially Europeanized by their experiences in the New World and in Great Britain, the Recaptives were liberated directly from slaveships. They were of heterogeneous ethnic origin, speaking a Babel of African languages, and had rarely known any European

---

1. From the Spanish *cimarron* and the French *marron*, meaning fugitive slave.

other than the slave dealer who bought them and the members of the British patrols who brought them to Freetown.

Initially, the tensions and disputes among the various immigrant groups were great. The Nova Scotians remembered vividly how their revolt against Sierra Leone Company rule in 1800 was suppressed by a unit of British troops aided by the newly arrived Maroons. For many years, these two groups lived in different sections of the city, generally attended separate churches, and openly expressed their mutual hostility. The Nova Scotians and Maroons were united, however, in their contempt for the Liberated Africans. This was especially so after the government drafted Recaptives into the Royal African Corps for no other reason, it seemed, than to subjugate the earlier settlers. The Nova Scotians and Maroons had a variety of pejorative names for the newcomers, calling them "cruits," "nata," or "Willyfoss niggers"[2] —the last as a reminder that the Liberated Africans had had their freedom secured for them by William Wilberforce and had not gained it through their own efforts. The Nova Scotians and Maroons, moreover, striving to live up to a European style of life which, in British eyes, would set them apart as a "superior class" of Africans, looked down on the Recaptives as boorish upstarts and were jealous of the attention they received from European officials, missionaries, and teachers. Chagrined by the willingness of the Liberated Africans to do hard, manual work and by their rapid acquisition of property and social graces, one Nova Scotian vented his feelings and, perhaps, those of other members of the community when he exclaimed: "It is my wonder dat we settlers do not rise up in a body and *kill* and *slay,* and *kill* and *slay*! Dem Spanish and Portuguese sailors are quite right in making slaves!"[3]

Among the Liberated Africans, too, unity was not easily achieved. Even after sharing experiences of enslavement and liberation, language kept people of different ethnic origins apart until a lingua franca became more widespread. Scuffles were not uncommon. Each ethnic group healed its own sick, took care of its old people, and found amusement in his neighbor's backwardness. Those Recaptives who were originally from Yoruba and known in Sierra Leone as "Aku,"[4] remained exclusive far longer than others by virtue of their numbers, retaining their own language, often espousing Islam rather than Christianity, and tenaciously holding on to their customs.

Elements drawing together the various black immigrants existed nonetheless. Whereas the first Liberated Africans had ordinarily refused to accept

2. "Cruit" was the lingua franca term for "recruit," "newcomer," or "greenhorn"; "nata" was probably taken from the Portuguese word for "cream," in reference to the newcomers cream-like separation from the rest of Sierra Leone society.

3. Quoted in A. B. C. Sibthorpe, *The History of Sierra Leone*, 2d ed. (London, 1881), p. 44.

4. From the Yoruba greeting *okushe,* meaning "welcome."

Sierra Leone as their country, recalling with bitterness that they would never again see their kinfolk in their own native homes, their children felt less alien or inhibited with one another. In spite of the fact that their elders often frowned disapprovingly, young people of all groups intermarried. Indeed, prejudices notwithstanding, the Nova Scotians and Maroons would permit their daughters to marry a Liberated African who had become "respectable" by assimilating the standards, values, and "cultured ways" which the older immigrants proudly displayed. And no matter how great their animosities had been at any time, all the settlers increasingly identified with each other in opposition to a mutual danger—the Africans indigenous to the hinterland of Sierra Leone.

By the 1870s the lines separating the Nova Scotians, Maroons, and Recaptives had virtually disappeared. The last of the original settlers from the United States and the West Indies were dying out.[5] The importation of new Liberated Africans ceased completely during the 1840s and the Creoles—the children of the settlers and recaptives who had been born in Sierra Leone—began to outnumber their parents and grandparents.[6]

Although the term *Creole* has on occasion been used to refer to the racially mixed offspring of a liaison between an African and a European, it is generally defined differently in Sierra Leone.[7] At first, *Creole* was only applied to the colony-born children of Liberated Africans. Intermarriage and cultural blending among the various groups, however, gradually erased the distinctions which had originally existed among them and *Creole* came to describe the descendants of *all* the black-African groups which were settled in Sierra Leone after 1787. The term *Creole* was taken from West Indian English, in which it had referred to any person or thing of West Indian origin and was used to differentiate between something native to the West Indies and something which had originated either in Europe, Africa, or continental America. West Indians might thus speak of "Creole" whites or "Creole" blacks, "Creole" corn or "Creole" rats to indicate that the whites, blacks,

5. The 1850 Census listed only forty-nine Nova Scotians and fifteen Maroons. But these may be misleading figures since a number of them may have been counted under the separate category, "Native Creoles." See Robert René Kuczynski, *Demographic Survey of the British Colonial Empire*, vol. 1 (London, 1948), p. 75; William Hamilton, "Sierra Leone and the Liberated Africans," *The Colonial Magazine and Commercial Maritime Journal* 8 (June 1842): 43; Christopher H. Fyfe, *A History of Sierra Leone* (Oxford, 1962), p. 378; Sibthorpe, *History*, preface.

6. "Religion and Other Statistics of Sierra Leone," *West African Reporter*, January 7, 1882; Letter from Thomas Raston, to the Methodist Missionary Society, March 7, 1843, in Sierra Leone Box (1841-1847), Methodist Missionary Archives, London.

7. Colonial Office Papers 267/22, Public Record Office, London, hereafter cited as C.O.; and Arthur T. Porter, *Creoledom: A Study of the Development of Freetown Society* (Oxford, 1963), p. 52.

corn and rats came from the West Indies and not from foreign soil. But, in Sierra Leone, the word *Creole* was used in reference to children of nonnatives born and reared in the colony and, in this respect, had a similar meaning to the Spanish word *criollo*. In South America, for example, the *criollos* were children born to Spanish parents in the colonies, as opposed to the *gachupines*, who were Spaniards born in Spain but who were living in America.[8] In Sierra Leone the designation paralleled this usage and pointed to the offspring of parents who were not indigenous to the colony.

Creole in Sierra Leone took on a wider, cultural definition as well. Besides those individuals who were biologically descendant from Liberated Africans or the earlier settler groups, the Creole community always included, and still includes, persons of black-African stock, usually from one of the neighboring ethnic groups or from the Sierra Leone hinterland, who emulated the "Creole way of life" by adopting the habits, standards of behavior, and outlooks with which Creoles identified. In the past, an up-countryman could "pass for Creole" if he sacrificed his ethnic identity and was willing to dress in European style, adopt a Creole name—that is, a European name—and cultivate certain Anglicized social manners. He would necessarily have had to be familiar with the English language and fluent in Krio, the vernacular of the Creoles. It would have helped had he become a Christian—but this was not essential since a minority of Creoles were practicing Muslims. And, if he were ambitious to penetrate the upper echelon of Freetown society, he would also have needed to acquire Creole prestige symbols such as literacy, real estate, and the baubles which indicated material wealth.[9]

Charity Balls and Awujoh: A Cultural Syncretism

From its inception until the last decades of the nineteenth century when racism polluted the atmosphere, the settlement at Sierra was infused with the philanthropic idealism of its founders. The Black-Poor, Nova Scotians, and Maroons had not been brought to West Africa merely to alleviate embarrassing situations in England, North America, and the West Indies, but rather to stand at the forefront of Britain's civilizing mission. Each settler, exposed to Western culture and engaged in a legitimate occupation, was considered by the British humanitarian ideologues who sponsored the Sierra Leone experiment as a living illustration of "the Blessings of Industry and Civilization" to

8. T. C. Luke, "Some Notes on the Creoles and Their Land," *Sierra Leone Studies*, old ser., no. 21 (January 1939), p. 53.

9. E. M. Richardson and G. R. Collins, "Economic and Social Survey of the Rural Areas of the Colony of Sierra Leone," a report to the Colonial Social Science Research Council, mimeographed (London: Colonial Office, 1952), p. 23.

Africans "long detained in Barbarism."[10] At the same time, in a situation where disease hindered large-scale European settlement, the black settlers were perceived as frontiersmen better able to adapt to the disease environment of West Africa—to the "climatic condition," in the language of the day—who would spread "civilization" beyond the line penetrable by Europeans.[11]

When the company transferred its control of Sierra Leone to the Crown and the Liberated Africans began to swell the population of Freetown after the British abolition of the slave trade, the special character of the humanitarian mission did not diminish. Educated and, whenever possible, converted to Christianity by missionaries, these Africans—but especially their colony-born children—were to continue the ennobling task of "civilizing" Africa in Britain's image. By their mere example the Creoles were to be beacons attracting indigenous Africans from the darkness of superstition and slavery.[12]

Europeans set the standards within the Creole social system, which was divided into several "classes." The greater the individual's success in achieving a style of living which, at least in its external aspects, approximated that of the white residents in Sierra Leone, the higher his status within the Creole community.[13]

Almost invariably the only non-African contact which the Creoles or their parents or grandparents had made in Sierra Leone was with government officials, missionaries, and merchants. Unless they were wealthy or fortunate enough to have traveled to England, they might never even have met a British manual worker. Their ideas were therefore biased in favor of middle-class, nonmanual occupations. The lowest class Creoles, therefore, were those whom circumstances forced to work with their hands—farmers, carriers, servants, laborers, builders, carpenters, tailors, laundresses, and seamstresses.

The Liberated Africans were initially relegated to the bottom of the social ladder. Many of them, however, combining determination, drive, and good

10. Instructions of the Sierra Leone Company Directors, in Sierra Leone Collection, Fourah Bay College Library, Freetown; Fyfe, *History of Sierra Leone*, p. 31.

11. See Kuczynski, *Demographic Survey*, 1: 185-187.

12. "If their [the Liberated Africans'] children are provided with the means of a Christian and religious instruction, as they grow up, so will religion, civilization, and industry advance and spread into the interior of Africa . . . ." Letter from Alexander Findlay to Viscount Goderich, Secretary of State for the Colonies, in Liberated African Department Letterbook, 1831-1834, Sierra Leone Government Archives, Freetown.

13. If a class is defined by its relationship to the means of production, as in Marxist theory, it would of course be incorrect to apply anything but the term *proletariat* to all colonized people. In a colonial situation the "owners" of the means of production—the Marxist "bourgeoisie"—are the colonizers or imperialists. Nonetheless, Creoles did perceive differences among themselves and between themselves and other people, distinctions which for lack of a better word can be called "class" differences.

luck, rapidly surpassed the Nova Scotians and Maroons in wealth and material possessions—evidence that Europeanization was more useful for purposes of status definition than for economic success. A pattern was soon established. Liberated Africans usually began in Sierra Leone as agricultural workers in the mountain villages behind Freetown—settlements which the missionary societies in partnership with the colonial government had established for the "Christianization" and "Europeanization" of the Africans fresh off the slave ships. Those persons with initiative would leave agricultural work and move to Freetown, where they would seek employment as laborers and servants. They would then save their money and set themselves up as petty traders or hawkers. By combining their capital with others in similar situations and by bidding shrewdly at public auctions, a number of them would purchase the cargoes, marine stores, and, occasionally, entire ships which had been condemned as slavers by the authorities at Freetown. In this way they were able to expand their trade and their wealth to acquire such prestige symbols as good European clothing, jewelry, a house, and advanced schooling for their children.[14]

The most rapid upward mobility in Creole society came about through education. In the Sierra Leone "experiment" the British departed from their own tradition of private education and sought to use public education as a means to bring about rapid acculturation. More school places paid for by public funds were available per capita in Sierra Leone in the early nineteenth century than were available per capita in Britain itself.[15] It was therefore relatively easy for an individual to acquire at least some European-type schooling in the colony, and many Sierra Leoneans were quick to take advantage of the possibilities which literacy in English offered. Education opened the doors to junior civil service positions and clerkships—higher salaried, white-color jobs commanding greater respect. Any individual who managed to reach the epitome of the educational ladder and receive a degree from Fourah Bay College or, even better, from a British university virtually guaranteed his standing among the patricians of Creole society. Professional men—doctors, lawyers, churchmen, newspaper editors, upper-level civil servants—along with wealthy merchants and other businessmen, occupied the top level of Creole society because they could most felicitously approximate the European good life.[16]

By the second half of the nineteenth century social life among the Creole

14. Hamilton, "Sierra Leone and the Liberated Africans," *The Colonial Magazine and Commercial Maritime Journal*, 7 (January 1842): 405-407.

15. D. L. Sumner, *Education in Sierra Leone* (Freetown, 1963), pp. 3-85.

16. See, for example, P. E. H. Hair, "An Analysis of the Register of Fourah Bay College, 1827-1850," *Sierra Leone Studies*, n. s., no. 7 (December 1956), pp. 155-160.

upper class in Sierra Leone was a self-conscious imitation of Victorian England. The governor and his lady were the focal points of Freetown "high" society and a person could gain must prestige by being invited to a dinner or a monthly "At Home" at Government House. Social events at the governor's residence were reported in minute detail, and the Creole press commonly published guest lists to spotlight those who had been favored by an invitation.[17]

One obvious way in which Creoles sought to emulate English middle-class manners was in the wearing of European dress. The Black-Poor, Maroons, and Nova Scotians, of course, had worn European-style clothing when they first settled in Sierra Leone. When the Liberated Africans began to arrive in the colony, however, they often were released naked from the captured slave ships, and received their first European-type clothing from the Liberated African Department. In time, when most of the Liberated Africans converted to Christianity and acquired Western education, they were encouraged—sometimes compelled—to imitate the dress worn by their European mentors. Their "English" costume—a discarded European outfit—was worn only on Sundays, holidays, and for weddings and funerals. On work days, men wore half-pantaloons and a vest, while women dressed in "cobberslots," petticoats, and short gowns. In the privacy of their homes, women wore only their *lappa*[18] of small country cloths which they either threw around their body across the shoulders or tied around their waist. Children, during weekdays, often ran naked in the streets.

As time passed, dress and bodily decoration became increasingly associated with "civilization" and the designation "lady" or "gentleman," and both sexes spared little effort or money in their acquisition of European clothing. The display of dress and jewelry was therefore often ostentatious and un- suited to Sierra Leone's climate. Because of their "superior keeping quali- ties," men came to prefer lounge suits made from wool instead of from lighter materials such as cotton. But some also wore kid gloves, swallow-tail morning coats, tall silk hats, shirts with standing collars, neckties, tie pins, and cuff links. Dashing young men with some cash to spare topped off this costume with a cigar. Women, too, copied European fashions as they were pictured in mail-order advertisements published in the Freetown press. They acquired bonnets and corsets, stockings and boots, and silk frocks when they could afford them, cotton when they could not.

17. One of these affairs and its honored guests was described in a poem, "Dinner at Government House," which appeared in the *Sierra Leone Weekly News*, hereafter cited as *SLWN*, April 21, 1888. This poem was in itself unique because it made the first extended use of Krio in the Sierra Leone press. See Eldred D. Jones, "Krio in Sierra Leone Jouranlism," *Sierra Leone Language Review*, no. 3 (1964), pp. 24-31.

18. Krio word deriving from the English "wrapper."

Figure 2. Freetown in 1898. The West Indian inspired-Creole architecture is in evidence. Many of the buildings in this photograph still stand today.

A poem in the Freetown *African Interpreter and Advocate* in 1868, written by a man who signed himself H.A.H., criticized the existing dandyism:

> Oh! there is something noble—
> Something sublime I know,
> In that nondescript creation
> A modern dandy beau. . . .
>
> I will tell you all about him,
> About his handsome vest,
> His pretty standing collar,
> The diamond on his breast.
>
> His primrose kids are faultless
> In fitting and in shade,
> You wonder at his necktie,
> And how that bow was made.
>
> His little hands are pretty,
> Soft, dainty, useless things,
> And on the fingers sparkle
> Most beautiful seal rings. . . .
>
> Speak kindly to the Dandy,
> And never give him pain,
> For softer than his pretty hands
> Is the poor Dandy's brain.[19]

19. "The Dandy by H.A.H.," *The African Interpreter and Advocate*, February 15, 1868.

Creoles were able to establish their social prominence and to exhibit their opulence on numerous festive occasions. The weddings of the wealthiest Sierra Leoneans were often celebrated on a grand scale, raising excitement in Freetown by several degrees. In 1896 the marriage of Laura Henrietta Thomas, daughter of the affluent Creole trader J. H. Malamah-Thomas, to Christopher Claudius Nichols, city councillor and contractor, was perhaps more splendid than most Freetown weddings, but it was certainly not unique. It was preceded by numerous banquets and parties in honor of the bride and groom. For the wedding-day festivities, J. H. Malamah-Thomas not only made use of his own stately "Malamah-House" but also of more than half a dozen of the nearest residences on the street. Malamah-House itself was decorated with flowers, wreaths, and flags, and illuminated with such brilliance that it drew the attention of the entire neighborhood. Thousands of additional persons were attracted by a spectacular fireworks display. The wedding ceremony, which took place in St. George's Cathedral and was officiated at by four priests, was witnessed by over one thousand persons crammed inside the church and, according to newspaper accounts, by no less than five thousand persons in the street outside. A report in the *Sierra Leone Times* captured the flavor of the occasion exquisitely:

> The Bridegroom as he entered the Church, attended by his Uncle Dr. Paris (Asst. Colonial Surgeon), excited great attention; the silver plaid striping on his nether garments on either side, arousing the curiosity of the male spectators almost to fever heat.
>
> But the excitement culminated when the Bride was driven by her father (similarly attired as the Bridegroom) to the main entrance in a carriage, the horse being tricked out with wedding favours. The Bride was met at the entrance by the bridesmaids, about 15 in all, her train (5½ yards long) being carried by 2 pages (splendidly dressed) in page-like equipment *Au Stuart*—in blue velvet with brown velvet capes—brown stockings and blue bonny caps with lace *Au Cavalier*, and 2 juvenile lady attendants.
>
> The Bride was richly attired in a costume of white Duchesse Satin, made in the style of Mary Stuart, embroidered with pearls and trimmed with Chiffon and Orange blossoms. The train . . . hung gracefully from the right shoulder and was of white brocaded satin, trimmed with tulle ruche and pearls. Her Veil had a border of Honiton lace. Her fan was of ostrich feathers and mother of pearl and the sunshade was of white satin edge with Devonshire lace.[20]

On the surface at least, the Creole "Establishment"—and this would

20. *Sierra Leone Times*, December 12, 1896, hereafter cited as *SLT*.

include the most Anglicized and, in terms of Freetown society, the most successful Creoles, both professionally and financially—manifested a characteristic Victorian prudishness and moral rigidity. Creole newspapers often commented about "naked aborigines" roaming the streets of Freetown. In 1899, for example, the editor of the *Sierra Leone Times* lamented the lack of enforcement of an ordinance which had prohibited people from appearing in the streets with insufficient clothing. "It was levelled against the aborigines especially," he wrote,

> . . . although many who pride themselves in being "Creole," stood just as much in need of some such prohibition. This Ordinance . . . was strictly enforced, and children found in the streets clothed in smiles and adorned with grease, were usually taken to the Police Station, and flogged a bit. Grown up men and women found in the same state of primitiveness as they are often seen now-a-days, were dealt with accordingly. But now, we appear to have got too enlightened for that sort of meddling with the liberty of the subject.[21]

Occasionally, the Creole press also attacked Europeans for improper dress. A great paroxysm occurred when a European appeared on his verandah in full daylight—for purposes of calisthenics it was granted—clothed in scarcely

Figure 3. Freetown market scene, c. 1898.

21. "One Thing and Another," *SLT*, March 11, 1899.

Figure 4. Freetown market scene, c. 1898.

more than nature's garb. According to a writer in the *Sierra Leone Times*, this action would surely have an injurious effect on less civilized members of the society for whom it was the duty of Europeans to stand as examples.[22] Having descended from people whose inhibitions concerning nudity scarcely existed, Creole indignation was a reaction against a past which European missionaries had told them was "undignified" or "uncivilized" and an assertion that they now "knew better."

Many Creoles—especially from the upper class—hoped to attest to their upright character through the practice and preaching of temperance. In 1876 a chapter of the International Order of Good Templars—a temperance and benevolent association which originated in England—was started in Freetown by a number of Creoles and British naval officers. The "Temperance Lodge," as it was called, where every member had to be a total, sworn abstainer, was extremely popular in the 1880s, published a *Temperance Record*, and was on the Freetown scene for a number of decades thereafter. A local chapter of the Women's Christian Temperance Union was also instituted. The *Sierra Leone Weekly News*, whose owners were closely related to one of the colony's leading teetotalers, the Reverend Joseph May, was especially concerned with this problem and, in the 1890s, ran a regular Temperance Column giving news about temperance activities. It editorialized about the need for enforcing the spirits ordinance so that the interior of Africa could be morally uplifted,

22. "One Thing and Another," *SLT*, June 4, 1892, March 11, 1899.

indicated with pride that many persons in the interior had given up drinking rum, and warned that, unless England and the United States stopped manufacturing "the poison," spirits would become so inexpensive that "a swelling of the mischievous current which flows into Western Africa" would ensue.[23]

The moralizing extended to sexual matters. Articles and editorials in the local newspapers contained warnings in oblique language about heinous deeds allegedly taking place in the dark alleys and approaches around Freetown—sites where, according to one writer, many young women received their "first lessons in a course of error."[24] The seducers, in these instances, were not Creole men but rather "outsiders"—aliens to Freetown society who lusted with evil designs after the virtue of Creole maidenhood. One poem, "For Dear Father Land," was explicit on this point, referring to Creole prostitutes as "Yoobas [Yubas] "—a Krio name for buzzards.

> Talk say—How dis ting go look,
> How he look to God and Christ:
> How he look to Bible Class;
> How he look to Sunday School:
> Girl lek me for turn to Yooba;
> Bad word Jenny—rotten Jane,
> Girl lek me for turn Rum-puncheon
> Creo boy for look me down. . . .
>
> O, de Yoobas,—ah, de Yoobas,
> Every day the number swell,
> Swell with blessed Creole girls;
> 18 year, 19 year, 14 year sef day join;
> Ah, me God—me Fader Jesus,
> Do yah sorry for dis land.
>
> Days gone by ting nor tan so:
> Those were days of modesty.
> Yase been day for yerry word:
> Shame been day for bad bad ting
> Ah de wait man—ah the aliens;
> Sa Lone nar dem yone te-day
> And dem mean for miss—*mash down*;
> Blessed Creole boys and girls. . . .

23. *The Independent*, February 10, 1876; *SLWN*, September 13, 1884, and regularly in the 1890s; *SLT*, March 11, 1899; J. Claudius May, *A Brief Sketch of the Life of the Reverend Joseph May, Wesleyan Minister to the Colony of Sierra Leone* (Freetown, 1896), pp. 18, 23; Fyfe, *History of Sierra Leone*, p. 409.

24. *The Artisan*, June 24, 1885.

O ye big men
O ye men who go to Church;
O ye men who get the money;
O ye men who get the voice;
Stand up—wake up—things day bad, mind
   Save de little girls from death;
   Save de Creole girls from ruin.[25]

As their status in Sierra Leone society grew, Creoles became increasingly sensitive to public activities which Europeans might label "barbaric." Many were inhibited about participating in dances such as "Gumbe" and "Shakee-Shakee"—dances which could be associated with the "lower classes," and

25. Anonymous, *SLWN*, July 13, 1907. Translation:

Say—How is this going to look,
How will it look to God and Christ:
How will it look to the Bible Class;
How will it look to the Sunday School:
A girl like me became a whore;
Bad word Jenny—rotten Jane,
A girl like me turned Rum-puncheon
Creole boy looks down on me. . . .

O, the whores,—ah, the whores,
Every day their number swells,
Swells with blessed Creole girls;
18, 19, even 14 year olds join;
Ah, my God—my Father Jesus,
Please feel sorry for this land.

In days gone by things were not like this:
Those were days of modesty,
Those were days for listening to the word:
Days when evil deeds caused shame
Ah the white man—ah the aliens;
Sierra Leone is not ours today
And they lead our girls astray;
Blessed Creole boys and girls. . . .

O you important men
O you men who go to Church;
O you men who have money;
O you men who have influence;
Stand up—wake up—things are bad, listen
   Save the little girls from death;
   Save the Creole girls from ruin.

On August 24, 1907, the *SLWN* published a sequel to the "yuba" poem called "Roselyn's Dialogues for Young Girls and Women." This poem took the form of a

which were frowned upon by some Europeans, especially missionaries, because of the drumming and suggestive gyrations involved in their performance. "Gumbay dancing in all its forms," stated an editorial in *The African*, "is notoriously the cause of many vices. It therefore behooves the wiser and better portion of the people to avoid it."[26] The Creole upper classes were fond of the more sedate and exclusive dances, sometimes called "Dignity Balls"—entertainments which A. B. C. Sibthorpe, the Creole historian and eccentric, labeled "the sole representative of the civilized dancing [in the colony]."[27] The occasions for holding one of these balls varied, as did their locale. Some were held at Fort Thornton, either at the initiative of a European administrator or his spouse or to celebrate an event such as the queen's birthday. Others were held anywhere a room large enough to accommodate a large crowd could be found: "One Dignity Ball" for a party of sixty was given by a wealthy Creole doctor at the West Africa Hotel.[28]

Less formal social gatherings took place at "soirées" and reunions and at the "Pleasant Sunday Afternoons" societies, where plays were staged and vocal and literary recitals held. A typical entertainment of this type was the

---

dialogue between Jane and her other sister. Both are members of a poor family. The older sister "is a good girl"; Jane is undecided about this matter. She wants to know what is wrong with the *sojer wer* (camp follower) type of life. The ensuing dialogue is worth quoting: "Sisse: 'The most dreadful reason, Janie, is this: Little by little you lose *shame*, and when *shame* don go—all ting go.' Jane: 'Thank you my Sissie. God bless you. But when you are hard up: or when you want dress, and are want money for spend, way are must do?' Sissie:

> Fry acarra: make you pancake.
> Cook agidee: turn you machine.
> Take one table nar big market,
> City market if you lek dat
> Go to Lemberg [Philip Lemberg, merchant], he go tell you,
> Good good woke way girl for do.
> But for God sake run from Barrick.
> Barrick life nar pure ruing,
> Ruin perfect, ruin clean:
> You go surely turn to yooba.
> You go surely turn rum-puncheon,
> And except the Lord have mercy
> You go surely die lek Abner . . . .

26. *The African and Sierra Leone Weekly Advertiser*, February 1858; Sibthorpe, *History*, pp. 22, 45.

27. Sibthorpe, *History*, p. 45.

28. Fyfe, *History of Sierra Leone*, p. 437. Europeans occasionally sponsored the balls but, especially in the last decades of the nineteenth century, there were complaints in the Creole press "that the native element might have been a little stronger" at a supposedly integrated affair.

"Grand Concert," presented by the pupils of the Educational Institute in 1892. It featured instrumental and vocal music, pianoforte solos, glees, and trios. A string band performed and was followed by an "English Recitation." As a novelty, quadrilles were sung, and a dramatic cantata received its premiere performance in the colony. The governor, Sir Francis Fleming, and Sir Samuel Lewis, the Creole lawyer, acted as patrons.[29] The "Conversazione" was another popular means for the Creole upper classes to pass an evening. It amounted to a kind of grand cocktail-less cocktail party for which tickets were sold and at which stimulating conversation was to take place. Since it was usually held at a private home it acquired a reputation for intimate social exchange and, as such, drew a regular following in Sierra Leone colony.

Most of the entertainments were put on by amateurs, and, in keeping with the Creole belief about performing "good works," many were promoted to raise funds for religious and charitable purposes. In 1882, for example, the money collected at one of these affairs supplemented the contributions raised for the purchase of an organ for St. George's Cathedral. On rare occasions, however, professional entertainers stopped off in Freetown for a few days while their ship was in harbor unloading and being outfitted. The sheer novelty of these visits invariably guaranteed their success. Professor Bertz and his troup of performers, prestidigitators, and acrobats arrived in Freetown in 1882, delighted the public, drew large audiences, and made plenty of money.[30]

Sawyerr's Bookstore on Water Street contained a wide range of books and sheet music for sale whose titles reflected the cultural tastes of the Freetown upper classes. Judging from the titles alone, there is nothing to suggest that Sawyerr's was located in tropical West Africa, catering to black Africans whose ancestors had been slaves, rather than located in the heart of London where white Victorian Englishmen formed its clientele. Among the music pieces sold at the bookstore in 1886 were: "An Arab's Farewell to His Favourite Steed," "Boosey's Twelve Christmas Carols and Hymns," "Chappell's Collection of Anthems," "D'you Know (I don't like London)," "Ehren on the Rhine," "Good-bye Sweet-heart good-bye," "Grandmother's Sweetheart," "Long Live the Prince of Wales," "Oh you girls," "Overture to Guillaume Tell," "Riding on the Top of an Omnibus," and "Wooing." Books included such titles as *Don Quixote, Bible Truths with Shakespearian Parallels, Arabic Koran, Boswell's Life of Dr. Johnson, Ball Room Guide, Biblical Reasons Why, English Journalism and the Men who have made it, Etiquette,*

29. "One Thing and Another," *SLT*, March 5, 1892.

30. *SLT*, May 28, 1892; Sibthorpe, *History*, p. 22; *Sierra Leone Guardian and Foreign Mails*, November 3, 1911; *West African Reporter*, January 6, 1883; Richardson and Collins, "Economic and Social Survey," p. 197.

or the Perfect Lady, England the English, Great African Travellers, Miss Misanthrope, Mrs. Burton's Best Bedroom Works, Queen's Necklace, Regent's Daughter, Uncle Remus, and the Agony column of *The Times.*[31]

Public lectures for popular instruction were common. When the Wilberforce Memorial Hall was finally completed in 1887, in time for Sierra Leone's centenary celebrations and Queen Victoria's Golden Jubilee, but more than twenty years after its foundation stone had been laid, it became the center for public meetings and entertainments. Clubs nevertheless continued to sponsor speakers and to serve as the organizational nuclei for social events of a more elevating nature. Many such clubs, generally limited in membership, existed in nineteenth-century Freetown. The City Literary Institute, established under the patronage of C. J. Lumpkin, in 1878 invited James Parkes, future secretary for native affairs, to read a paper on "The Prospects of the Youth of Sierra Leone."[32] A. B. C. Merriman-Labor, a bright young Creole then working in the colonial secretary's office, read his paper, "The Story of the African Slave Trade in a Nutshell," in 1900 before the Greensfield Club. This organization sponsored lectures, occasional dramatic shows, a yearly picnic, and had as its objectives the promotion of a love of literature and the encouragement of social intercourse in the Freetown community. The Eccentric Circle, a multi-racial coterie, was at its peak in the 1880s and supplemented its regular fare of dances and charity work with "mind-uplifting" concerts. Edward Wilmot Blyden delivered a lecture in 1892 on "Study and Race" to the Young Men's Literary Association—an organization founded to raise the culture of the "corrupt" youth of Freetown. Another, the City Club, pledged itself "to aid and foster all enterprises which may tend to the amelioration of the young and the improvement of the youths of this Colony."[33] For the athletic-minded, a Cyclist club was formed in 1892 to promote outings and social mixing, and as a benefit society for its members. Chess was a distinct favorite, especially among the less active men, and the Freetown Chess Club offered them the opportunity for cerebral as well as social interchange.[34]

31. See *Sawyerr's Bookselling, Printing and Stationery Trade Circular and General Advertising Medium*, February 27, 1886, in British Museum Newspaper Library, Colindale, hereafter cited as *Sawyerr's*.

32. *The Watchman and West African Record*, October 16, 1878. C. J. Lumpkin, the patron, was a son of Henry Lumpkin, Aku Recaptive, wealthy merchant, and member of the Legislative Council. C. J. Lumpkin went on to Europe, where, in 1884, he became an M.D. after studying at University College, London, and in Brussels. See Fyfe, *History of Sierra Leone*, pp. 366, 423.

33. *The Watchman and West African Record*, October 16, 1878; *The Artisan*, Feburary 25, 1885; *SLT*, May 27, 1893, May 12, 1894; A. B. C. Merriman-Labor, *The Story of the African Slave Trade in a Nutshell* (Freetown, 1901).

34. *SLT*, May 27, 1893, May 12, 1894.

Generally the Freetown clubs were extremely short-lived. Dramatic societies suffered the fate which seems inherent in their genre: they lasted only through one performance. Literary societies, drawing on a limited audience, often pedantic if not boring, and with a complacent regard for minimal achievements, did little better. Michael Denway, a European observer writing in the *West African Reporter* in 1877, analyzed their failure as the result of a singular lack of interest in self-improvement among the majority of Creoles and a great want of unity in their society.[35] This assertion, however, was only partially true. The groups and clubs failed because, unlike other organizations such as the Freetown press which also sought to improve Creole standards, they remained the exclusive domain of the upper level of Freetown society. Since this level comprised no more than a few hundred persons, all organizations tended to draw from the same group. Men like Samuel Lewis and Cornelius May were members of a half a dozen societies and clubs and were officers in most of them. Membership lists no longer survive for the majority of Freetown organizations but, in those that did appear from time to time in the newspapers, the names of the same group of people turn up again and again. Given this limited source of possible members, any antagonisms that developed between individuals could easily cause the demise of the entire organization. And because most clubs offered much the same fare in the form of activities, no individual felt the need to devote his entire allegiance to any particular society.

It was easy to see these Creole entertainments and organizations as pretentious and singularly philistine in taste. In the increasingly hostile colonial atmosphere in which Creoles found themselves in the last quarter of the nineteenth century, however, their social and literary activities became the outward manifestation of their apparently successful adoption of European customs and manners—a transformation which the Creoles had made in a period of little more than one generation since the majority of their parents had been landed in Sierra Leone as ex-slaves. As European attacks on Creole capabilities became more blatant, Freetown social and intellectual clubs and organizations became the vehicles through which Sierra Leoneans consciously hoped to impress critics that Africans were just as capable of "culture" and "refinement" as any European.

It is essential to understand that to most Creoles, including the overwhelming majority of the upper class, culture was not an either-or situation. Adoption of one way of life did not mean rejection of another. While having become genuinely Anglicized in their outlook toward education, wealth, and upward

35. "Societies and Clubs in Sierra Leone, An Essay," *West African Reporter*, July 11, 1877.

mobility, they continued to adhere to beliefs which were founded in the customs of their pre-Creole ancestors.

Sierra Leoneans, whether Christian or Muslim, generally believed in the power of their ancestors and in their continuing influence among the living. This belief was exemplified in a feast called *awujoh*—of Yoruba origin—by means of which Creoles hoped to gain the protection of the ancestral spirits for a new-born child, to acquire their blessings for the success of a marriage, or to ease the transition from life to death. Likewise, most Creoles believed that misfortune was caused by angered ancestral spirits and, consequently, held an *awujoh* to gain forgiveness.

The *awujoh* usually took place in the home or yard of the person wishing to invoke the ancestors. That person, several days before the rite was scheduled, called upon his ancestors by name and notified them of the forthcoming event. His intention was to put them in a receptive mood for the favors which would be requested during the ceremony.[36] For the *awujoh* itself, he invited family and friends and, according to his wealth, slaughtered chickens, goats, or even a cow for the feasting. Then followed an elaborate ritual. A portion of food was kept separate and cooked in palm oil without salt. This portion belonged to the dead. Vultures, who were thought to represent the ancestors, were fed a small part of this reserved food and it was considered bad luck if these birds failed to appear. Since garbage-ridden Freetown abounded with vultures, however, the probability of their absence was remote. At one point in the ritual festivities, the person communicating with the ancestors—usually the oldest female member of the family, because in age she was nearest to the ancestors and had had the longest contact with them—knelt next to a freshly dug hole and, according to whether the person was a Christian or Muslim, imbiber or teetotaler, poured either alcohol or water on the ground while, at the same time, praying to the dead. These liquid offerings were extremely important because the assumption was that the dead were always thirsty. All liquids of this sort, alcoholic or not, were generically called "cold water."[37]

The following invocation, recorded by Professor Harry Sawyerr at an *awujoh* in 1963, probably differed little from a prayer as it might have been said in the nineteenth century:

Grandma X, Papa Y, Uncle B, you all who have gone, see what a

36. Victor Williams and M. A. Deen, personal communication to the author, January 1966.

37. Victor Williams and M. A. Deen, personal communication to the author, January 1966. Also see Harry Sawyerr, "Sacrificial Rituals in Sierra Leone," *Sierra Leone Bulletin of Religion* 1, no. 1 (June 1959): 3; Harry Sawyerr, "Ancestor Worship—The Mechanics," *Sierra Leone Bulletin of Religion* 6, no. 2 (December 1964): 27.

great occasion this is [coming]. Here is cold water, drink. . . .
Here are your grandchildren and great grandchildren. See to it
that everything takes place by the power of God. Look at H, the
whole family, the grandchildren and the great grandchildren.
Guide us all—all of us. Here is your cold water to gladden your
hearts. Pray for us, you all who have gone before. Here is D. Look
upon us all here present, and those who [of the family] are not
able to be here with us. You know us all in the spirit (being
spirit). M is at her own home, please do not forget her; Z, M's
husband is overseas, he is your grand-son-in-law . . . . Take good
care of him, don't leave [neglect] him, by the power of
God . . . .[38]

After the "cold water" had been poured, the individual invoking the dead
placed a part of the ancestor's food in the hole in the ground and covered it
with plantain leaves. As this food was associated with good luck, a mock
struggle (*nyoleh*) took place in which everyone tried to grab a bit of the meat
that was left over. The *nyoleh* emphasized the communal nature of the
worship.[39]

When a child was born, family and friends gathered together to rejoice.
Some Creoles hung charms over the doorway to keep out unwanted spirits
and tied others around the neck and waist of the newborn child to protect it
from the "evil eye." "An owl," according to one source, "dared not make a
sound near where the child was born; if it did it would be stoned or even
shot, as it was the belief that witches attack babies in the forms of owls."[40]
Among the Aku, as was the custom among the Yoruba from whom they
descended, twin children received special attention because they were
thought to have the power to work great mischief upon their parents. To
placate them and to insure their favor and good will, friends and neighbors
were frequently invited by the twins' parents to feast and make merry.[41]
And, because it was believed that a woman who had just given birth to a child
was more vulnerable, a wooden pestle was placed in the middle of the floor in
the family room to safeguard her from evil. No stranger was permitted to visit
the new mother.

The most important ritual associated with the birth of a child was the

38. Sawyerr, "Ancestor Worship—The Mechanics," p. 28. Translated from Krio by
Professor Sawyerr.

39. Victor Williams and M. A. Deen, personal communication to the author, January
1966; Dulcie Nicolls, "The Effects of Western Education on the Social Attitudes of the
Creoles in Sierra Leone (thesis, presented to the University of Durham for the Diploma in
Education, 1960), pp. 18-19; Sawyerr, "Sacrificial Rituals," pp. 6-7. *Nyoleh* is a Krio
word of Yoruba origin.

40. Nicolls, "Effects of Western Education," p. 8.

41. *SLWN*, May 24, 1902.

komojade, or *pull na doe,* in which the baby and its mother were taken from the place of birth into public view.[42] Female children, because they were believed to mature more quickly than males, were brought out seven days after birth, while the latter had to stay in an extra two days. The morning of the *komojade,* among Christian Creoles, the baby was bathed, dressed, and brought to the parlor, where it was met by relatives, guests, and the pastor. After someone read a passage from the Scriptures, the company recited a prayer and sang a hymn. This was followed by the pastor's address, in which he instructed the parents about the training and upbringing of the infant and asked for God's blessing on the entire family. One of the older women then picked up the child and took it on a tour of the rooms in the house. Later, she brought it outside and walked about the neighboring streets pointing at buildings and familiar objects. Presently, she took the child back to the house and, speaking aloud, told the baby that there was no place like home and that no matter where it wandered in life it could always return there. When this ceremony was finished, the visitors gave presents to the baby—gifts meant to ease the pain of a male child's impending circumcision and a female's piercing of the ear lobes for earrings. The hosts then brought on what Creoles call "small refreshment"—rice bread, sweet biscuits, canapes, salad, and, depending on circumstance and wealth, stout, beer, gin, and other beverages. Beans and *akara,*[43] food especially associated with placating the ancestors, were invariably part of these refreshments.[44]

Both the ideal and reality of romantic wedlock obviously existed among some Creoles. For the majority, however, marriages were arranged by the parents of the couple. Such arrangements not only corresponded to practices in Victorian England but also to African traditions in which marriages were normally contracts between families rather than individuals. Usually the young man's parents chose a woman for him—one who ideally possessed good looks, a polite manner, and an ability to work hard. Wealth and social standing of the bride's family were also important considerations. For their part, the groom and his parents were expected to give a substantial sum of money to the bride's family—an amount known as the "trousseau." This arrangement, even though given a European name, undoubtedly derived from the "bride-wealth" practice which had completed the premarital formalities among most of the African groups from which the Creoles descended. Like "bride wealth," the "trousseau" had to be returned if an unsuccessful marriage could be blamed on the wife. Although the amount of the "trous-

42. *Pull na doe,* Krio for "take outside the door." *Komojade* is a Krio word of Yoruba origin.
43. A mashed bean paste often served with hot sauce.
44. Victor Williams, personal communication to the author, February 1966; Nicolls, "Effects of Western Education," p. 9.

seau" was not generally disclosed to outsiders, news sometimes "leaked" to the public if the sum was especially large, a sign that the groom showed respect for the bride and her family.[45] A poem which appeared in 1888 in the *Sierra Leone Weekly News* commented on this practice:

> If a young lady should marry for love,
> Her friends all immediately say,
> We cannot but pity the innocent dove;
> Poor thing: she is quite thrown away.
> But should she mate with an ugly old man,
> If with bright gold he is mettled,
> They spread the good news wherever they can,
> That she's comfortably settled.[46]

Creole couples who could not manage the preliminary financial arrangements because the man lacked cash for the "trousseau" often lived together out of wedlock, sometimes for years, until they could save enough to legalize their match.[47] Others were kept apart until they could fulfill all the requirements of marriage. In such cases the young man was permitted to visit his fiancée occasionally. He did not stay later than early evening, however, and the couple was never left unchaperoned because the parents believed that if the man became too familiar with their daughter he would no longer look forward to the novelty of married life. When a young man or his parents felt that they had earned enough to pay the "trousseau," they informed the parents of the bride that they would soon be coming to ask for her. A "put stop" day was fixed in which the man's parents would ask for the girl and in which the girl's parents had to "put-to-a-stop" her interest in other fellows.

The "put stop" ceremony itself was quite stylized, striking in its mixture of Victorian formalism with African ritual, and the people involved in it performed like actors speaking the lines of a well-rehearsed play. It was usually a woman's affair which took place in the evening but, sometimes, the older men of the family stayed and watched the proceedings. At an agreed time, just before the arrival of the groom's relatives, the bride-to-be and some of her younger female relatives were locked in a room while her parents and the older women remained in the parlor. When the groom's family knocked

---

45. Richardson and Collins, "Economic and Social Survey," pp. 188-189, 204-205.
46. Anonymous, "Comfortably Settled," *SLWN*, November 3, 1888.
47. See Abioseh Nicol's short story, "The Truly Married Woman," in *The Truly Married Woman and Other Stories* (London, 1965), for a charming depiction of this tendency. Among the less well-to-do, financial circumstances often forced less formal conjugal arrangements. The ideal, however, was that a wedding take place in church as soon as there was enough money for all the preparations.

on the door, the oldest female relative went to it and, without opening the door, asked:

> Bride's relation: "Who is it, friend or foe?"
> Groom's relation: "I lead a band of travellers
>   and am a friend."
> Bride's relation: "What do you want?"
> Groom's relation: "As we passed we saw a rose in
>   your garden and have come to ask permission
>   to pluck that rose."
> Bride's relation: "Will you cherish that rose if
>   I give it to you?"
> Groom's relation: "I promise to care for it as
>   best as possible."[48]

The relative of the bride then opened the door and the delegation entered the house. They were told to look around the room for the "rose" that they desired. Since only the older females were sitting in the parlor the "rose" was, of course, not to be found. The room in which the bride was kept hidden was then unlocked and her female companions stepped into the parlor, one at a time, with the bride staying behind until the end. As each one entered the parlor, the bride's relatives asked the groom's delegation, "Is this your rose? Is this your rose?" Each time they answered in the negative until, at last, the bride-to-be stepped into the room. Then they shouted, "Hurrah, we have found our rose!" One of the women then gave the bride's mother a calabash containing a Bible (or Koran)[49] inscribed with the girl's initials, and a ring in symbolic payment for the "rose." At this point, the bride's father chose a passage from the Bible and read it aloud and, after a prayer, the girl put the ring on her finger. The groom's relatives then began to dance and sing, proclaiming that the bride's mother had given her consent:

> Hibbi-hibbi-hurrah
> Hibbi-hibbi-hurrah
> Yawo mammy don answer yes-o![50]

After some "light refreshments," the bride was taken to the groom's house, where she was formally introduced to his relatives.

After the "put stop" day, the groom's parents sent an elderly lady relative

---

48. The description and much of the information about prenuptial arrangements closely follows Dulcie Nicolls' thesis, "Effects of Western Education," and Abioseh Nicol's *The Truly Married Woman*.

49. Nicolls, "Effects of Western Education," p. 10; Oral communication, M. A. Deen, August 1965.

50. Nicolls, "Effects of Western Education," pp. 10-11.

to the girl's parents with the "trousseau." Then both the bride's and the groom's mothers picked out different materials for the dresses they would wear on the wedding day and sent sample swatches to all relatives and friends. This was known as the *ashoebi.*[51] The actual engagement ceremony, however, did not take place until a few days before the wedding date. Again, it was a highly stylized ritual, between the two families. A number of the groom's older female relatives, accompanied by young girls dressed in blue and white to symbolize peace and love, were sent to the home of the bride-to-be. They brought two calabashes with them—one usually containing a bottle of whisky or gin and the other filled with peppers, kola nuts,[52] some coins, a needle, and, sometimes, another ring. These items were to indicate that the bride would lack nothing in her new home, an assurance of her future well-being. But the inclusion of the peppers and the needle also implied that she would be expected to be a good housekeeper. The ceremony thus acted out a contract between the families of the groom and bride—the groom's family promising security for the girl in return for the training in homemaking skills which she had received from her own family. Such family contract arrangements were extremely common among the groups from whom the Creoles had descended.

In Freetown, as in Britain, the evening before the wedding was "Bachelor Eve" for the groom. All of his friends congregated in his home and, in what was supposed to be the groom's last "fling" before his marriage, much wining and dining, dancing, and merrymaking took place.[53]

On the wedding day, the bride was dressed by her attendants so that she be spared from looking in the mirror—considered extremely unlucky on this occasion. She was also told not to look back after she had left her house for this too would be unfortunate. After the wedding, the couple went directly to the bride's house. They were greeted at the doorway with shouts complimenting the bride. The oldest female member of the family then proceeded to make a good luck speech and asked that both the bride and groom be faithful to their marriage vows and work for their mutual well-being. After some refreshments, the groom and his family went to his house for a celebration of their own. In the evening the groom called for his bride and took her to a temporary abode called a "farm," where they spent their honeymoon. She was usually accompanied by two bridesmaids and by an elderly woman related to her whose job it was to cook for the couple and to

51. Ibid., p. 12.
52. Kola is a chestnut-size, bitter nut, rich in caffeine content. The nuts reduce hunger pangs and are chewed as a stimulant. They have great ritual significance throughout West Africa. See Ellen Gibson Wilson, *A West African Cookbook* (New York, 1972), pp. 31, 239-246.
53. Nicolls, "Effects of Western Education," p. 13.

keep house during the honeymoon. On the day after the wedding, members of the bride's and groom's families visited the "farm," bringing food along, in order to inquire whether the groom had found his wife virginal.[54] If he had, there was much rejoicing and the bride was rewarded with gifts and was excused from housework during her entire stay on the "farm." The groom's family also congratulated the bride's mother for keeping her daughter virtuous and presented her with a calabash—called "tie calabash"—filled with presents and, usually, some money. If, however, the bride was not found to have been a virgin, she was sometimes beaten by the bridegroom and her mother for having disgraced them. Her bridesmaids also left the "farm" immediately, and, instead of enjoying a leisurely honeymoon, she was assigned menial tasks. Sometimes, undoubtedly depending on the temper of the groom, she was forced to leave the "farm" before the prescribed honeymoon was over, and sent to her husband's home where she had to begin doing housework at once. Under more normal circumstances, the bride and groom dressed in their wedding outfits on the Sunday after the weeding, attended church, and visited their friends and relatives. These visits marked the formal end of the wedding ceremony.[55]

Funeral and mourning ceremonies showed even more Creole retention of the traditional customs of their ancestors. At the point of death, relatives removed the corpse from the bed and placed it on the floor. They stripped the feather pillows and blankets from the bed because these were thought to prolong the dying person's struggle with the forces of death. All framed pictures and mirrors were turned to the wall or covered, as in the Orthodox Jewish practice, so that the dead person's image could not be seen in them. As it was believed that the spirit of the dead might frighten children under six, their foreheads were marked with a line of coal-dust to protect them.

The wake took place on the night before the funeral. Relatives, friends, and acquaintances came to the home of the bereaved family to offer their sympathy and to join the mourners. By nine in the evening, they began to sing spirituals, church hymns, and, among the Aku Creoles, occasionally songs in Yoruba:

Ai-ye-ye	This world
Ai-ye yi	This world
Ko sha ta wa	Is not ours

54. Ibid., p. 14. Given the rather liberal attitude of Creoles to less formal conjugal arrangements, particularly among those who lived together out of wedlock until finances would permit them to marry, this inquiry was probably intended figuratively. When I asked my informants to clarify this point, they chuckled.

55. Nicolls, "Effects of Western Education," pp. 15-16.

Mo gba pe ti ti ti	If you live long-long-long
La-ye wa ku	You will die
Mo gba pe	If you live
Mo gba pe	If you live
Ti Ti Ti Ti Ti Ti	Long long long long long long
Ti Ti Ti	Long long long
La-ye wa ku.	You will die.[56]

The singing was usually loud and accompanied by much handclapping—noises which were designed to rouse the body in case it was only in a trance and not dead. All those present were served a loaf of bread and as much coffee as necessary to keep them awake. Alcohol, although frowned upon by many, was also used to boost sagging morale. The singers had leaders, sometimes professionals, whose job it was to keep the wake alive by repeatedly introducing new songs. Through these means, while a candle was left burning continually in the room where the corpse lay, the wake stretched out into the early hours of the morning.

By one o'clock of the next day the relatives washed and dressed the corpse in expensive shrouds, if they could at all afford to do so, and laid the body on a bed in the middle of the parlor so that everyone could have a last glimpse of the departed. The corpse was then placed in a coffin and taken to the church for a service and, finally, to the cemetery for burial.[57]

The period of mourning, which lasted one year, was highlighted by special celebrations on the third, seventh, and fortieth day after death and by the one-year anniversary commemoration. Here again there is correspondence with practices among groups from whom Creoles descended, particularly the Yoruba.[58] Creoles believed that the spirit of the dead rose from the grave on the third day. They therefore prepared a small *awujoh* for which only the nearest relatives were invited. They cooked the traditional meal for such an occasion, including beans and *akara,* and, after eating, placed a portion of the food plus some kola nuts and water on a table and left these standing overnight. In this way, when the spirit visited the house in the night, it would know that it had been remembered. On the seventh day the relatives held another *awujoh* similar to the three-day celebration except extended to a larger crowd of people.

56. F. W. Butt-Thompson, "Handwritten Notes and Clippings in Army Book 129," in Sierra Leone Museum, Freetown.

57. An excellent description of a Creole burial, describing the ceremony and illustrating some of the mourners' fears that their practices would be thought of as "too Native" by European observers, can be found in Abioseh Nicol's short story, "Love's Own Tears," which appears in his *The Truly Married Woman.*

58. Geoffrey Parrinder, *West African Religion, A Study of the Beliefs and Practices of Akan, Ewe, Yoruba, Ibo and Kindred Peoples* (London, 1961), pp. 106-111.

The "fortieth-day" celebration was by far the most elaborate, for it was believed that this was the deceased's last day on earth and all relatives, friends, and acquaintances were therefore invited for his "send off."[59] A big meal, usually consisting of Jollof rice, rice and sauce, foo-foo and palava sauce,[60] salad, cake, rice bread, ginger beer, drinks of all types, as well as the ritual foods, was served. Unless the family of the deceased was quite well-to-do, the guests contributed to the success of the festivities in kind or cash.

In the early evening the merriment was called to a halt and everyone was invited to the yard where a hole had been dug for the *nyoleh* ceremony. Portions of all the food that had been prepared and cooked for that day, including a beverage and kola nuts, were placed into this hole so the dead might share in the day's festivities. The family and relatives of the deceased were then free to talk into the hole, either to ask for advice and help or to unburden themselves to the dead on any matter that bothered them. After speaking, they split two or three kola nuts in half and cast them on the ground. If they landed with all their flat sides turned either upwards or downwards, this was taken as a sign that the dead had heard. If, however, the nuts landed with some of the flat sides turned downward and others upward, then the dead had not listened, and the supplicant had to continue pleading and throwing the kolas until they landed in the desired manner. This went on until everyone who wanted to speak to the deceased had had his turn. The hole was then covered up and the celebration resumed until late at night.

Soon after the "fortieth day," among Christian Creoles, the family of a deceased relative chose a Sunday when mourning service was being held in church and, dressed in black, attended the service as a unit. Later, they all proceeded to the house of the deceased where, after saying prayers, preparations were made for the reading of the will. Among many of the African peoples from whom the Creoles descended, all deaths were regarded as the potential result of unnatural causes such as witchcraft, curses, or foul play.[61] Some Creoles continued this belief. After reading the will, the mourning party left for the cemetery, and, at the grave site, one member of the group poured "cold water" on the ground. He then took three kola nuts, split each into two, and threw them on the grave. If the flat side of each kola landed face upward it was concluded that the decedent had died of natural causes. If,

59. See M. J. Herskovits, *Trinidad Village* (New York, 1947), for the West Indian counterpart to this "fortieth-day" celebration.

60. Jollof Rice is a "one pot" dish, common to West Africa but most probably of Wolof origin. Foo-foo is a Creole staple dish made from cassava and always eaten with a "Palaver Sauce" or "Plassas"—a spicy, delicious, green leaf dish which usually includes tripe, fish, beef, salt pork, and chicken. For excellent recipes of these foods see Wilson, *West African Cookbook*, pp. 56, 64-65, 68-71.

61. See Parrinder, *West African Religion*, pp. 106-107.

on the other hand, all the flat sides landed face downward, and continued to do so each time for three tosses, then the party was convinced that "foul play" had been involved in the death—either from malicious thoughts or evil doings—and left the cemetery.[62] Since it was not a common Creole practice to seek out and punish the guilty, the mere discovery of wrongdoing sufficed to placate the dead.

Mourning terminated with the one-year anniversary. On the Friday before this anniversary the family held another *awujoh.* For Christians, the Sunday that followed was *pull mohning* day—the day mourning officially ended. All the members of the family attended church services wearing white clothes. They then walked to the cemetery as a group, visited the grave, and returned home for food and entertainment. From that day on the mourners stopped wearing black.

Rituals like *awujoh*, and the degree of ostentation with which they were celebrated on joyous and solemn occasions, clearly indicated the duality of Creole outlook—a duality composed of elements which seemed to inherently antagonistic as to make European and African critics believe that Creoles were hypocrites, false both to the world of traditional African practices and to that of Victorian Britain. Creole actions in these ceremonies, however, were neither hypocritical nor callous. Instead, they were a sincere attempt to do justice to two worlds without appearing to infringe on the rules of either. In the *awujoh* and other rites having to do with ancestral worship, they were true to the African beliefs about the continuity between the living and the dead, about the extended family as a unit broad enough to include ancestors long deceased, and in life as a series of stages—birth, marriage, and death—through which all individuals progressed in a journey that brought them ever nearer to their deceased relatives. On the other hand, these rituals and the festivities associated with them had their "European" aspect as well. They satisfied the religious requirements of Christianity and, while taking care of the basic human need for companionship and entertainment, were also opportunities for the display of material wealth—especially of possessions like "English" furniture, knick-knacks, and clothing—which were concrete proof of an individual's status within a society whose top standards were set in Europe. And, in this respect, by balancing between their commitments both to the African and European worlds, Creoles were defining themselves and their culture and arriving at a way of life which would permit them to develop and progress most satisfactorily.

62. Nicolls, "Effects of Western Education," pp. 17-18.

Part II: A Deteriorating Relationship

Chapter TWO
England Through Creole Spectacles:
Love and Betrayal

"We must lay a good foundation," he said, adding, "when you start school you must study hard, and if you do, who knows but you may go to England one day!"

England! I was really interested now. For even in those my early days, England was a magic word to us. It was the country where our bishop, our governor, the women missionaries, and the white men in the shops all came from, and where our own people had to go to become doctors and lawyers. It was almost as far as heaven in our imagination, except that heaven was above the clouds.

Cole, *Kossoh Town Boy*

It is Our Will that so far as may be, Our Subjects, of whatever race or creed, be fully and impartially admitted to offices in Our Service, the duties of which they may be qualified by their education, ability, and integrity duly to discharge.

Queen Victoria's Proclamation, November 1, 1858

Love

Creoles were long called "Black English."[1] Initially, Sierra Leoneans understood the term to have no pejorative connotations. Upper-class Creoles took it as a confirmation of fact: they were black and they felt English, and to be English during the reign of Queen Victoria was something of which to be

1. A. J. Shorunkeh Sawyerr, "The Social and Political Relations of Sierra Leone Natives to the English People," *SLWN*, April 15, 1893.

proud. To be called "Black English," moreover, was recognition of their successful Anglicization—of having shed the customs which they and Europeans associated with the "less civilized" peoples of the African interior. For a large number of Creoles, living, dressing, speaking, and acting like Englishmen—or as they believed the English to do these things—was "the inevitable outcome of the civilization and enlightenment" which had been brought to bear on Sierra Leone colony since its inception.[2] The Sierra Leone experiment, after all, had originally set out to create "Black English"—persons who were educated in the European manner, preferably Christian, disdainful of superstition, abhorrant of slavery, and willing to accept the values of Victorian England and to keep its faith.

England was the focus of attention for educated Creoles. They were drawn to the island physically and, like true lovers when given the chance, tended to idealize her virtues and minimize her faults. For many of the wealthier Creoles England was a second home—a place to which one could journey during the rainy season, a country where one completed his education, where young women were polished into genteel ladies and young men became gentlemen. "No African—impressionable as we are," commented an article in *Sierra Leone Weekly News*,

> . . . coming into close contact with European civilization and refinement can see Englishmen in their homes, and meet other European people in their own climes, listen to their speech, watch their actions and observe their movements, free from the heat and inconveniences of the tropics, without learning a great deal from what one sees and hears. The ideas of many in our colony are "narrow, crabbed and confined," and a few months' residence in England among Englishmen will tend to round off those angularities in our character which only mixing with refined people can effect. . . . If each one of us must contribute our quota towards the elevation of our colony, the more we see and know of the patriotism, philanthropy and liberality of Englishmen at home, the better.[3]

And, indeed, Creoles attended some of the best schools in Britain, graduated with degrees from Oxford and Cambridge, studied law and medicine, joined societies like the Royal Colonial Institute, dressed in the latest fashions, and mixed freely, if at times self-consciously, with the English on the latter's home grounds.[4]

2. "Our Native Manners and Customs," *SLT*, June 23, 1894.

3. *SLWN*, June 6, 1885.

4. For examples, see M. C. F. Easmon, "Sierra Leone Doctors," *Sierra Leone Studies*, n.s., no. 6 (June 1956), pp. 81-96; Fyfe, *History of Sierra Leone*, pp. 406, 433.

At a time near the mid-nineteenth century when the color bar and racial discrimination in Britain were as yet relatively uncommon, it had been easy for Sierra Leoneans to see England as Utopia achieved. Creoles had felt then that theirs was a special association with Britain—that their relationship had been made exceptional by historical events. Proud of Sierra Leone's place among the oldest of British possessions, Creoles came to view their homeland as somehow more loyal to the British Crown than other colonies. The *Sierra Leone Weekly News* explained that Creoles, unlike other colonial peoples, had not been conquered. "We are a people born and fostered . . . by the British Nation," an editorial stated in 1890, "whom we regard and own as our parents and to whom we look for instruction, advice, guidance and advancement in the same manner as the other British subjects born in England."[5] They were grateful to British philanthropy for freeing their ancestors from slavery, for educating them and placing them at what they believed to be the vanguard of black peoples on the African continent. It was reassuring to imagine themselves as Britain's favorite and favored Africans.

Queen Victoria had a special place in their hearts, symbolizing all that was good in the relationship between Britons and Sierra Leoneans. Locally she was called "We Mammy"—"Our Mother."[6] The queen's Golden Jubilee in 1887 coincided with the centenary of the first settlement of Sierra Leone by the ancestors of the Creoles and both events were celebrated in the colony with an enthusiasm bordering on ecstasy. E. W. Blyden composed a centenary ode and wrote a historical play depicting the settlement of the colony. Fireworks, parades, balls, and entertainments marked the festivities. Many female children born during 1887 were named "Jubilee" or "Victoria." Articles about the "Good Queen" appeared frequently in the press.

In 1897 the queen's Diamond Jubilee was similarly celebrated with dancing and delight, occasioning a debate over whether Sierra Leonenas should commemorate Her Majesty's august reign by erecting a statue depicting the monarch, at a cost of £1000, or a statue of a lion, at a cost of £500. Perhaps because busts of Victoria were not unusual in the colony, gracing the homes of many prominent Creoles, this debate extended to include the possibility of setting up a public garden in Freetown which could be used for rest and recreation.[7] The extended proposal ultimately was approved, talk about lions and queenly busts subsided, and the Public Works Department was ordered to lay out Victoria Park, complete with benches and bandstand.[8]

A number of the more enlightened deputies of the British government in the colony were also regarded with great affection. Sir Charles MacCarthy,

5. *SLWN*, May 10, 1890.
6. *SLWN*, June 10, 1911.
7. *SLWN*, January 9, 1897.
8. *SLWN*, June 23, 1900.

who eventually lost his head fighting the Ashanti, was called "We Daddie"—
"Our Father"—during his sixteen years in Sierra Leone.[9] Sir Arthur Kennedy,
who had begun his career as an unpopular governor, presently redeemed
himself and was commemorated by the "Kennedy Leaf"—an indispensable
home remedy whose medicinal good effects were beyond question, and by
the song popular among women:

> Who reign? Governor Kennedy!
> Who reign? Beloved Kennedy![10]

Sir John Pope-Hennessy, perhaps the most popular of all Sierra Leone
governors not only for his abolition of the resented house and land tax but
also because of his championing of African capabilities, was remembered long
after his death with a yearly celebration of "Pope-Hennessy Day," a public
holiday, and with the Krio song:

> All dem Governor do bereh well
> All dem Governor do bereh well;
> Pope Hennessy do pass dem,
> Pope Hennessy—Pope Hennessy do pass dem.[11]

Creole sympathies for Britain, however, went even beyond their near
adulation of Queen Victoria and the handful of British governors that had
pleased them. After the Congress of Berlin and during the accelerating
scramble for Africa, for example, many educated Sierra Leoneans felt a
genuine identity with the aims of British imperialism and the white man's
burden. Creole children recited Kipling by heart and sang "Britannia Rules
the Waves."[12] Similarly their parents, who had grown up learning a great deal
about European history and geography and little or nothing about Africa and
its past, took pride in Britain's imperial victories and mourned her defeats.
Many Creoles, including Muslims, were genuinely saddened when General
Gordon lost his life at Khartoum, displaying not the slightest sympathy for
the aims of the Mahdi, a fellow African. Generally they approved the
sentiments of Major A. M. Festing, who, in a poem published for the *Sierra
Leone Weekly News*, implored Britain to recoup herself and to rise to new
heights of conquest:

9. *West Africa*, February 28, 1920, p. 185; Sibthorpe, *History*, p. 23.
10. Article by D. T. Akibo-Betts, *SLWN*, October 27, 1934.
11. Recorded in Freetown at the home of Victor Williams, September 1965.
12. Robert Wellesley Cole, *Kossoh Town Boy* (Cambridge, 1960), p. 91.

> Wake, Britain, wake! yea, Greater Britain arise!
> And teach the world this lesson of today;
> The little Isle beneath the western skies
> Is but the centre of a vast array.[13]

Creoles rationalized their sympathy and support for Britain's imperial aims in a number of ways. Foremost was their gratitude for what Britain had done in the past for their ancestors and for Sierra Leone colony. Not only had Britain put a stop to intertribal wars that had been a by-product of the slave trade, but also, according to some Sierra Leoneans, "by patience, perseverance, by sacrifice, by expenditure, by wise administration, in spite of some deplorable mistakes," Britain restored order and peace to Africa, stopped the trade in human beings, and gave the opportunity to millions of Africans "for growth in civilization." "We are largely indebted to England," argued an editorial in the *Sierra Leone Weekly News*, "for material, intellectual, and it may be, ultimately, spiritual salvation."[14]

In the biblically oriented Sierra Leone society, support for British imperial actions inevitably derived also from interpretations of the Testaments. A. B. C. Sibthorpe judged Britain's role in abolishing slavery and imposing a *pax Britannica* on Africa to be a literal fulfillment of Isaiah's prophecy about the peace which would exist in Christ's kingdom. According to Sibthorpe, any nation approaching the Creator in acts of benevolence would always be pre-eminent among men. "What nation can stand before almighty England?" he asked rhetorically. "Not one. Not, however, as is commonly said or sung, 'They have the *men*, they have the *ships*, they have the *money too*.' No. 'God is in the midst of her; therefore she shall not be removed.' The Ark of God, lost to the Jewish nation, is now tabernacled in England."[15] Another opinion was that European—and particularly British—conquest and domination were part of a divine plan in which the various races of man followed a preordained role. In accordance with the prophecy that "God shall enlarge Japhet," the white race, which was believed to have descended from Japhet, would therefore dominate the other races of man even though it was numerically the smallest.[16] The price, however, was the white man's burden, which editorials in Creole newspapers defined in much the same way as it was defined by leading British defenders of imperial expansion—to protect the "weaker races

---

13. *SLWN*, April 11, 1885.

14. *SLWN*, November 25, 1899.

15. A. B. C. Sibthorpe, *Sibthorpe's Oration on the Centenary of the Abolition of the Slave Trade by the English Government* (London, 1907), pp. 108-109.

16. Editorial, *SLWN*, November 25, 1899.

against the unchastened impulses of arbitrary power," to reclaim and evangelize the world, and to lead the darker races to advancement and a "higher civilization."[17] Creoles judged their role in this divine plan to be one of sympathy and judicious cooperation.[18] According to some of the most Westernized Creoles, moreover, it was not difficult to extend this support since Britain ruled for the good of Africa, impartially and with justice. Where occasional deviations from these standards took place, she was willing to correct herself and make redress.[19]

Most important of all, however, Creoles were favorably inclined toward the imperial movement because they still liked to see themselves in much the same way as the missionaries and philanthropists had viewed them in the early decades of the nineteenth century: they were an important and privileged arm of British penetration into and "civilization" of the interior of the continent, living proof of successful British ideas and actions in Africa. Some Creoles realized that Britain was "but a bird of passage" in Africa and that European rule would eventually end. A number of articulate Sierra Leoneans concluded, nevertheless, that the very thought of their homeland no longer being under British rule was terrifying enough to make their blood curdle.[20]

The possibility of British withdrawal from Africa was discussed in a series of articles which appeared in the *Sierra Leone Weekly News* beginning September 7, 1901, entitled "When Sierra Leone Ceases to be British." The writer, who signed himself only as "Columbus," perhaps to symbolize his daring in opening up this question, anticipated that a day might come when Britain, compelled by circumstances, would abandon Sierra Leone to her own resources.[21] Editorial reaction was indignant. It dismissed independence from Britain as "an event which may never take place for centuries to come" and chided the writer:

> Our correspondent surely does not . . . expect us to establish a government of our own within the British Government and so prepare ourselves for an event, such as he has forecast. The reference made by him to the conquest of Great Britain by Julius Caesar, and of its subjugation in consequence to Rome for nearly 500 years, after which the transactions between the conquerors and the conquered ceased, does not appear to be pertinent to Sierra Leone. The Britons were a people in their own country,

17. *SLT*, March 11, 1899; *SLWN*, November 25, 1899.

18. *SLWN*, November 25, 1899.

19. Editorial, "British Rule in West Africa," *SLWN*, November 16, 1895; *SLWN*, November 25, 1899.

20. Editorial, *SLWN*, July 29, 1899.

21. Columbus, "When Sierra Leone Ceases to be British," *SLWN*, September 7, 1901; also see *SLWN*, October 12, 1901, and letter to the editor in the issue of November 30, 1901.

but we as Sierra Leoneans were brought from various parts of the Guinea Coast to settle in this Colony which, though in Africa, is England's by right of purchase. *Our settlement here is by sufferance and not as a matter of right, humiliating as such a statement might be.*[22]

Betrayal

The Creole attitude toward Britain had its obverse side as well. Love stood back-to-back with hate. Throughout the nineteenth century Europeans had equated "civilization" with "Westernization." This feeling of cultural superiority had existed even among the British philanthropists who worked for the abolition of slavery. They believed that Africans, as fellow creatures of God, had the right to be free. At the same time, they rarely questioned the premise that African blacks were culturally inferior to Europeans.[23] But most significantly, while these Britons were certainly cultural chauvinists, they were not racists: they did not believe that race determined cultural attainment and found nothing inherent in blacks to prevent their "civilization." Indeed, the Sierra Leone experiment was a testament to the philanthropists' faith in the power of cultural conversion.

Having for decades been nurtured in the belief that they were somehow special—better than those Africans who had never been exposed to the benefits of European culture and as good as any Englishman who, like them, was a Christian and a gentleman—Creoles were psychologically unprepared for the changes that took place in European ideas about Africans after the 1860s. With racist ideas coming into vogue, few in Europe still believed that "lower races" could even grasp the complexities of the European "way of life"—to say nothing of mastering it well enough to act as carriers of European culture among their own people.[24] While physical anthropologists proclaimed the inferiority of black peoples, and Darwin's work was used to bolster the proposition that superior races were marked by their material superiority, the "noble savage" stereotype was replaced by the popular image of an ape-like black man in top hat and dark suit. As paternalism came to displace the ideal of equality through conversion, too many Britons made Creoles feel like parodies rather than equals. Under these circumstances, it was difficult for Creoles to maintain their love for Britain without blemishes or disillusionment.

When British deeds and attitudes toward Africans became more negative as the century progressed, educated Creoles increasingly deviated from their

22. Editorial, *SLWN*, September 7, 1901. Italics mine.

23. Philip D. Curtin, *The Image of Africa: British Ideas and Actions, 1780-1850* (Madison, Wis., 1964), pp. 238-240.

24. Ibid., pp. 414-415, 425-426.

starry-eyed idealization of Britain and her aims. They began to feel betrayed, scorned. By 1887, the year of Queen Victoria's Golden Jubilee and the centenary of the Sierra Leone settlement, a number of Creoles were certain that things had changed—that the days of beneficent British philanthropists who had worked along with other Europeans for the cultural transformation of Africans through christianity, education, and commerce, had become obscured if not forgotten. "Now-a-days," complained a writer in the *Sierra Leone Weekly News*, "we may expect to meet with antipathy where in by-gone days we met with support. The successors of those who forty years ago believed in giving us every opportunity to rise in the world, now believe that every effort on our part should be nipped in the bud or regarded with indifference bordering on contempt."[25] Having striven for an identity with Britain and Britons in all phases of their lives, these Sierra Leoneans repeatedly saw themselves relegated to subordinate positions, spurned by the very people whose cultural wards they had become.

Even those Creoles who were physically and emotionally most attracted to the British Isles could not fail to perceive the growing disparity between their image of Britain and the reality. A. B. C. Merriman-Labor, for instance, who had been drawn away from his job at the colonial secretary's office in Freetown to visit England, and ultimately remained there to study law at Lincoln's Inn, attempted to dispel the overblown notions his countrymen held about Great Britain.[26] He did this first in a series of articles published in the *Sierra Leone Weekly News* entitled "Through the United Kingdom—My Wanderings and Impressions" and, later, in his book *Britons Through Negro Spectacles*.[27] In the latter, Merriman-Labor described how he would warn Authur Adventurer, a fellow Sierra Leonean, about London:

> My dear Adventurer, London is not paved with gold. It is paved with stone—stone hard and cruel to those not used to paved roads. Instead of gold, we see on the roads something which for our purpose must be nameless, something left behind by the thousands of horses drawing vehicles along. If ever you get here, your first difficulty will be to prove that you understand the English language. Even the sewage-man whose English is as bad as his job, will consider himself better spoken than you, although

25. *SLWN*, February 26, 1887. Also see "Some of Our Drawbacks," February 5, 1887; "My View of Things," June 25, 1887, *SLWN*; "Origins and Purpose of Sierra Leone," *West African Reporter*, June 4, 1888.

26. *SLWN*, March 12, 1904, May 22, 1909.

27. *SLWN* began publishing the series "Through the United Kingdom" on November 25, 1904; *Britons Through Negro Spectacles or A Negro on Britons* was published in London in 1909. See Eldred Jones, "Turning Back the Pages (No. 1)," *The Bulletin of the Association for African Literature in English*, no. 2 (1965), pp. 19-26.

you have graduated at a British university with high honours in English.

Still do not expect that in this country your university degree will carry you far. Such degrees are too *beaucoup* here. Every other person you meet in the street is a Bachelor or Master of Arts. Even, as a chance is, you will find that the otherwise unemployed little daughter of your possible landlady here—an under-age lass who will have to clean your boots, has graduated at a leading university with double honours in Classics and treble honours in Hebrew. . . .

Apart from the people's disbelief in your knowledge of your language, you will have tremendous difficulty to get a chance to prove yourself a capable clerk. There is absolutely no chance on this side. No one, not even a Briton, can get a chance here, unless he is able to do an old work in a new way. You, being Black, cannot get on here, unless you can start a new work of your own in a novel manner, or can do an old work three times better than the best.

Are you prepared to expend the tremendous energy which the nonrecognition of our race entails on those who would succeed? If not, you had better stay where you are. Even in your own home, I know, colour puts impediment in your way. Still, I think with a little sense and tack, you will get on as a clerk or schoolmaster better there than you can in Britain.

Besides, never you reckon on the charity of British individuals here as a means of bettering your personal education or position. Remember that the Negro has been completely weaned from the suckling period of sympathy and philanthropy. He has now to creep, stand, or walk for himself and that without the help of a nurse's hand.[28]

Creole awareness of the unfavorable attitudes toward Africans that were gaining prominence among Europeans was heightened by events both at home and abroad. One clear indication that the wind had shifted in Britain was in the abuse heaped upon educated Africans in the writings of European travelers and ex-colonial servants. Richard Burton's books, *Wanderings in West Africa* and *To the Gold Coast for Gold*, G. A. L. Banbury's *Sierra Leone, or The White Man's Grave*, A. B. Ellis' *West African Sketches*, and A. F. Mockler-Ferryman's *British West Africa* all had one thing in common—that derogation of Creoles and their scorn for African capabilities.[29] Written in a racy, popular style, these books lampooned "ultra-civilized black loaf-

28. Merriman-Labor, *Britons Through Negro Spectacles*, pp. 127-129.
29. Richard F. Burton, *Wanderings in West Africa, from Liverpool to Fernando Po. By a F.R.G.S.*, 2 vols. (London, 1863), vol. 1; R. F. Burton and J. L. Cameron, *To the*

ers" and made pronouncements about "niggers" which, much to the chagrin of educated Sierra Leoneans, generally received approval from the British public.[30] Burton, for example, wrote with scathing sarcasm about two educated Africans, one a Creole, who traveled with him on the ship from England to Sierra Leone:

> The second, our Gorilla, or Missing Link, was the son of an emancipated slave, who afterwards distinguished himself as a missionary and a minister. His—the sire's—name has appeared in many books, and he wrote one himself, pitying his own "poor lost father," because, forsooth, he died in the religion of his ancestors, an honest Fetishist. Our excellent warm-hearted ignorant souls at home were so delighted with the report of this Lion of the Pulpit, that it was much debated whether the boy, Ajai, had not been providentially preserved for the Episcopate of Western Africa.[31]

The "Missing Link," Burton's traveling companion, was none other than Samuel Crowther, son of Samuel Ajayi Crowther, a Creole who had become bishop of the Niger Territory and one of the best known Africans of his time. Sierra Leoneans who read *Wanderings in West Africa*, and their numbers included many who published or wrote for newspapers and whose contacts with less informed Creoles throughout the colony were substantial, could not ignore such insults.

Equally disheartening were the letters to the editors of British newspapers and the lectures delivered in England by Europeans who had been in Africa, for varying lengths of time and for obscure reasons, and who now felt qualified to generalize about Africans. Typical of this genre was the letter by Hal Dane which had been published in the *London Daily Graphic* and reprinted in the *Sierra Leone Weekly News*. Dane, who had been in Sierra Leone but briefly, returned to England and complained about the "poor-spirited race" there:

> They peacock as fine fellows within our boundaries, but have not dared to push civilization beyond the safe borders among the more war-like tribes of the interior. To these folk came governors like Sir John Pope Hennessy, who taught them that they were as good as white men, but failed to explain to them how to prove it.

Gold Coast for Gold (London, 1883); G. A. L. Banbury, *Sierra Leone, or The White Man's Grave* (London, 1881); A. B. Ellis, *West African Sketches* (London, 1881); A. F. Mockler-Ferryman, *British West Africa* (London, 1900).

30. Abiose, "Review of *British West Africa*," *SLWN*, April 20, 1901.
31. Burton, *Wanderings in West Africa*, 1: 207.

Consequently, Mr. Habakkuk d'Eresby Willoughby struts forth in fine clothes, with broad, self-complacent smile on his black face, and Mrs. H. d'E. W. does all the work. The highest aim of this creature is to insult the whites, remembering that it is an assault to strike him in return, but forgetting that if the troops were withdrawn from the barracks, he would find a speedy end as a tolerable roast for the appetite of the more manly and warlike tribes on the borders.[32]

The Sierra Leone press was especially sensitive to European criticisms of Creoles. Perhaps because the newspapers' publishers, editors, and writers—as the best educated, Europeanized, and among the most influential members of Creole society—felt they had more to lose than others, they were quick to publicize the changes in British ideas and attitudes toward Africans in general and Creoles in particular. In this respect the Creole press served a dual function: to inform and to act as the leading vehicle for the expression of Creole hopes, aspirations, disappointments, and exasperations.

Initial Creole reactions were mild, designed to counter insults with humor, logic, and a somewhat defensive indignation. Creoles laughed about the "Instant Experts" on Africa—men who wrote volumes about black Africans on the basis of one quick sea voyage down the western coast of the continent, a short punitive expedition, or a fast trip to the interior:

> It would appear that any and every adventurer on the coast, who can handle a pen, feels himself competent to abuse West Africa and its people. The climate is no doubt in a great measure to be blamed for this not uncommon phenomenon. The liver of foreigners in this climate is subject to such melancholy vicissitudes, that a great deal may be said in palliation of the execrating (and execrable?) proclivities of "roving" penny-a-liners. Let intelligent natives remember and console themselves, when they take up the writings of any of these men, that they have sat down to a study of a case of climatic monomania, if not of hereditary but latent insanity, developed by new conditions and unaccustomed environments, and allow this thought to temper their amazement or indignation at all the "sound and fury, signifying nothing."[33]

A number of Sierra Leoneans sought to rebut a common European contention that Creoles, as descendants of slaves, were bound to be inferior to those Africans, such as the Mende and Timne in the Sierra Leone hinterland,

32. *SLWN*, March 14, 1891.

33. Editorial, *Methodist Herald*, December 9, 1885. Also see Merriman-Labor, *Britons Through Negro Spectacles*, p. 121.

who descended from free-born persons.[34] Resentment and some bitterness were certainly beneath the surface, but the most obvious characteristic of these reactions was the attempt to rationalize British behavior toward edu-cated Africans, to safeguard their image of the English as basically decent people, understanding toward black men in general and especially Sierra Leoneans. George Gurney Nicol, for example, in his *Essay on Sierra Leone*, hoped to strike a balance between the views of European travelers who returned from the coast of Africa with too high an opinion of its inhabitants with those whose opinions were too low. The former, Nicol concluded, were generally of a better class and went to West Africa thinking that they would find highly educated and civilized people. The latter went with the expecta-tion of finding only savages with whom they could deal in any manner they pleased. Both kinds of travelers were thus disappointed by what they found in the colony. Sierra Leone "turns out to be what it really is," wrote Nicol, "neither a community which has reached the acme of European civilization and refinement, nor, on the other hand, a conglomeration of rude and untutored boors, huddled up together in one unshapely mass; but a race, forming and not formed."[35]

As the catalogue of actions unfavorable to Creoles expanded in the 1890s, however, Sierra Leoneans found it ever more difficult to rationalize British behavior. Some of the iniquities in the catalogue were minor—a haughty tone of voice, a murmured insult, a shove in the streets, an arrogant gesture.[36] They were inflicted on an individual basis, person-to-person, and their impact, although cumulative, was not sufficient to arouse a mass response. Such occurrences deviated markedly from the good will, courtesy, and tact which Creoles believed to have characterized interracial relationships in former days; still, many upper-class Sierra Leoneans excused these incidents as the product of a "lower type of Englishman," less educated and certainly more boorish, but to be pitied for his actions if not forgiven altogether.

Other incidents, however, either affected or became known to a greater number of people and were less easily dismissed as uncharacteristic slips. Creoles met discrimination in the professional fields, in the civil service, and in commerce. Each aberration added fuel to a fire which, for a significant element of Creole society, was consuming the old associations between themselves and the British. Events at the turn of the century were even leading to the physical separation of the European and Sierra Leone commu-nities in Freetown.

34. *SLWN*, March 28, 1891.
35. George Gurney Nicol, *An Essay on Sierra Leone* (Sierra Leone, [1881]), p. 5.
36. See *SLWN*, February 16, 1896, for a Creole reaction to the word "nigger."

From the very beginnings of the settlement in the Sierra Leone peninsula, through moments bright and troubled, through years of depression and prosperity, through periods of idealism and disillusionment, Europeans had lived and died in the midst of the African community. Because they had rarely come there as permanent immigrants but were transients who governed, traded, taught, evangelized, and ultimately tried to return to Britain, the white inhabitants in Freetown rented houses from Creoles and lived side-by-side with African neighbors.[37]

Frequent interaction with persons of a different race was unavoidable: men met each other at work; women shopped together in markets and stores; hawkers approached all houses to sell their wares. Europeans, moreover, had African servants and cooks. And socially, segregation was unacceptable. Persons belonging to the upper reaches of Creole society mingled freely with European officials and their wives at the afternoon teas, "conversazione," "at homes," balls, and entertainments which frequently highlighted the Freetown scene. Even dinners at Government House and small-talk visits with the governor's lady were arranged on the basis of color-blind invitation lists.

It was a pleasant world, if not the best of all possible ones. Pretension and occasional tokenism marred its honesty; whispered racial slurs against "Black Englishmen" disrupted the surface harmony. Cliques formed along divisions of black and white. Few genuine, intimate friendships were formed between Europeans and Africans. Nonetheless, so long as Creoles and Europeans continued to live in the same neighborhoods, under analogous conditions and facing similar problems, their proximity bred familiarity if not understanding, knowledge if not sympathy. "Togetherness with reserve," in the Creole view, was preferable to a separation which altogether denied them a belief in their own cultural equality with Britons.

For Europeans, death had been an invisible companion and constant spoiler in Sierra Leone, with the danger of being struck down by fatal diseases measurably greater than in Europe. Freetown was so reviled that insurance companies refused to insure the lives of Europeans going there. The deduction made by the Colonial Office as a contribution to the "Widow's Fund" was higher for Sierra Leone officers than for those serving in any other place.[38] The range of killers was large, calling forth, in an age of less sophisticated medical knowledge, dreaded images of Sierra Leone as the "White Man's Grave." For at least the first half of the nineteenth century,

37. I have published a modified version of the following section as an article, "The Mosquito and Segregation in Sierra Leone," in *Canadian Journal of African Studies* 2, no. 1 (Spring 1968): 49-61.

38. See Burton, *Wanderings in West Africa*, 1: 200; Leslie William Charles Pearce Gervis, *Sierra Leone Story* (London, 1956), p. 12.

blame for the high mortality was laid on everything from the climate, which differed dramatically from that in Great Britain, to bad air from tropical marshes, to imbalances of the fluids of the body. These were impersonal factors, not attributable to the African inhabitants and, therefore, without effect on the relationship between Africans and Europeans.[39] With advances in tropical medicine in the last decades of the nineteenth century, however, the true causes for malaria and yellow fever were discovered. The decision of the Colonial Office and the Sierra Leone government to act upon the suggestions for health improvements made by the scientists, reinforced by the prevailing racism of the epoch, upset the long-standing integration of Creole and European society in the colony. Among the remedies explicitly proposed was the physical separation of European living quarters from those belonging to the African population.

The background and the catalyst for this departure from established social patterns were intimately connected with researches and discoveries in the field of tropical medicine, particularly those dealing with the disease-carrying mosquito. British interest in tropical medicine had grown in the 1890s—the result of the increased publicity given to British military involvement in the tropics and the heavy casualties suffered by British troops in campaigns such as in Ashanti. With British prestige in the competition for empire at stake within Europe, and the white man's burden and the glories of imperialism capturing the popular imagination, Britons became conscious of the dangers posed by tropical diseases. Money for medical research suddenly was appropriated by the Colonial Office and donated by private individuals. This infusion of funds permitted research of unprecedented intensity, especially at two institutions newly established in the 1890s—the London and Liverpool schools of tropical medicine.

In 1899 Doctor Ronald Ross, a lecturer at the Liverpool School of Tropical Medicine, was sent to Freetown along with other scientists seeking ways to decrease the incidence of malaria. Earlier, while in the British Army in India, Ross had discovered that the malarial parasite, in one stage of its life cycle, had the Anopheles mosquito as its host, but he had not been able to prove Anopheles the universal culprit. Freetown gave him this chance.[40] The Liverpool expedition remained in Sierra Leone for seven weeks. In the course of that time, working mainly at Tower Hill and Wilberforce Barracks with West Indian soldiers, who had been in Sierra Leone for only a short time and

39. Curtin, *Image of Africa*, pp. 76-79; Philip D. Curtin, " 'The White Man's Grave': Image and Reality, 1780-1850," *The Journal of British Studies* 1 (1961): 94-110.

40. "The Malaria Expedition to Sierra Leone," *British Medical Journal*, September 9, 1899, p. 675; Ronald Ross et al., *Report of the Malaria Expedition of the Liverpool School of Tropical Medicine and Medical Parasitology* (Liverpool, 1900), pp. 1-2, hereafter cited as *Report of Malaria Expedition*.

many of whom were suffering from malaria, Ross and the other scientists were able to conclude that Anopheles was the principal genus of mosquito carrying the malarial parasite.[41] Ross would later win the Nobel Prize for his pioneer work in this field. The Freetown experience demonstrated, moreover, that unlike the nonmalarial Culex mosquito, which could breed in any vessel of water, the West African species of Anopheles would breed only in small pools of stagnant water which formed in rocks, in ditches, in tubs or pots, or in containers.[42] Having come to these conclusions, it became possible to consider the ways in which the incidence of malaria could be cut down.

Two solutions became apparent. The first, based on the discovery that Anopheles bred in small pools, sought to eliminate the disease at its source by killing off the larvae before they hatched. Instead of draining the whole of an infected area at great cost as had been done in the past, it now seemed sufficient to concentrate on eliminating puddles, mires, and similar containers of stagnant water. But this method was more easily conceived than accomplished. While Dr. Ross and the Liverpool expedition were still in Sierra Leone, Acting Governor Matthew Nathan sent out fifty Africans, with a European overseer, to map and destroy the mosquito breeding places. It soon became apparent that it was a gigantic and expensive task to clear up debris that had accumulated for decades.[43] Freetown enjoyed well-deserved notoriety for atrocious public sanitation practices. Neither drainage nor removal of night-soil existed; garbage-filled deep wells and ruts abounded. Refuse was thick and noticeable, especially during the dry season when its aromatic presence became inescapably accented by the breezes.[44] The colonial government's enthusiasm for a clean-up campaign faded rapidly when the expedition departed. Ultimately, the support of public officials for concerted action against mosquitoes waned as well, and only partial measures were taken.[45] Ross, in his *Memoirs*, complained that officialdom did not want to be bothered with public sanitation drives; they were satisfied to take their daily quinine and to rationalize their attitudes by saying that "nothing was to be attempted against mosquitoes until the native population was sufficiently educated."[46]

But a second way to whittle down the high incidence of malaria also became apparent. This method, in the short run, would be costlier in terms of

41. *Report of Malaria Expedition*, pp. 3-10; Ronald Ross, *Memoirs* . . . (London, 1923), pp. 367-386.

42. *Report of Malaria Expedition*, p. 5; "The Malaria Expedition to Sierra Leone," *British Medical Journal*, October 14, 1899, pp. 1034-1035.

43. W. R. E. Clarke, *The Morning Star of Africa* (London, 1960), pp. 61-63.

44. *Report of Malaria Expedition*, p. 46.

45. Ross, *Memoirs*, pp. 434-442; C.O. 270/35, Medical Report, 1902.

46. Ross, *Memoirs*, pp. 443, 490; S. R. Christophers, "The Prevention of Malaria in Tropical Africa," *Thompson Yates Laboratories Report* 3, pt. 2 (1901): 169.

energy and money than an all-out drive to eliminate the Anopheles larvae. Unlike sanitation operations, however, which would have to be checked and rechecked after every rainy season, this would only have to done once, thoroughly, and never again. And its greatest advantage was that it fit contemporary racial prejudices. This was the principle of "sanitary segregation."

Ross had been shocked to find that Europeans in Sierra Leone, unlike their compatriots in India, had not learned how best to live in the tropics. Not only were *punkahs* (fans) and mosquito nets not used in Sierra Leone as in India, but houses in the colony were small, crowded together, not located on the most elevated site available, and poorly built from the point of view of light and ventilation. "Serious attention," the report of the Liverpool expedition stated,

> . . . ought to be given to this question of the houses of Europeans in the tropics. If employees are sent at all to dangerous climates, it is the manifest duty of their employers—whether these employers be the government or private persons—to see that they are housed in a manner most likely to preserve their health. If the nation wishes to maintain colonies in intensely malarious localities, the least it can do is to protect its servants as much as possible from the disease.[47]

Worse still, from the point of view of the effect that his visit would have on the relationship between Europeans and Creoles, Ross attributed much of the high European death rate in Sierra Leone to the fact that they lived in houses which were not segregated from those in which Africans lived. His experience in India, where the British officials and troops were "nearly always housed in separate locations and frequently spared infection from neighborhood crowded native quarters," contrasted favorably with what he found in Sierra Leone. Since the total eradication of mosquito breeding areas seemed unlikely, Ross concluded—on pragmatic rather than racist grounds—that the segregation of Europeans in Sierra Leone would be the most immediately effective measure for preserving their health. And many of the individuals who were intimately involved in tropical medicine research concurred with this opinion.[48]

47. *Report of Malaria Expedition*, pp. 45-46. The report stressed "employer-employee" responsibility because Sierra Leone, like India, was not a European settlement colony; Europeans went there for particular governmental or private business purposes, not as colonists.

48. Ronald Ross, *The Prevention of Malaria* (London, 1910), pp. 285-286. For concurring opinions see Christophers, "Prevention of Malaria," pp. 169-176; Dr. Henry Strachan, Chief Medical Officer for Lagos, "The Health Condition of West Africa," paper

Government officials in Sierra Leone had in fact long considered the mountainous area beyond Freetown peculiarly salubrious for Europeans. In the period of Sir Charles MacCarthy's governorship, government officials and Church Missionary Society missionaries frequently had retired to Regent village to recuperate from attacks of fever. Governor Pope-Hennessy— "beloved Hennessy" to many Creoles—had become so upset by the high European mortality which he associated with Freetown's unsanitary condition that in 1872 he urged the entire colonial government to pack up and move to the mountains. His proposal, which did not envision the separation of Europeans from Africans but simply the removal of the former to a healthier environment, was rejected, but the suggestion appeared again in later administrations. Each time the move was thought to be impractical and expensive.[49]

Ross's recommendations, however, came at a time when Europeans were building a color-bar against educated Africans in a wide range of social and economic areas. The racist reasoning of many who embraced Ross's ideas was, of course, camouflaged by the arguments pertaining to health. The Colonial Surgeon, Doctor William T. Prout, contended that not only had ill-health brought on mental and physical deterioration of many European officials, but government suffered a measurable annual monetary loss because of the illness and death of its colonial servants. Sir Charles King-Harman, the governor at the time, concurred. He too felt that if a European area were built Sierra Leone could be transformed from a "blot on the Empire" to "the bright jewel of the Crown for which its natural wealth and capabilities befit it." The initial monetary outlay would certainly pay off in the future.[50] The atmosphere in England was attuned to any suggestions which would safeguard British administrators and keep the empire running smoothly, so their arguments received a favorable hearing.

The rationale behind health segregation was based on the perceived differential tolerance to malaria between Africans and Europeans. It appeared to any observer that Europeans in the tropics seemed more susceptible to malaria than Africans. This was not so in fact but this misconception gave rise to the various myths about the Africans' superior qualities of survival in the tropics and, consequently, their preference as labor on new world plantations.

---

prepared for the African Trade Section of the Incorporated Chamber of Commerce of Liverpool in 1901, quoted in Kuczynski, *Demographic Survey*, 1: 17.

49. Dispatch of Gov. Hennessy, December 31, 1872; dispatch of Gov. Berkeley, 1873, p. 151; dispatch of Gov. Cardew, 1900, p. 95 in Governors' Dispatches to the Secretary of State, Sierra Leone Government Archives; Fyfe, *History of Sierra Leone*, pp. 394, 603.

50. See B. W. Fitch-Jones, "Hill Station," *Sierra Leone Studies*, old ser. no. 18 (November 1932), pp. 4-5.

Whereas Europeans usually came to Africa as adults and, lacking immunity, suffered the toll of the disease at this stage of their lives, Africans were first infected in childhood—a fact reflected in their high infant mortality but not generally appreciated either by Africans or Europeans at the time.[51] If African children survived the initial infection, however, subsequent attacks of the same strain of the parasite built up their tolerance. Those Africans who survived were then constant carriers of the disease parasite in their blood, and any Anopheles mosquito that bit them would become a source of infection to any person who was thereafter attacked. With the disease endemic in the African population, it would take only one hungry Anopheles to spread illness and death to newly arrived Europeans. This was what prompted the proposal that European quarters be removed—separated—out of the range and vicinity of the African "carriers."[52]

It was initially planned that segregation only take place at night for this was the time when the mosquitoes generally attacked their victims. During the day Europeans could work on their jobs in Freetown, then retreat to the hills in the evening to escape "the bite" which, according to Dr. Ross, was "as much to be dreaded as that of a mad dog."[53] The area selected was to be large enough to contain all of the European homes in the colony. It was to be surrounded by a strip of land cleared of trees, plants, and houses, about a quarter of a mile wide, or "of a width sufficient to defy the powers of flight possessed by the average mosquito." Within the segregated area itself, care was to be taken that no place existed where mosquitoes could deposit larvae. Most important of all, the number of African servants in the area during the day was to be reduced to a minimum, African children were to be totally excluded, and, during the evening and night, all non-Europeans were to be kept outside the cantonment. To prevent the encroachment of the African population, squatting, house building, and cultivation of land within one mile of the residential area was not to be allowed. Warning signs and fences were to proclaim that trespassing was forbidden.[54]

The hills surrounding Freetown were ideal for the establishment of a European enclave. The mosquito population thinned out considerably as the land became more elevated and, except for a few cultivated patches, the areas of planned settlement were free of existing African habitation. A precedent for a location in the hills, moreover, had been set years earlier when a missionary society rest house was established on Leicester Peak.

51. African infant mortality was, of course, increased by factors other than disease, such as malnutrition and bad general care.

52. Curtin, " 'White Man's Grave,' " p. 46; "Segregation in Theory and Practice," *West Africa*, July 9, 1921.

53. "Segregation in Theory and Practice," *West Africa*, July 9, 1921.

54. Kuczynski, *Demographic Survey*, 1: 305; Fitch-Jones, "Hill Station," p. 11.

Figure 5. Hill Station soon after its completion in 1904.

A site was finally chosen on a plateau about 750 feet high between the villages of Regent and Wilberforce, about four miles from the center of Freetown. Workmen began to clear the bush early in 1902 and, using prefabricated building materials sent from England, completed twenty bungalows and a hillside residence for the governor by 1904. For the sake of maximum ventilation and protection from the insects and elements, the residences uniformly faced north and were raised high above ground on columns. The area beneath the building was covered with cement to prevent the formation of Anopheles breeding pools. And, like its India counterpart, this segregated settlement became known as Hill Station.[55]

The transportation problem had yet to be considered and solved. The only way to get to the hills at the turn of the century was by walking on bush paths or by being carried in a hammock. Since Europeans living in the enclave would need to commute to Freetown and back daily, however, the success of the settlement depended on rapid, mechanized transport. In 1902, therefore, workmen began to lay track for an adhesion railroad between Freetown and Hill Station.[56] The "Mountain Railroad," as it came to be known, running on

55. The cost of the first twenty bungalows and their water supply was over £46,000. Twenty additional bungalows were built after 1911, not including those constructed by the war department and the African Cable Company. A new Governor's Lodge was built in 1928, replacing the old residence, which became part of Hill Station Hospital. European and Lebanese residential suburbs also grew up at nearby Hill Cot and Railway Hill. See Fitch-Jones, "Hill Station," pp. 13-14.

56. To countervail objections based on its expense, the colonial administration successfully argued that this railroad could be valuable for military purposes, since it passed close to the Signal Hill lookout post and would benefit Africans living near the

Figure 6. Hill Station terminal soon after its completion in 1904.

one of the steepest grades ever attempted for its type of locomotive, opened for goods and passenger traffic early in 1904. From that time until passenger service ceased in 1929, after road-building and car transport had made it a costly anachronism, the train made the round trip three or four times daily with two or three carriages separated by class.[57]

Initially, the idea of health segregation did not offend Sierra Leone Creoles. The most Europeanized and influential among them, with the best formal education and greatest intercourse with Europeans both socially and professionally, gave such a project their qualified support. These also tended to be the more vocal elements of Creole society, men who made their opinions known in the newspapers or in other public forums. Even before the Liverpool expedition's first visit to Freetown, a letter to the editor of the *Sierra Leone Times* suggested that Europeans move to the hills and that they use Freetown only for business purposes during the day. "Sierra Leone is not so bad a place," the writer concluded in a ditty:

> As some folks try to make it;
> Whether you live or whether you peg-off
> Depends upon how you take it.[58]

line as well as providing easy access to Freetown markets for the farmers from the mountain villages and the residents of the seaside villages. Sierra Leone Legislative Council Debates, November 24, 1925, in Sierra Leone Government Archives; Fitch-Jones, "Hill Station," p. 57.

57. The tracks were pulled up in 1931. Fitch-Jones, "Hill Station," pp. 5-10; Clarke, *Morning Star of Africa*, pp. 61-63.

58. Letter to the editor by "Well Wisher," *Sierra Leone Times*, November 19, 1898.

During the construction of the Mountain Railway and Hill Station and, for a time, even when they were finished, the *Sierra Leone Weekly News*, the colony's leading newspaper, viewed health segregation as a necessity for the growth and development of the country. "It is to be hoped," stated an article in that paper, "that the residence on the hills will prove . . . healthy . . . to enable European residents to have the company of their wives and their family."[59]

But the seeds of dissatisfaction with the scheme had already been sown with the initial ground-breaking. At first, only two sectors of the Creole population felt sufficiently aggrieved to grumble: those persons who owned houses and other property on the streets where the railway was being constructed and who felt that they were not being favorably compensated for their lands, and the inhabitants of the mountain villages—especially of Wilberforce—who had claims to land on the plateau where Hill Station was being built.[60] The complaints of the second group were certainly more valid—a judgment which by no means eliminated the grievances of the other sector. Official policy was based on the lack of extant title deeds and records for this area; the government thought it extremely unlikely that land so far removed from Wilberforce village would have been granted to the Liberated Africans who had settled there originally. Given the haphazard way that lands were promised and distributed to Africans in the colony at the beginning of the nineteenth century, however, this lack of documentary evidence was in fact no proof that the people had not been using it for generations. In this case, moreover, the government was particularly obtuse in not realizing that Creoles in the villages followed traditional African cultivation practices, rotating their crops and leaving some portion of land to lie fallow while recovering its fertility. Thus, while some claimants who resided on the land and regularly cultivated it did receive compensation, the government refused to pay persons who cultivated but did not live there, and did not pay anyone who claimed ownership of fallow land.[61]

The expenditure for Hill Station, a stark contrast to the paltry sums spent by the government for the physical improvement of Freetown, brought forth criticism as well. "All that fine work enables us to judge what a splendid thing the government could have made of our streets and public buildings if the inelasticity of the funds did not prevent," wrote the editor of the *Sierra Leone Times*. "Then again, it would be of no use to beautify our thoroughfares when the Segregation Party is going to live elsewhere."[62]

59. "A Review of the Year 1904," *SLWN*, January 7, 1905.

60. Editorial, *SLWN*, March 7, 1903.

61. See T. F. V. Buxton, "The Creole in West Africa," *Journal of the African Society* 12, no. 48 (July 1913): 387; Fitch-Jones, "Hill Station," pp. 10-11.

62. "One Thing and Another," *SLT*, January 16, 1900.

In addition to these grievances, the segregation plan eventually aroused a different kind of dissatisfaction among Creoles. It was less tangible, more emotional, and yet was the most indicative of the feelings of betrayal and bitterness with which Sierra Leoneans came to view Hill Station. That group of Creoles who had begun by supporting a segregated settlement in the hills for purposes of health had second thoughts. Taking into account rising European discriminative acts and racist attitudes, they reconsidered what mosquito extermination, segregation, and other hygienic arrangements might mean for the future of West Africa. Creoles feared that their "climatic estate"—the natural protection which disease and climate had given their land—would be overridden and large-scale colonization by Europeans could take place, with adverse social, economic, and political consequences.[63] Already concerned over faulty census reports which showed the Creole population to be in numerical decline, these people viewed with alarm the possibility of an influx of Europeans who would be able to compete with and displace Sierra Leoneans from all their fields of endeavor.[64] Hill Station, therefore, acquired a Machiavellian shadow, potentially providing the means to transform Sierra Leone into a settlement colony much like Kenya, Southern Rhodesia, or even the American frontier during the destruction of the American Indians. Indeed, more than forty years after Hill Station's founding, when health segregation had proven a practical failure and the number of Europeans in the colony did not appreciably increase, Creoles continued to look on this Eruopean reservation with suspicion.[65]

It did not take long, furthermore, for Hill Station's iniquities to surface. A mentality which considered separating groups according to race for one purpose, no matter how rationally conceived, would not hesitate to separate these groups for other purposes as well. Accordingly, socializing between Europeans and Creoles in Hill Station, on other than a master-servant basis, was nonexistent in all the facilities associated with the European enclave. Hill Station Club, for instance, used for lesiure largely during the daylight hours, did not darken its membership list by a single black face.[66] The Mountain Railway similarly discriminated against Africans. J. A. Fitz-John, the nimble-witted Creole editor of the *Sierra Leone Times*, in his typical caustic manner, described the racial segregation which took place at the inauguration of the track. The railway had made two inaugural trips: one especially for Euro-

63. "The Future of Africa," August 18, 1900; "When Sierra Leone Ceases To Be British—Another View," October 12, 1901; Editorial, September 28, 1901, *SLWN*.

64. For example, see "One Thing and Another," *SLT*, June 24, 1893, August 28, 1897; letter to the editor by Abdul Mortales, January 8, 1898; editorial, January 4, 1902, *SLWN*.

65. Article by Thomas Decker, *Daily Guardian* (Freetown), March 8, 1945.

66. See Roy Lewis, *Sierra Leone* (London, 1954), p. 13.

Figure 7. Reception at the governor's residence in the first decade of the twentieth century. Tower Hill Barracks is in the background. While Africans were still invited, there were noticeably fewer present as racial discrimination heightened in official British colonial policy. (From the albums of James Carmichael Smith, post-master general of Sierra Leone, 1900-1911, in Royal Commonwealth Society, London.)

peans—the "Segregation Party"—in which, according to Fitz-John, "there was nothing tawney [*sic*] to come between the wind and the divinity of anyone of the party—not even the Mayor," who, at this time, was C. E. Wright, a Creole; the other trip was "exclusively for natives." "Let us trust," Fitz-John commented, "that the authorities fumigated the carriages afterwards, in order to run no risks."[67] Sixteen years later this color bar still continued, its strength undiminished. One persistant complaint was that the train's "official" coach was usually reserved for Europeans, whether they were "officials" in the true sense of the word or not, while Africans, whatever their status, had to ride in the other carriages.[68] Hill Station, moreover, gave birth to a series of little "suburbs"—Hill Cot, Railway Hill, Regent Road—each exclusive to Europeans, in practice if not by edict. There, no pretense of segregation for purposes of health was made; it was pure and simple voluntary separation from the African community in Freetown. And while settlement in these areas might have been motivated by conscious racism in only a minority of cases, Creoles could not but resent the trend by which Europeans were insulating themselves as if disdainful of Freetown and its inhabitants.[69]

Judging from its overall effectiveness, the Hill Station complex was more harmful to the relationship between Creoles and Britons than it was influential in keeping Europeans healthy. Interracial social events in Freetown itself also became less common. The Freetown press in the first two decades

67. "One Thing and Another," *SLT*, January 2, 1904.

68. "Things We Want To Know," *Colonial and Provincial Reporter* (Freetown), March 13, 1920.

69. Fitch-Jones, "Hill Station," pp. 13-14.

of the twentieth century mentioned relatively few "at homes," soirées, balls, or other entertainments where the Creole and European communities could mix informally. European mortality, to be sure, did decrease in Sierra Leone, but it had already begun to do so in the last years of the nineteenth century thanks to better medical care, advancements in the treatment of tropical diseases, and improved sanitary measures. No existing statistical evidence indicates that Hill Station was in any way involved.[70] Indeed, Hill Station can be considered a failure in accomplishing its goal. The colonial government miscarried miserably in bringing private companies to the enclave. The African Cable Company was the only one to build a bungalow on the Hill; a mere 1 percent of nonofficial European residents lived there in 1913. Among government officials recruiting was not much more successful. No more than one-quarter of their total contingent lived at Hill Station nine years after it had been started. Anopheles mosquitoes, furthermore, managed to breed on the Hill, and the Europeans who lived there suffered the discomforts of malaria almost as though the segregated enclave had never been built. In 1914, for example, ten of forty-eight government officials residing at the Station came down with malaria.[71]

The entire scheme, in fact, was misconceived from the beginning. Segregation for health purposes had to be all or nothing. But the colonial situation made it impossible to bring about the complete withdrawal of the European community into truly antiseptic sectors. Europeans were in West Africa to work, either privately or for the government, and this made contact with Africans necessary. They had to leave their quarters, go up-country or to Freetown to carry out business or government transactions, and, occasionally, returned to Hill Station with malaria. So long as mosquitoes were not totally eliminated everywhere, these Europeans then became the carriers who infected other inhabitants on the Hill, destroying whatever advantages segregation might have offered. Similarly, by establishing the practice of periodically keeping African servants overnight, a flagrant infraction of the rules of health segregation, Europeans violated the very reason for Hill Station. In spite of Hill Station, therefore, European interaction with Africans was self-perpetuating.

Ironically, Ronald Ross, the man who indirectly had provided the justification for the separation of the races in Sierra Leone with his discoveries about malaria, changed his views about health segregation later in life. He realized that this type of separation protected only one section of the public and came to feel that money would have been better spent to protect the entire population.[72] As the scheme proved imperfect, it did not give potential

70. Kuczynski, *Demographic Survey*, 1: 17-18, 304.
71. Ibid.; Fyfe, *History of Sierra Leone*, pp. 610-611.
72. Editorial, *Aurora* (Freetown), July 21, 1921.

propagandists in Britain an opportunity to advertise it and entice the would-be settlers whose appearance in Sierra Leone the Creoles feared. The European minority remained small, and the complexities of colonial administration and business demanded the participation of educated Africans. Its multiple failure notwithstanding, Hill Station nevertheless continued to exist as a limited white preserve—the most visible manifestation of Britain's rejection of the Creoles. High above Freetown, it stood as a monument to the deterioration of the British experiment in philanthropy and racial equality which had led to the original founding of Sierra Leone.

In the mercantile field, the old established relationships between Sierra Leoneans and Europeans were also changing rapidly. Formerly, European firms had been wholesalers, satisfied to sell imported goods still in original packing to African middlemen—of whom many were Creoles—and to buy from them native produce for shipment to Europe and America. They dealt in large quantities, hardly ever broke bulk, and left the retailing to Creoles. European firms, however, gradually assumed the role of retailers as well as wholesalers. This changeover, to be sure, had little if anything to do with an increase in racial prejudice on the part of European firms. Rather, merchants were loathe to see the healthy profits being reaped by middlemen, and, attempting to outstrip competition, decided to streamline their commercial practices to capture a wider market. The Creole intermediaries were badly hit.

The delineation of Anglo-French boundaries between the areas that became the Sierra Leone Protectorate and French Guinea in 1895 further damaged Creole commercial interests. Because of unfavorable export tariffs, caravans from the far interior carrying a rich trade in ivory tusks, raw gold, bullocks, and sheep were diverted from Freetown and found their way up the coast to Conakry and other French ports, resulting in a general decline in revenue for Sierra Leone. The major effect of this was to intensify the feeling among Sierra Leoneans that the British were not "doing right" by them economically: first by standing back while European merchants displaced Africans and prevented their financial advancement, and, second, by ceding the best portions of the hinterland to France.[73]

These commercial setbacks, moreover, reinforced the already strong preferences Creoles possessed for white collar occupations and for professional careers in the legal and medical fields. In the past, Liberated Africans and settlers who had become financially successful as merchants and traders had encouraged their sons to seek an education, preferably in Britain, which would

73. T. J. Alldridge, *A Transformed Colony* . . . (London, 1910), pp. 73-74; A. Howard, "Economic History," in J. I. Clarke, *Sierra Leone in Maps* (London, 1966); "One Thing and Another," April 14, 1894; editorial, February 9, 1895, *SLT*.

prepare them for more prestigious occupations. The children came to act as status symbols for the parents. As Arthur Porter has pointed out, the merchants not only sought to give more validity to their own social position but also hoped that their children, possessing an English degree and entering occupations highly valued by Europeans, would thereby attain "that component of upper class status" which their parents had been unable to reach.[74] In the last decades of the nineteenth century, however, not only were the avenues for individual Creole enterprise in the mercantile field fast closing but, in the professional and white collar occupations as well, changing European attitudes led to the erection of barriers for Sierra Leoneans where they had never existed before.

In the 1890s a great deal of dissatisfaction arose among educated Creoles who felt that they were being discriminated against in civil service appointments, promotions, and salaries. They wanted the establishment of a system of salary increases based on a graduated scale and on seniority, and sought a fixed method whereby top grade vacancies would be filled from the ranks of those "already in the Service" while lower rank vacancies would be filled through recruitment.[75] During the administration of Governor Frederick Cardew in particular, Creoles became extremely outspoken regarding civil service practices. Writing that "the employment of educated Natives is an eyesore to Governor Cardew," the *Sierra Leone Times* criticized Cardew's handling of the service, and his recruitment of Europeans at high pay with housing and rent allowances, while successful Creole candidates received salaries that were so piteously low that they amounted to less than those received by boatmen, Survey Yard laborers, or low-ranking constables. Further, when African subordinates asked for a salary increase they were told that the financial condition of the colony did not permit such action. The *Sierra Leone Times* postulated that these practices brought on "the suspicion that merits and demerits have little or no influence over racial prejudice, engendered in the swamps of Zululand and elsewhere."[76] Sierra Leoneans were justified in making some of these charges, but not unequivocably so. It was long-standing policy of British colonial governments to give housing allowances and higher salaries to European colonial servants while not doing the same for Africans. The rationale was that the Europeans not only had to keep up their living standards in the colonies, but also often had to support families back in Britain. Creole employees, on the other hand, had but a single household to maintain—in Sierra Leone. What the European officials who set the dual salary scale were unable or unwilling to understand was that

74. Porter, *Creoledom*, pp. 113-115.
75. *SLT*, April 15 and 22, 1893.
76. "On Educated Africans," July 25, 1896; "The State of the Colony, Article No. 4," July 18, 1896, *SLT*.

"white-collar" Creoles were usually responsible for their own immediate families plus an extended range of relatives, near-relatives, and wards who looked to them for sustenance, school fees, and other financial support—outlays which drained an already meager paycheck.

A definite tendency existed in Cardew's administration to "Europeanize" the civil service by cutting back reliance on Creole staff. After the protectorate was established and after the Hut Tax War of 1898, for instance, official opinion was set against using Sierra Leoneans as district commissioners in the up-country.[77] The number of Europeans in Sierra Leone colony grew in the last decade of the nineteenth century, from 210 in 1891 to 351 in 1901, as a result of the expansion of business and trade, to be sure, and as an effect of the "Europeanization" effort.[78] This tendency was tempered only by the fact that a complete takeover by Europeans in all spheres of the administration—the virtual transformation of Sierra Leone into a European settlement colony—would have been tremendously expensive and would have become even more so with the establishment of the protectorate, the railway, and an increasing number of public works projects. No matter how much British attitudes about the capabilities of Africans changed, racism carried to its ultimate logical conclusion—the separation of the races—was costly and conflicted with the long-established British tradition of keeping a tight rein on colonial expenditures. Creoles therefore continued to hold the majority of the civil service positions and were even appointed to some of the top ranks. This, however, in no way decreased their feeling that the old order had changed.[79]

Discrimination in the government medical service, even though affecting only a few Creoles directly, was of critical symbolic value to all those who were concerned with the professions as a means of upward social mobility and superior status, which meant the most educated and vocal members of Creole society. In the past, the colonial medical service had been one vehicle which guaranteed social recognition and was open to any African who had attended British medical schools and received his degree. Throughout a great part of the nineteenth century, African doctors had served on a basis of equality with European medical men in the government service. William Broughton Davies and James Africanus Beale Horton, both sons of Liberated Africans, were among the best known of many Creoles doing outstanding

77. C.O. 267/422, 22 July 1895; C.O. 267/427, 6 November 1896; J. D. Hargreaves, "The Establishment of the Sierra Leone Protectorate," *Cambridge Historical Journal* 12 (1956): 64.

78. Sierra Leone Census Report, 1891 and 1901, in Sierra Leone Collection; Fyfe, *History of Sierra Leone*, p. 611.

79. Fyfe, *History of Sierra Leone*, pp. 357-358; Gov. Cardew, September 23, 1896, minute; Gov. Cardew, dispatches nos. 1, 116, 352, in 1896 Letter Book, Sierra Leone Government Archives.

work and achieving high rank in the medical service in Sierra Leone and other parts of British West Africa.[80] By the end of the nineteenth century, however, the medical service of the several West African colonies was gradually being converted into an all-European preserve.

In 1901 a committee of the British medical service, appointed originally to investigate a scheme for the amalgamation of the medical services for the various West African colonies, decided in addition to consider the question of the *employment* of persons native to West Africa and India as medical officers and, in its report, advised strongly against it. According to the committee, the British government administering the colonies in West Africa was duty bound "to provide only the best medical assistance for their European employees, especially when [European women were] stationed in the bush or at out-stations." Except in very rare instances, however, the members of the committee did not think that such assistance could be supplied by non-European doctors because they neither possessed the confidence of European patients on the coast nor were they professionally on a par with European doctors. This judgment would have been more believable had it not been for the fact that African doctors studied and received their degrees in Britain, at the same or superior institutions than their European counterparts, and that a respectable percentage of them graduated with honors. Drs. Horton, Robert Smith, Michael Lewis Jarrett, Joseph Spilsbury Smith, Obadiah Johnson, C. J. Lumpkin, John Randall, Tom Bishop, Albert Whiggs Easmon, and John Scotland had done part or all of their medical training at Edinburgh; J. F. Easmon won six gold medals and silver medals in his last year of study.[81] Clearly the committee report was not based on an objective evaluation of the credentials and abilities of the African doctors but was a reflection of the medical service's increasing color-bar mentality. Thus the report continued:

> Social conditions, particularly in Southern Nigeria, where European officers live together and have their meals in common under the "mess system," and in Northern Nigeria, where a large proportion of the European staff consist of officers of the regular army, make it extremely undesirable to introduce native medical officers into those Protectorates. They have already been tried in Southern Nigeria without success.
>
> It is possible that in a few isolated cases, e.g., at hospitals where patients are always, or practically always, natives, it may be desirable to employ a native doctor, but such cases may be regarded as exceptional. . . .

80. See Easmon, "Sierra Leone Doctors," pp. 81-96.
81. Ibid., pp. 82-83.

The Committee are certainly of the opinion that, if natives either of West Africa or of India are employed, they should be put in a separate roster, that they should not be employed on military expeditions, and that European officers should in no circumstances be placed under their orders.[82]

Drawing upon witnesses with local experience in Africa and offering the "Indian Subordinate Medical Service" as an example of a medical corps that was racially segregated, the committee proposed that nonwhite West African doctors be made subaltern to Europeans and that they be employed in a medical service of lower rank.[83]

Pressured by recruiting difficulties and the need for more doctors in West Africa and convinced that only a segregated medical service would attract good doctors from England, the Colonial Office eventually accepted the committee's recommendations.[84] A West African Medical Staff was formed whose membership requirements stated that "candidates must be of European parentage" and in a later amendment also "British subjects." A subordinate category was established for African doctors employed in government service—that of Native Medical Officers—whose senior member would be definition rank below the most junior member of the all-white West African Medical Staff. Salaries, of course, which in the past had been set according to a color-blind scale, were now to be lower for Africans.[85]

Creoles did not react immediately. The changes were not well-publicized in Sierra Leone and, initially, affected few people. Although the Legislative Council, which contained some Creole "unofficial" members, briefly discussed the issue in 1902, soon after the newly remodeled West African Medical Staff came into existence,[86] the press was silent. Only in 1905 did

82. The British Medical Association to the Colonial Office, December 10, 1901, in C.O. 879/99, 918, 1901-1908.

83. Great Britain, Parliament, *Parliamentary Papers*, vol. 61 (House of Commons and Command, 1909), "Report of the Departmental Committee appointed by the Secretary of State for the Colonies to enquire into the West African Medical Staff," July 1909, p. 715, par. 53.

84. Fyfe, *History of Sierra Leone*, p. 614. In 1902-1903 the University of Edinburgh made strong protests to the effect that a number of West African doctors had been certified by this institution and that to discriminate against these men as was planned was, in fact, an attack on the accreditation of the university.

85. Easmon, "Sierra Leone Doctors," p. 86. Thus men like Dr. William Awuner-Renner, who had received an M.D. (Brux) "avec la grande distinction" and had served as Assistant Colonial Surgeon, were excluded from the West African Medical Staff. To be sure, these exclusions affected others than Sierra Leoneans. Doctors like Quartey-Papafio in the Gold Coast and African medical officers from Lagos also fell victim to this reorganization of the medical service. See C.O. 879/99, 918, 1901-1908.

86. Sierra Leone Legislative Council Debates, October 21, 1902.

the *Sierra Leone Weekly News* reprint an article that had appeared in *West Africa*, written by a "well known West African" and drawing attention to the inequities and disadvantages that existed for Africans in the segregated version of the West African Medical Staff.[87] There was still little rancor in the tone of this article. The author gave the British public the benefit of his doubt, implying that racially motivated schemes of this sort were unsportsmanlike and, as such, very un-English.[88] But four years later, in 1909, after a White Paper was published to explain the changes in the medical service to the public, the tone of the Sierra Leone press changed considerably. An editorial in the *Sierra Leone Weekly News* clearly reflected the degree to which the medical service discrimination deviated from the Creole image of their relationship with Britain. According to the editorial, this relationship had been premised on Creole eligibility to fill offices and receive emoluments under the Crown according to their "education, ability, and integrity"; now race was the only qualification. This was unfair, especially since Creole doctors were as well trained as their European counterparts. "We see many signs," the editorial concluded,

> ... which seem to indicate what we must describe as a nefarious intention on the part of many Europeans serving on the W. Coast of Africa to lose no opportunity of creating the impression upon the minds of the British public, that Creoles—educated Africans— can never become qualified to occupy the superior, highly paid, or governing position in any one of the Governing Departments, and that, therefore, such positions should be reserved exclusively for Europeans . . . . The Foundation of the nefarious intention is Race-Prejudice, which is against all human reason.[89]

By 1909 the protests were too late. Racial separation in the medical service had become a fact long before the White Paper was published. In 1912 all but seven out of some two hundred medical men employed in the West Africa Medical Staff were white, in spite of the fact that many Africans were still trained in English medical schools.[90] Tardily, Creoles sought action, contacted the Aborigines Protection Society in England, and won the sympathies of some members of Parliament, but to no avail.[91] For the most

87. *SLWN*, June 10, 1905, reprinted from *West Africa*, May 6, 1905.

88. The writer concluded that "the conversion of the Medical Service of the several West African colonies, which was formerly open to British subjects of any nationality, into an European preserve or monopoly does not seem to be conducive to the best interests of the colonies . . . ." Ibid.

89. *SLWN*, October 30, November 6, 1909.

90. Buxton, "The Creole in West Africa," p. 389.

91. "West African Medical Men: 1912, Dr. Easmon's Case," in Aborigines Rights Protection Society Papers, Mss British Empire, S22, vol. G248, Rhodes House Library, Oxford.

Westernized Creoles, this was but another indication that the good old days were over. The means to advancement were being closed even to those with years of education and with qualifications matching those of any European. In total, the crescendo of rebuffs and insults could not but leave Creoles with a feeling of betrayal and a touch of bitterness. "In the days of our good Queen Mother Victoria," read an editorial in the *Colony and Provinical Reporter*,

> . . . we were accustomed to fairness in her dealing with her subjects. It was an accepted axiom in the West African Colonies that every subject of her late Majesty . . . , be he of whatever nationality or creed, provided he was loyal and fit, might aim at any position under her gracious rule. But, we have got into the age of Imperialism—Chamberlain Imperialism—in which coloured races have no part. Since the good Queen died, coloured races, especially West Africans, have been gradually driven to the wall.[92]

92. *Colony and Provincial Reporter*, September 14, 1911.

Chapter THREE
Creoles and Up-Countrymen: The Gulf

The beginnings of this Colony of Sierra Leone appear to be on all fours with the beginnings of Canaan or Palestine with the Jews in possession.

The Timanees who are now rushing into the Colony and . . . say that the Colony is theirs by right, were thrust out more than one hundred years ago and our ancestors were put in possession by God through the valour and philanthropy of the British Nation.

And for certain the thought of God was, not that the offsprings of these ancestors of ours should be elbowed out in time by a pagan population but that they should always be in the ascendant, being God's light-bringers and His powerful instrument for the regeneration and uplifting of those who are in darkness. If we have forgotten this we who are called "Creoles" have quite forgotten or chosen to ignore the purpose of God for settling us in this land which in very truth is a land flowing with milk and honey.

Sierra Leone Weekly News, quoted in *West Africa*, April 30, 1938

The Molding of an Attitude

The Sierra Leone peninsula is only twenty-five miles long and ten miles wide. These dimensions alone afford sufficient contrast to the much greater area of land which is still commonly called the "up-country," and to which the peninsula connects in appendage-like manner.[1] But nature, almost as if to emphasize the differences between the two, erected physical barriers dividing the land within itself. Mountains on the peninsula, thickly dressed in rain-

---

1. See A. M. Howard, "Administrative Boundary Changes," in *Sierra Leone in Maps*, ed. Clarke, pp. 30, 31.

forest greenery, rise abruptly from the sea to nearly 3000 feet and, like green walls, impede movement to and from the inland coastal plain. Dangerous ravines and abyss-like dry moats act as a second line of resistance which, when reinforced by obstacles inherent in mangrove and sedge swamps and seasonally flooded grasslands, cut off the peninsula from its hinterland. Indeed, before railway engineering conquered topography in the first decade of the twentieth century, land communication between the peninsula and the hinterland was so difficult that most travel took place on water. The peninsula was like an island, vulnerable by sea, yet apart and distinct from the rest of its surroundings.

Freetown, lying at the northern end of the peninsula at the base of the Lion Mountains, between them and the ocean-like estuary of the Sierra Leone River, accented the separation between the peninsula and the up-country. Endowed with one of the finest harbors in the world, its outlook was that of a coastal town—toward the Atlantic Ocean rather than the hinterland. Geography, in this case, underscores a theme which runs throughout the history of Sierra Leone: the gulf, first physical and later psychological and cultural, between the African peoples of the interior and the Creoles on the peninsula.

Even though they were racially akin to the local inhabitants, the ancestors of the Creoles were "settlers" in an alien land—men and women who had colonized an area already occupied by indigenous peoples. As such, they faced a double challenge: to interact successfully both with the British, under whose protection and aegis they lived, and with the Timne, Mende, Sherbro, and other peoples who were their neighbors in the peninsula and its hinterland.

Characteristically, in settlement colonies where Europeans lived as racial and cultural minorities, their fear of being overwhelmed by indigenous peoples was complicated by xenophobia. The histories of South Africa, Rhodesia, and Kenya—the so-called "white settlement colonies"—contain numerous illustrations of this phenomenon. To protect their community from real or imagined dangers posed by the nonwhite peoples among whom they lived, the European settlers retrenched, withdrawing into mental and physical laagers which they hoped to keep inviolate through color bars and actual physical segregation. In doing this, the xenophobia based on racial differences tended to be strengthened. Once having withdrawn, it became easier for the Europeans to eliminate from their minds the individual variations among indigenous people and to see them collectively in terms of dehumanized stereotypes such as the "Kaffir Hordes" or the "Black Menace." Furthermore, needing to rationalize their behavior toward the people whom they had colonized and, on occasion, enslaved, these Europeans generalized about the barbarity of their neighbors, about their treachery, cruelty, brutishness, and inferior mental capabilities.

Unlike the European colonists in southern and eastern Africa, however, the ancestors of the Creoles were racially indistinct from the people among whom they had settled. Being as black as their neighbors, they need certainly not have feared or despised them on the basis of physical differences. And yet the attitudes of these settlers and their Creole descendants toward "upcountry" Africans gradually became comparable with that of Europeans to nonwhites in the "white settlement colonies." Sierra Leone literature of the later nineteenth century yields many illustrative examples.[2]

Dr. James Africanus Beale Horton, the Creole son of a Recaptive Ibo carpenter who had lived in Gloucester village near Freetown, was one of the first Sierra Leoneans to be trained and to qualify in England as a doctor. He was a man of many interests, a prolific writer who published books and pamphlets on topics ranging from tropical medicine, his specialty, to the political condition of the British settlements in West Africa, his preoccupation. His first book, based on his Cambridge University thesis, appeared when he was twenty-four.[3] He was a member of the Royal College of Surgeons and often served in positions of great responsibility in connection with British military and colonial departments. He was appointed civil commandant at posts in the Gambia and Gold Coast and, upon his retirement in 1880, he had reached the rank of surgeon major.[4] In spite of his outstanding accomplishments—his brilliance as a medical man, his literary ability, and his passionate desire to erase European misconceptions about Africa and Africans—Horton was typical of his fellow Creoles in one respect: he was guilty of drawing stereotyped and unflattering descriptions of the peoples from Sierra Leone's hinterland. Horton described the Timne people as

> ... somewhat an industrious race .... They are by no means speculative .... When they land at Freetown they seem to be great cowards; a little boy of ten years of age would frighten and drive away the men. Here [in Freetown] they are peaceful, quiet, dirty in their dress and person, and walk about in Indian file. ...
> As soon as they leave they become cruel and domineering. ...
> Whilst in their country they are very treacherous, and for the least provocation they would fall on the stores of the trader and

2. For instance, see *SLT*, particularly the "One Thing and Another" column, in the decade prior to the Hut Tax War of 1898.

3. J. A. B. Horton, *The Medical Topography of the West Coast of Africa* (London, 1859).

4. *CMS Record*, 1856, p. 26; *West African Reporter*, January 15, 1881, October 20, 1883; *Methodist Herald*, October 26, 1883, obit.; *Freetown Express*, October 19, 1883; Dr. Davidson Nicol, principal of Fourah Bay College, public lecture on Horton given at the college, Freetown, February 7, 1966. For the best biography of Horton see Christopher Fyfe, *Africanus Horton, West African Scientist and Patriot* (New York, 1972).

pillage them of every article. They are excessively cruel in their treatment of one another. . . . In war they are great cowards, but extremely cruel . . . . Christianity makes but little progress among them; they are hardy, and incapable of an advancing civilizing progression.[5]

The Susu and Mende people Horton described as "allied nations to the Timnehs, but . . . very warlike and troublesome . . . . Attempts at civilizing them have hitherto failed, so that the saying has become proverbial, 'Teach a Korsor [Mende] man howsoever you like, he will ultimately return to the bush.' "[6]

Other Creole writings equalled Horton's in their unfavorable descriptions of up-countrymen. A. B. C. Sibthorpe, a teacher, historian, and eccentric-about-town, wrote about hinterland Africans in his *Geography of the Surrounding Territories of Sierra Leone*.[7] He saw the Yonni as "warlike and cruel"; the Susu as "lazy and proud," to whom begging was no disgrace; the Timne as "stupidly shrewd"; the Mende as "decisive," taking "knowledge by intuition"; and the Limba as "only half-man from long servitude."[8] Likewise, James A. Fitz-John, who later became editor of the influential *Sierra Leone Times*, won a 17s. 6d. first prize in 1876 from *The Independent* for his essay "Our Native Manners and Customs," which contained some fascinating stereotypes about up-countrymen. In it he spoke about the "shrewd and inquisitive Mandingoes," the "treacherous and greedy Foulahs," the "brutal and bragging Kossohs [Mende]," "the clean though rascally Sossoss," and the "indolent and much abused Timnees."[9] Even J. Augustus Cole, a Creole who became firmly convinced that the future of Africa lay with the interior and not with the Europeanized coastal settlements like Freetown, referred to up-countrymen as "barbarous and wild, ungodly, superstitious, and wicked."[10] The stereotype developed to the extent that up-country names such as "Sorie" and "Fatimatah" acquired pejorative implications and were used in the press or in everyday conversations as general epithets for non-Creole,

5. J. A. B. Horton, *West African Countries and Peoples, British and Native. With the requirements necessary for establishing that self government recommended by the Committee of the House of Commons, 1865; and a Vindication of the African Race* (London, 1868), p. 93.

6. Ibid., p. 94.

7. A. B. C. Sibthorpe, *The Geography of the Surrounding Territories of Sierra Leone* (London, 1892).

8. Ibid., pp. 8, 34.

9. *The Independent*, 1876. Fitz-John continued to hold a derisive view of up-countrymen throughout his life and frequently used the *Sierra Leone Times* to express it.

10. J. A. Cole, *The Interior of Sierra Leone, West Africa; What Can It Teach Us?* (Dayton, Ohio, 1887), p. 7, passim.

hinterland Africans.[11] The term "aborigine," with all of its connotations of primitiveness and lack of sophistication, was similarly and frequently used by Creoles to describe up-countrymen and to emphasize the cultural differences between themselves and the original inhabitants of the land.

Why did Creoles fall prey to the mentality associated with white settlement colonies? Why did they come to disparage non-Europeanized Africans? How did the gulf between themselves and up-countrymen develop?

The ancestors of the Creoles and the Africans indigenous to Sierra Leone were usually ethnically unrelated and, from the beginning, did not mix freely with each other. Exceptions existed of course. Some of the Liberated Africans belonged to ethnic groups living in the hinterland of Sierra Leone but, upon their release in Freetown, made their way back to their homes as soon as possible.[12]

The Nova Scotians, Maroons, and Black-Poor from Europe and America were usually Christian, literate, and conversant with Western ways. They wore European-style clothing, built European-style houses, and identified with the British, who had brought them to Africa. For the most part they had been long removed from traditional African life by the time of their arrival in Sierra Leone and made little effort to bridge the gap which existed between themselves and the indigenous people.

The Liberated Africans, on the other hand, upon first landing in Sierra Leone, did not find the cultural practices among up-country peoples entirely unfamiliar. Most of the Recaptives had originated in West Africa and had not been removed from their traditional environment long enough to forget what it had been like. In spite of the diversity of languages which were spoken in this part of the continent, both the religious beliefs and certain of their political and social practices were comparable, if not interchangeable, with those of the Sierra Leone up-countrymen. The Yoruba, Ibo, and Ewe, for example, from whom many of the ex-slaves descended, like the indigenous Mende and Timne, all believed in a supreme God who created the world and then retired from it, in ancestral spirits who determined the fortunes of the individual and his lineage, and in a series of personal religious rites, similar in their purpose and execution, connected with birth, puberty, marriage, and burial.[13] Eventually, however, after their conversion to Christianity and their

11. See "One Thing and Another," SLT, February 22, 1896, for an example.

12. Jean Herskovits Kopytoff, A Preface to Modern Nigeria: The "Sierra Leonians" in Yoruba, 1830-1890 (Madison, Wis., 1966), is the best for Sierra Leonean emigration.

13. See Parrinder, West African Religion; M. McCulloch, The Peoples of Sierra Leone, Ethnographic Survey of Africa, Western Africa; pt. 2 (London, 1964), pp. 39-46, 70-74; Philip D. Curtin and Jan Vansina, "Sources of the Nineteenth Century Atlantic Slave Trade," Journal of African History 5, no. 2 (1964): 185-208.

education along European lines, the Liberated Africans also came to see themselves as different from up-countrymen. Like the Nova Scotians, Maroons, and Black-Poor who had preceded them and had established the standards for cultural acceptability, they became increasingly concerned with the projection and maintenance of their image as "civilized" Africans. For this reason they were careful not to appear to condone practices in public which would permit Europeans to include them among the "barbarians."

The Creoles, descending from marriages between the various settler groups, continued in this tradition. "Our claims to be regarded as a civilized community," stated an editorial in the *Sierra Leone Times*, "must be weak, untenable, and even ridiculous, so long as we continue to tolerate and participate in practices which cannot be reconciled to any of the beliefs, tenets, or principles which we profess to hold as civilized Christians."[14]

At first, as if defensively, Creoles attacked "uncivilized" practices within their own group. They assailed "superstition," "witchcraft," "idolatry," belief in "fetishes" and magical medicines—any religious conduct which suggested heathenism. They decried "barbaric" social customs—drumming and dancing in abandon, nudity, "howling" and shaking at wakes, polygyny, and membership in secret societies like Bundu and Agugu.[15] In proportion to their Europeanization and acceptance of an ethos in which social mobility depended on a successful imitation of Western culture, the now Christian, missionary-influenced Creoles came to look upon up-countrymen as unregenerated models of themselves—reminders of a past which they had been taught to abhor as primitive and undesirable. The latter were seen to possess customs which were not only inherently "evil" but which, like a disease, infected the "weakest" and least acculturated members of Creole society, leading them to backslide from Christ to the Devil. "Having no religion of their own," wrote the editor of the *Sierra Leone Times*, "they help us to spoil ours, and to rob us of the only crown we had."[16] Furthermore, taught by philanthropists and missionaries that they were black agents of "Christian

14. Editorial, *SLT*, December 17, 1898.
15. W. A. B. Johnson, *A Memoir of the Rev. W. A. B. Johnson, 1816-1823* (London, 1852), pp. 214-216; "The Life and Experience of Joseph Booth May, by himself"; Moses Renner, "The Best Means of Improving the Social and Industrial Conditions of Sierra Leone," Sierra Leone, 1850, in Sierra Leone Box, 1845-1866, Methodist Missionary Archives; News, February 4, 1882; editorial, February 11, 1882, *West African Reporter*; editorial, June 30, 1894; "Varia," August 17, 1895; "Public Nuisances," February 29, 1896; "Our Native Manners and Customs," January 23, 1897; "Freetown Day by Day," December 18, 1897; "Bondohism," March 18, 1899; editorial and "One Thing and Another," October 28, 1899, *SLT*; editorial, September 13, 1884; letters to the editor, September 20, 1884; "My View of Things," March 5, 1887; "Superstition in Freetown," November 23, 1889; "Passing Topics," September 27, 1890, *SLWN*.
16. "One Thing and Another," *SLT*, May 25, 1895.

civilization" in "heathen Africa," Creoles gladly accepted the designation as a "Chosen People"—a "light unto the Gentiles"—better than the indigenous Africans who lived in darkness and superstition. It was common for Creoles to refer to the up-countrymen as the "Unto Whom"—pagans "unto whom God swore in his wrath, that they should not enter in his rest."[17] In spite of the fact that Christian Sierra Leoneans retained certain traditional rituals such as the *awujoh*, they were entirely sincere when, in church, they sang that "the heathen in his blindness bows down to wood and stone."[18]

Although they envisioned themselves as "civilizing" agents, charged with bringing "light into the darkness" of the interior, educated Creoles often directed their thoughts and energies not to the hinterland of Sierra Leone but overseas, either to England or to other places in Africa. A man who signed his articles in the *Sierra Leone Weekly News* with the pseudonym "Czar," for example, coined the terms "Little Freetonians" and "Greater Sierra Leoneans" to illustrate this Creole propensity. Accordingly, "Little Freetonians" were defined as "the pigmy-souled, little-minded, stay-at-home, conservative folks" while "Greater Sierra Leoneans" went "over the seas to build up the reputation" of Sierra Leone and to undertake "the noble task of assisting the Westerner in his grand work of reformation and civilization" as "the principal agents in the transformation from wildness and savagery to civilization and religion [of] such large areas as the Gambia down to Sokoto."[19] Editorials in the Freetown press occasionally boasted about Creole involvement and interest abroad. In one of their frequent moments of introspection, for instance, Sierra Leoneans examined their own role in the development of West Africa and found it favorable. "All along the West Coast," declared an 1890 editorial in the *Sierra Leone Weekly News*,

> . . . the influence of this Colony is felt and recognized. The man from Sierra Leone, bent on improving his condition, adventures whereever he has reasons to believe that his labour, intellectual or manual, his intelligence and enterprising spirit, may meet with encouraging remunerations. He has left his footprints in the Sands of Senegal. He dips his hands into the waters of the Congo. He followed in the train . . . to the conquest of Ashantiland. He colonises Lagos and makes it a prosperous settlement. He was present at all the explorations of the Niger from the earliest. He has largely contributed to the development of the Niger trade. The Niger Mission—its conquest, . . . its conversions, are mainly his work.[20]

17. Nicolls, "Effects of Western Education," p. 7.
18. Max Gorvie, *Old and New in Sierra Leone* (London, 1945), p. 74.
19. Article by "Czar (or Floode)," *SLWN*, August 5, 1905.
20. "The Sierra Leonean Abroad," *SLWN*, November 15, 1890.

Ironically many Creoles, especially the trend-setting and articulate upper classes, sophisticated in their awareness of Britain and other parts of Africa, were sadly lacking in knowledge about the hinterland of Sierra Leone, its geography, character, resources, and the ways and behavior of its native peoples. The European-oriented educational experience which the Creoles underwent in Sierra Leone was partly to blame. J. A. Fitz-John related how he, as a young student, could answer extremely detailed questions about the geography of Europe but failed miserably when asked to identify the Rokel River—one of the main bodies of water flowing from up-country into the Sierra Leone River northeast of Freetown.[21] But the deficiency could be explained in other ways as well. "Our knowledge of this area [the up-country]," stated an editorial in the *Sierra Leone Weekly News*, "has until recent years, unfortunately, been very limited, and even at present the expense and difficulty incidental to traveling has been a barrier to our obtaining that wide knowledge which we should have of it."[22] Sir Samuel Lewis, successful lawyer, member of the Legislative Council, mayor of Freetown, and the first African to be knighted, observed that most Sierra Leoneans based their opinions about the hinterland and its inhabitants on secondhand information, reports supplied by travelers and traders. In a speech to the Legislative Council, he pointed to the crux of the problem—the lack of inexpensive and quick communication between the colony and the interior:

> Speaking on behalf of the intelligent natives of the Colony whom the duties of life compel to remain day after day in the immediate neighbourhood, where they obtain their means of livelihood, it would be folly . . . in the absence of the means of quick transit, to explore the interior of their own country either for pleasure or profit when in the present state of travel the expense for a single individual would be counted by tens if not hundreds of pounds.[23]

Communication between the colony and the hinterland remained deficient well into the twentieth century. The rivers, during the dry season when they were low enough to be navigable, and those bush paths wide enough for hammock transport were the only "roads" between the peninsula and the interior throughout most of the previous century.[24] The greatest improve-

21. *SLT*, March 1, 1904; Fyfe, *History of Sierra Leone*, p. 461.
22. Editorial, *SLWN*, January 30, 1897.
23. Minutes of the Legislative Council, May 3, 1895, in C.O. 270/33, fols. 259, 441-444.
24. On the peninsula itself, a circular hammock road had linked up all the main villages on the Atlantic coast. A road also crossed York Pass from Waterloo to York and

ment came with the construction of the Sierra Leone Railway and the opening of the Freetown-Songo stretch in 1899. Eventually the two-and-a-half foot gauge railroad, which the *Sierra Leone Weekly News* hailed as the "leading civilizing agent of the interior," ran at a top speed of eighteen miles per hour from Freetown to Makeni in the north and Pendembu in the south. It was not until the First World War that the main hammock roads were improved for motorized transportation and not until the beginning of the Second World War that the road systems between the colony and the protectorate were connected.[25]

To be sure, in spite of the natural obstacles which impeded communication between the peninsula and the hinterland, numerous Creoles—traders for the most part, but some missionaries—had gone up-country and became well-informed about the land and people among whom they worked.[26] But it was not merely a matter of contact between individual representatives of the two groups, one Europeanized and the other not, that was pertinent. It was also a matter of perception. Creole traders who habitually traveled up-country or resided there for long periods neither controlled communications media nor strongly influenced the established value system. The Creoles' stereotypical image of up-countrymen had been formed from preconceptions, mainly under European influence, which had built up over a long period of time. It took conscious efforts to modify or alter it—even by those most ready to view with sympathy and learn to understand the manners and customs of their hinterland neighbors. The transport and communication difficulty between the colony and the interior impeded the free flow of information which might alter the image and, as such, was one of the factors which helped to maintain it. Moreover, the image, once formed, was self-reinforcing. Reports about "savage" hinterland practices such as cannibalism, for example, were frequently circulated and exaggerated. The *Sierra Leone Times* published a letter from a Creole trader which detailed the kidnapping of his domestic servant and the latter's subsequent victimization. Fitz-John in

---

roads existed between Freetown, Leicester, Gloucester, Regent, Charlotte, and Allen Town—all of which had been kept in repair by the Liberated African Department. During the war in British Koya in 1861-1862, a hammock road was built between Waterloo and Songo for troop transport. The War Department built a road from Leicester Sanatorium to Wilberforce in 1894. See Richardson and Collins, "Economic and Social Survey," p. 25; *SLT*, February 24, 1894.

25. See Arthur T. Porter, "The Development of the Creole Society of Freetown, Sierra Leone. A Study on Social Stratification and the Processes of Social Mobility" (Ph.D. diss., Boston University, 1960), p. 35; Sierra Leone Colonial Report, 1955, p. 88, in Sierra Leone Collection.

26. C. H. Fyfe, "European and Creole Influences in the Interior of Sierra Leone before 1896," *Sierra Leone Studies*, n.s., no. 6 (June 1956), pp. 113-123; Hargreaves, "Establishment of the Sierra Leone Protectorate," passim.

his "One Thing and Another" column worried that well-fed Creoles would become the dinner objects of some "savage gourmand." He accused stipendary chiefs, particularly in Sherbro, of having been bribed not to punish offenders, and he concluded with the hope that his article would encourage Creoles in the various districts to make vigilant efforts to Protect themselves against the "greedy propensity of blood-thirsty savages."[27]

A key factor in establishing and then prolonging the cultural differences between Creoles and up-countrymen was education, which came to Sierra Leone through the peculiar medium of evangelical Christianity. The various early black settler groups as well as the Liberated Africans had shown an overwhelming desire to have their children receive an education from the Christian missionaries in Sierra Leone. They quickly had learned that European education was a valuable acquisition, that a person who possessed it not only differentiated himself from a slave past filled with indignities, but also was able to acquire the tools which could bring material and social rewards. Their eagerness was reflected in the high enrollment figures for schools. In 1842 a commission of inquiry reported that nearly one-fifth of the total population in the colony attended elementary school.[28] This was a proportion which compared favorably with enrollment figures in many European countries at the time.[29] In the hinterland of Sierra Leone, on the other hand, where missionary schools were scarce throughout the nineteenth century, very few Africans had the chance to receive an education of the Western type.[30]

Because of the educational advantages over up-countrymen, moreover, Creoles were able to take jobs at relatively high rates of pay, as clerks for the colonial government or mercantile firms, as artisans, or as teachers and churchmen. Their Europeanization also gave them an entrance as middlemen in trade—an opportunity which a number of them exploited effectively. They bought European imported goods such as cloth and ironware and sold or

27. *SLT*, March 26, 1892.

28. J. C. May, *Semi-Jubilee of the Wesleyan High School, Freetown, 1899* (Freetown, [1899?]), p. 87; Sumner, *Education in Sierra Leone*, pp. 51-52.

29.

Country	Approx. no. enrolled in primary schools	Approx. total population	Ratio
Prussia (1843)	2,328,146	16,285,013	1: 6.9
Austria (1838)	1,674,788	23,652,000	1:14.1
France (1843)	3,164,297	34,230,178*	1:10.8
Holland (1846)	382,370	3,053,984	1: 7.9
England & Wales (1851)	2,108,473		1: 8.5

*Population figure is for 1841.

See Henry Barnard, *National Education in Europe*, 2 vols. (New York, 1954).

30. Sumner, *Education in Sierra Leone*, pp. 59-61.

traded them in the hinterland at a profit. There they bought palm oil, rice, kola, palm kernels, and various other products to sell in Freetown at another profit. In time, they were able to build large houses, to buy European clothing, furniture, and fineries, and to send their children to England for advanced study in the professional fields. More important, however, from the standpoint of their relationship with up-countrymen, Creoles became economically able to employ hinterland Africans as "month boys"—domestic servants, cooks, and agricultural laborers who were paid once a month.[31] A "master-servant" relationship thus emerged between Creoles and up-countrymen as well—one which reinforced in economic terms the Creoles' belief in their cultural superiority.[32]

Occasionally, Creoles lived with up-countrymen on terms of equality. A Timne trader, for example, would sometimes send one of his sons to live with a Creole merchant to create a feeling of trust in commercial transactions or credit dealings. Numerically—and in terms of psychological effect—this practice was of less significance than the ward system—an arrangement whereby non-Creole children were entrusted to the care of better-to-do Creoles for whom they would perform household chores in return for the opportunity to go to school. In so far as the indigenous Africans were concerned, this system fit well into their traditional concepts of the extended family and was not abhorrent. In the hinterland it was common for children, at least those who were the first born, to be raised by their maternal grandparents or by other people more experienced in child-raising than the parents.[33] A. B. C. Sibthorpe noted in his *History of Sierra Leone* that neighboring chiefs "deem their sons in favour with fortune" if they obtained employment and were brought up by Europeans. Dalla Mahomadoo was thus brought up by Sierra Leone Company agents. Macaulay Wilson, son of King George of Yongoro, was raised, first by Zachary Macaulay, and afterwards by Dr. Thomas Winterbottom. It was one indication of the success of British missionarism that up-countrymen entrusted their children to Creoles as a substitute for Europeans.[34]

31. Richardson and Collins, "Economic and Social Survey," p. 29.

32. By virtue of the original settlement arrangement in Sierra Leone, Creoles owned large portions of land in Freetown and the nearby villages on the peninsula. This meant that up-countrymen who moved to the colony and who wanted to farm either had to squat or had to rent or buy land from Creoles—a situation which also immediately placed them in a subordinate position vis-a-vis the Sierra Leoneans. See Richardson and Collins, "Economic and Social Survey," p. 44.

33. Oral communication from Allen Howard, Livingstone College, Rutgers University, September 1969; H. E. M. Lynch-Shyllon, "The Effect of the Ward System on the Schools in the Colony of Sierra Leone" (Thesis for the Diploma in Education, University of Durham through Fourah Bay College, 1953), p. 11.

34. See Sibthorpe, *History*, pp. 44-45.

Although nothing was inherently evil in the ward system, all too frequently its positive aspects were perverted. Wards complained about harsh treatment from their guardians and frequently felt like slaves, exploited, with little time for formal study and unable to take advantage of their exposure to Freetown life.[35] Even under the best of circumstances, the ward system was paternalistic. Based on the premise of a "teacher-pupil," "superior-inferior," relationship, it buttressed the Creoles' already strong belief in the relative supremacy of their own way of life. An editorial in the *Sierra Leone Weekly News*, which complained about the "Alien Registration Ordinance" requiring a twenty-shilling fee for the registration of up-country children brought into the colony as wards, makes this explicit:

> It is, in fact, to the benefit of aliens themselves that as many as possible, without restriction or hindrance, be brought into the Colony, no matter what they learn, even if it is the English language alone. Generally, however, these aliens when in the Colony, are sent to some school, or, in a few cases, are taught at home: the boys afterwards become servants, cooks, etc. and the girls are taught sewing, washing, house-keeping, and all kinds of domestic work. Surely, this is preferable to their being left in their own homes where they see and learn nothing. As a rule the aliens are quite capable of taking care of themselves, and in cases of ill-treatment, which occur only on rare occasions, the laws of the land are quite sufficient, without the necessity of any special alien act; besides, they ought to be able to live here without being placed under the special care of the Government, and will thrive better without being spoon fed.[36]

Both the ward system and the economically based "master-servant" relationship could, and many times did, work as powerful vehicles for the integration of hinterland Africans into Creole society. The exposure of up-countrymen to colony households often led them to imitate creole manners and to adopt Creole standards in clothing, house-building, furnishing, and religion. Many up-country children added the last name of their Creole guardian to their own, learned Krio, and served as human links to bridge the cultural gap between the inhabitants of the colony and those of the hinterland.[37]

But the "Creolization" of the up-countrymen can easily be overemphasized. Many up-countrymen who came to the colony as adults settled into their own insulated communities or "fakais," either in Freetown or the

35. Lynch-Shyllon, "Effect of the Ward System," pp. 15-33.
36. Editorial, *SLWN*, September 27, 1890.
37. Richardson and Collins, "Economic and Social Survey," p. 185.

villages nearby, continued to maintain their own way of life, and remained little exposed to Creole customs.[38] For that matter, even those Creoles who lived close to an up-country family tended to know little about their neighbors. According to one source, Creoles acting as guardians of up-country wards or employing up-countrymen as "month boys" often did not know the ethnic group to which the wards belonged, nor such personal facts as their marital status or place of origin.[39]

The cultural distance between Creoles and up-countrymen was further intensified by the growing influx of hinterland Africans into the peninsula, especially in the last two decades of the nineteenth century. Between 1871 and 1881 the population of the entire peninsula, including Freetown, had grown by less than 5000 persons.[40] In the following decade the population increase of the peninsula, excluding the capital, was 4,586—from 53,862 to 58,448.[41] Freetown, however, grew by 8,102 persons.[42] In the decade 1891-1901 Freetown again increased by some 15,000 persons, while the colony as a whole grew by 25,000. As deaths in the colony appeared to exceed births, the registrar general felt that the increases were almost entirely due to the "constant stream of immigration on the part of male persons coming from the Protectorate in search of work in the Colony."[43] In fact, this was probably not true. According to R. R. Kuczynski, births may in all probability have exceeded deaths since the registration returns were incomplete.[44] Creoles in Freetown, however, agreed with the registrar general and considered the immigration of up-countrymen as a menace to their own ascendancy in the colony.

The population movement does seem to have fluctuated with the seasons.

38. Ibid., pp. 185-186.

39. Ibid., p. 194.

40. Kuczynski, *Demographic Survey*, 1: 275; Sierra Leone Census Report, 1881, pp. 4, 6, in Sierra Leone Collection.

41. These figures exclude Quiah.

42. Kuczynski, *Demographic Survey*, 1: 275.

43. Sierra Leone Census Report, 1901, p. 4, in Sierra Leone Collection.

44. See appendices A and B. It is extremely difficult to gather accurate statistics about the composition of the African population in the colony for most of its history. No data exist for the twenty-year period between 1861 and 1881 and, for the earlier periods, the population of Africans other than the Liberated African-Settler-Maroon group tended to fluctuate so that the figures which do exist are quite uncertain. Many Fulah and Mandingo traders passed through the colony, temporarily adding to its numbers, but as transients staying only from one to six weeks. Numerous Kroo were in the peninsula as well, employed on ships, at the harbor, in merchant stores, and as domestic servants, staying for about three years and then being replaced by others of their ethnic group. Occasionally, moreover, Creoles were misclassified as "Natives" in the population counts and, since the error could run as high as 10 percent, the number of up-countrymen in the peninsula would consequently be unduly inflated. Kuczynski, *Demographic Survey*, 1: 157n5, 161, 163n5.

Annually, after their crops had been harvested at home, up-countrymen migrated to Freetown in search of employment as manual laborers. Illiterate and unskilled, the majority of them competed for jobs with laboring class Creoles, arousing considerable resentment. The Freetown newspapers blamed the emigration of young Creoles who left the colony to seek jobs elsewhere on the fact that up-countrymen were undercutting their opportunities at home. They suggested that the government adopt a registration scheme to note the arrival and departure of hinterland Africans and set up a labor bureau to control their employment.[45] In the decade 1881-1891 many came to work on the fortifications which were being built for the defense of the harbor and on the additional barracks which were being constructed on Tower Hill. Several were also employed by the Sierra Leone Coaling Company.[46] A substantial number of up-countrymen, especially Mende, were recruited by private contractors in Freetown and shipped as indentured labor to Fernando Po and for public work projects in the Congo Free State. Many died there, while others suffered ill treatment under conditions of disguised slavery.[47] Some of the immigrants to the colony went back to their land in time to prepare the ground for the next crop. A great number, however, like the characters in the World War I song who found it difficult to return to "the farm after they've seen Paree," remained in the peninsula permanently.[48]

Aside from the direct economic threat, labor emigration awoke fears among *all* Creoles—old fears inherited from their parents and grandparents who, on many occasions in the early years of the Sierra Leone settlement, had met open hostility from up-countrymen. Until 1807, when a final settlement was negotiated with the Koya Timne and the colony acquired undisputed control over the peninsula, battles between settlers and indigenous Africans had been frequent.[49] Granville Town, the first capital of the settlement in Sierra Leone, had been burned to the ground in 1789 by the Timne chief, King Jimmy. The burning, to be sure, had been done to avenge the destruction of a Timne village by the black settlers, but the Creoles only seemed to remember King Jimmy's deed and not the circumstances surrounding it.[50] Again, in 1801, Timne and Susu warriors had attacked the second Granville Town, rushed Fort Thornton, and killed about thirty settlers,

45. For example, see editorial, *SLT*, May 16, 1896.

46. Kuczynski, *Demographic Survey*, 1: 275; Sierra Leone Census Report, 1891, p. 4, in Sierra Leone Collection.

47. *SLT*, July 7, 1894, May 16, 1896; Fyfe, *History of Sierra Leone*, pp. 504-505, 546-547.

48. Kuczynski, *Demographic Survey*, 1: 276.

49. Fyfe, *History of Sierra Leone*, pp. 96-97, passim.

50. Sierra Leone Company, *Report of the Court of Directors of the Sierra Leone Company to the General Court*, 7 vols. (title varies) (London, 1791-1808), 1: 6-7.

including women and children, before they were eventually driven off by a combined force of Maroons and British sailors from the H.M.S. *Wasp.*[51]

Attacks such as these, distorted by time and inflated in the retelling, strengthened the lingering insecurity Creoles felt in face of the sheer numerical superiority of their African neighbors.[52] Their insecurity, moreover, was intensified by the belief, occasionally aired in the Freetown press, which held that Creoles were "outsiders" in Sierra Leone—descendants of an alien minority—whose survival depended largely on British protection:

> It may seem an irreconcilable, but nevertheless it is a bold fact that Sierra Leone is not our home. Our home and our own land are far beyond the distant seas. There are more than a dozen nations and tongues constituting the aboriginal tribes of Sierra Leone and its Protectorate. From which of these do we claim descent? From none whatever. Between the white man and the aboriginal native, we are just like parasites to the one, and mushrooms to the other. The former despises us, and the latter both despises and ridicules us. The white man regards us as mere *aping* creatures of the highest type, and the aboriginal native regards us as interlopers and homeless wanderers—children of slaves from beyond the seas, and has no confidence in us.[53]

Knowing that the up-countrymen frequently referred to them contemptuously as "slave *pikin*"—children of slaves—or as "white men," Creoles would naturally dread the potential results of any major dispute which might occur between themselves and the interior peoples.

With more and more up-countrymen arriving in the colony, it was easy, given Creole trepidation, to magnify the menace out of all proportion. Haunted by the specter that Freetown would again be overrun by the "aborigines," the local press prophesied imminent disaster. Thus one commentary stated:

> We are in trouble and we are not. The influx of aboriginal tribes is a matter of serious concern to right thinking minds. These people live with and among us, they watch our movements, hour and out; they "play cutlasses" in the streets without any molestation whatever; they are finding out our weak points, and are longing for the time when they would become masters of the situation. . . . The threat is there. And unless proper precautions are

51. Fyfe, *History of Sierra Leone*, pp. 89-90.

52. See A. B. C. Sibthorpe, "History of Sierra Leone, Volume II," found in the *Artisan* beginning with the issue of February 25, 1885, for his comments about "native invasions" and the fear of irreconcilable hostility which they had left behind.

53. "Random Jottings by Marillia Van," *SLWN*, January 15, 1916.

taken in time, I fear that on some fine Sunday evening, when our souls are "magnifying" the Lord in our churches and chapel, "the sound of trumpet and the alarm of war" would be all to tell each man, woman, and child of this city that the Timanees have put into practical shape, the cowardly suggestions of their savage ancestors.[54]

Another writer was even less subtle. He stated: "What we desire to direct special attention to is the numerical increase of the aboriginal population who, by their . . . blood-thirsty disposition, may one of these days be inspired to think that it is their sacred mission to bring about a revolution in a wholesale massacre of the inhabitants for the purpose of possessing their property."[55] And still another article in the *Sierra Leone Weekly News*, written in 1886 when the migration of up-countrymen into Freetown had noticeably grown, clearly reflected the state of mind of many Creoles:

> "Do you know," said a Limbah man to a Sierra Leonean, "why we aborigines are thus pouring into the city and making our abode with us? It is because we sincerely believe that this colony was wrongfully wrested from the hands of our ancestors; and we thus come to stay with you, in order that we may learn the secret of your present greatness." Depend upon it, therefore, that we shall ere long hand Sierra Leone back to the sons and successors of NYAMBANA, TOM, YAMIE, and PA DEMBA. The question naturally arises: Are we safe?[56]

Commentary in the Creole newspapers about "the aborigines" appeared to increase in direct proportion to the number of up-countrymen that appeared in the colony. Creole writers blamed immigrants for perpetrating "atrocious crimes" in Freetown, for making life and property insecure, for ambushing "peaceful and unobtrusive travellers," and for burglarizing homes and stores. These accusations were sometimes justified. Up-countrymen coming into the colony occasionally included people on the run—escaped domestic slaves, voluntary and involuntary exiles—individuals who were not always the best representatives of life as it was led in the interior. Away from the checks and obligations which had existed back in their home villages, ordinary men faced both new freedoms and great frustrations. Under the unsettling conditions of urban life, during periods of unemployment and disorientation, they sometimes resorted to illegal activities in order to survive. During the rainy season especially, thievery was common. Stripped naked and covered with palm oil,

54. "My View of Things," *SLWN*, October 22, 1887.
55. "The Imperial Government and Our Aboriginal Population," *SLWN*, March 2, 1889.
56. "My View of Things," *SLWN*, March 13, 1886.

the thieves had triple protection: falling rain camouflaged their footsteps; nakedness made them practically invisible in the dark; and the palm oil covering allowed them to slip out of grasping hands like eels in the mud if, by chance, they were seized.

The newspapers also reflected Creole concerns about the danger of rape and kidnapping by Africans from the interior. With up-countrymen viewed as barbarians—outside the realm of Christian morality and, as such, not liable to the same restraints as Christian Sierra Leoneans—little would appear to keep them from overstepping the bounds of propriety. "Are our children safe on the streets of Freetown with all these aborigines about?" questioned the editor of the *Sierra Leone Times* bluntly.[57] Might they not also take advantage "of specimens of Creole womanhood to enrich their father-land?"[58] In language startlingly reminiscent of that used by white settlers in plural societies like Rhodesia and South Africa, Creole writers declared that a continuing influx of indigenous Africans into the peninsula, accompanied by their cohabitation with Creole women, would bring about the "degeneration of the race" and the "overthrow of civilization and the erection of barbarism."[59]

Furthermore, exemplifying a Victorian prudishness and a missionary fervor worthy of more recent converts, Creole writers warned of the danger of "superstitious customs brought to Freetown by the unwashed aborigines" and complained about their nakedness and promiscuity:[60]

> Dressed, or rather undressed in a style which would have been considered scanty even in the days when Adam delved and Eve spun, they go about our thoroughfares offering silent and *nude* reproaches to the existing local regulations, our civilisation and ideas of decency.
>
> The Kossoh folks—or as they like to be called, Mendies—file along the streets, all in a row, like skewered herrings, clothed for the most part with hideous grins and adorned with dirt; the lower apparel or rather appendage, which they ought not to wear, only rendering the absence of those which they ought to wear more conspicuous . . . .[61]

Various remedies were offered. Some Creoles recommended that a home mission be established in the colony, supported both financially and morally

57. "Abduction of Girls" and "Kidnapping," *SLT*, August 12, 1893.
58. "One Thing and Another," *SLT*, August 19, 1893.
59. "One Thing and Another," *SLT*, January 21, 1893, June 17, 1893; "The Government and the Aborigines," *SLWN*, February 17, 1900.
60. "One Thing and Another," *SLT*, January 21, 1893.
61. Editorial, *SLT*, April 1, 1899.

by the government, which would educate and convert up-countrymen to Christianity in order to incorporate them into the body politic.[62] Another possible solution—advocated by young, unemployed, laboring-class Creoles who most keenly felt the economic competition posed by the up-country-men—was the direct intimidation of the immigrants. Banding together on Christmas, Sports Day, or most any day when the spirit moved them, they roamed Freetown in gangs and, in a practice which they called "whisco," thrashed any up-countryman on whom they could lay their hands.[63] But "whisco" quickly backfired when up-countrymen lost their initial bumpkin greenness about life in the colony and formed gangs of their own for self-defense and retaliation.[64]

Equally drastic in its conception, another suggestion called for the forma-tion of a volunteer Creole militia or police which would be well armed and would patrol Freetown in ten-man companies to keep it free of immigrant troublemakers.[65] When the government refused to acquiesce in this proposal, it was modified so that "exemplary" up-countrymen would be included in the companies with the rationale that they would be interested in keeping their own neighborhoods safe. A letter to the editor of the *Sierra Leone Times*, however, which seemed to make public what many Creoles probably thought privately, warned that "the employment of the services of an aborigine for the detection of the crime of his own countrymen, is, to say the least of it, perfectly unsafe."[66] The proposal was dropped.

By far the most common suggestion was a call for government to regulate immigration into the colony and to supervise the African immigrants care-fully after they had arrived. A writer for the *Sierra Leone Weekly News*, in a column entitled "Insecurity of Life and Property," asked for a law, similar to one already in existence in the French colonies, which would "forbid the protracted residence of waifs and strays, without any regular legitimate means of subsistence."[67] An editorial appearing in the same paper at a later date, and perhaps influenced by legislation passed by whites in South Africa to regulate Africans coming to work in the gold and diamond areas, suggested that the colonial government ascertain the reasons why up-countrymen came to the colony. If they came to work and reside permanently their location might be fixed to one particular area of the peninsula, such as the wastelands

62. Editorial, *West African Reporter*, September 29, 1883.

63. Lawson, May 20, 1884, pp. 103-194; December 22, 1886, p. 174, December 23, 1886, p. 175, Government Interpreter's Letter Book, in Sierra Leone Government Archives.

64. *SLT*, January 8, 1898.

65. *SLWN*, February 21, 1898.

66. Letter to the editor from Kossoh Town, *SLT*, July 9, 1892.

67. *SLWN*, February 21, 1891.

in the Western District. If they came without fixed goals or merely to sojourn they might be issued a pass to that effect but would have to leave the colony as soon as their permit expired.[68]

As immigration continued and Creoles seemed to grow desperate, they more frequently suggested that up-countrymen in Freetown be segregated from the rest of the population. A writer in the *Saturday Magazine*, for instance, was convinced that the segregation of up-countrymen according to their ethnic origins would solve the problem of thievery and violence in the city. His reasons showed insight into the problems of intercultural contact. The hinterland Africans, he felt, resorted to their unpleasant city habits because of their bewilderment upon confronting a Europeanized population for the first time. By segregating up-countrymen along ethnic lines, therefore, they would feel more like they were in their own "countries," and, under conditions and laws native to their place of origin, they would become honest and industrious.[69] The more common reason for proposing a segregation scheme, however, was that up-countrymen were unsanitary and brought disease to the colony—a rationalization which, ironically enough, was exactly the same as the excuse later used by the Europeans in Sierra Leone for their own segregation scheme at Hill Station. An editorial in the *Sierra Leone Times*, commenting on the impossibility of effecting a fusion of the Creoles and up-countrymen in the peninsula, declared the isolation of the hinterland Africans in the colony to be of such momentous importance to the health of the Creoles "that the approval and disapproval [of the up-countrymen] did not even matter." The editorial stated:

> The city on three sides abounds with waste Crown Lands which could be utilised for such a purpose, and when we contemplate the immediate salutary effect the withdrawal ... of the hetero-geneous groups of *filth-loving and filth-abiding country people* to localities of their own—under competent managers—must have upon the health prospects of Freetown, we cannot but indulge in the hope that the necessity for it will soon force itself upon the Government.[70]

68. "The Government and the Aborigines," *SLWN*, February 17, 1900; "One Thing and Another," *SLT*, January 21, 1893; *SLT*, April 1, 1899, June 17, 1893.

69. *Saturday Magazine*, September 21, 1907.

70. "The Health of Freetown and the Aborigines," *SLT*, August 15, 1896. Also see *SLWN*, August 8, 1896, for a letter signed "A Citizen" which suggested that the prevalence of disease in Freetown at the time was due to the large numbers of "aborigines" crowded into town, living under unsanitary conditions. The author observed that in earlier days, when the "aborigines" only came to sell their goods and then went away again, these "hard times" had not occurred. He felt that hinterland Africans would be "happier in their own town" and suggested that a separate section of the city, on bush ground, be reserved for them.

So convinced was the *Sierra Leone Times* of the validity of their solution that they ran exactly the same editorial twice, once in 1897 and again in 1899:

> Freetown swarms with a vast horde of these unwashed gentry . . . . Ill lodged in hovels which might be regarded as being unservable even for animals, they add to the difficulties which the Sanitary Dept. have to contend with.
>
> It is no uncommon thing to find over eighteen of them, males as well as females dwelling together in one hut barely large enough for four persons; dwelling together promiscuously.
>
> It is also notorious that in the majority of cases, no cess-pits or latrines are provided in their premises; open fields, public springs of water, street gutters and even highways, furnishing objectionable alternatives for these filthy people. So disgusting are their habits, that in these localities where they reside mostly, the rentable value of decent houses had depreciated; no citizen who could help it, caring to dwell within 100 yards of such abominable filth . . . .
>
> There ought to be a distinct and separate legislation for these people, a legislation that might include a trial, at least, of the plan suggested a few years ago, viz.—to locate them in quarters apart by themselves, under the careful supervision of the Sanitary Authorities.[71]

War in the Interior

The Hut Tax War of 1898 in the Sierra Leone Protectorate, in which several hundred Creole traders, missionaries, and officials were murdered, was the single most detrimental event in the relationship between Creoles and up-countrymen.

Sierra Leoneans had been present up-country for a long time. Practically from the moment of their initial settlement in the eighteenth century, enterprising black settlers who felt confined by the limited potential of the peninsula began to exploit the hinterland commercially. Before the abolition of the slave trade by the British in 1807, the more unscrupulous among them joined with slave traders operating in the rivers and islands, both north and south of the peninsula and in the Sierra Leone and Sherbro estuaries. Others traded for rice and eatables, which the settlers could not provide in sufficient quantities on their own plots of land, as well as for agricultural products which could be exported.[72]

It is difficult to estimate how many Sierra Leoneans were involved in up-country trade throughout the nineteenth century. Probably the total was

71. Editorial, *SLT*, February 13, 1897, April 1, 1899.
72. See Fyfe, "European and Creole Influences," pp. 113-123.

not greater than two or three thousand.[73] The hinterland of the peninsula was certainly less attractive to many of the Liberated Africans and their Creole children than Europe and America and those parts of the African continent from which their ancestors had originated before being enslaved.[74] It was in the coastal region from the Gambia to the Bight of Biafra, rather than in the hinterland of Sierra Leone, that the Creoles made their main contribution to commercial, missionary, and governmental endeavors.

But the penetration of Creole traders and missionaries into the Sierra Leone hinterland, small at first, increased as the century progressed, and the search for new commercial horizons drove Sierra Leoneans to new frontiers. Initially, the majority of traders had stayed close to the rivers—practically the only viable highways. Gradually, however, individuals moved farther inland, and compatriots soon followed in their footsteps.[75]

In the Susu, Limba, and Timne regions of the north, where traders from Sangaran and Futa Jallon (in what is now Guinea) had long been bringing their goods, their religion, and their culture along well-established trade routes to centers like Kambia, Port Loko, and the surrounding areas, the physical presence of another group of trading "strangers" such as the Creoles caused relatively little commotion. Resentment only built up when the more enterprising Creole traders moved beyond the established market towns to buy produce and caravan goods directly from the producers and, in this process, undercut the native middlemen.[76] At this point local northern chiefs did attempt to stop the scattering of Creoles throughout their territory—but sound economic reasons motivated their actions, not xenophobia.

In the southern hinterland, on the other hand, not far beyond the Sherbro estuary, where Fulbe traders did not generally operate, Creoles were more often than not the first "intruders" in the region. Racially, of course, they were similar to the local inhabitants but culturally they were far removed, especially when Creole missionaries attacked traditional practices and disturbed the order of society. The penetration of Creoles into the south—less exposed to outsiders and to the type of cultural interchange that had been occurring in the north for generations—was undoubtedly more shocking to the indigenous inhabitants. The resentments which built up here against the Sierra Leoneans were much more xenophobic in nature than, for example,

73. See Kuczynski, *Demographic Survey*, 1: 1-18, 154-161, for a discussion of the problem of census-taking in West Africa.

74. Kopytoff, *Preface to Modern Nigeria*, passim.

75. Basing his evidence on two maps, one military and one naval, Fyfe estimates that by 1865 the traders had not penetrated much beyond Tikonko, Bumpe, and perhaps Taiama—about forty miles northeast from Bonthe. See Fyfe, "European and Creole Influences," p. 120. The maps are found in C.O. 267/271, and in Algernon Montagu, *Ordinances of Sierra Leone*, 6 vols. (London, 1857-1881), vol. 4.

76. Fyfe, *History of Sierra Leone*, p. 411; Fyfe, "European and Creole Influences," p. 121.

among the Timne. Ultimately, the reaction which occurred here against the Creoles during the Hut Tax War, in contrast to that which took place in the north, was violent and irrational.

War between the various up-country ethnic groups and the disruption it brought to the countryside were one of the two main factors hindering Creole trading ambitions. The other was the territorial expansion of the French, who, unchecked by the British authorities, had by the 1860s already annexed the Mellakori River region and then slowly started to entice the Futa Jallon trade caravans to look on Conakry rather than Freetown as the ultimate outlet for their goods.[77] Beginning in the late 1870s, therefore, and continuing for almost two decades, the Sierra Leone traders and their sympathizers back in Freetown concerned themselves with the "disruption of the up-country," the "depression of trade," and accordingly, with efforts to influence the British government to annex the hinterland and to make it safe for "civilized" endeavors.

Even when all statistics showed otherwise, the "depression of trade" remained a favorite topic. In newspaper editorials, at mass meetings, in petitions to the secretary of state, Creoles repeatedly urged the British to interfere, to stop the French advance, and to end the "reckless habits of the surrounding tribes" who, in the words of one writer in the *Sierra Leone Weekly News*, were "disturbing the cause of Christianity, civilization, and progress."[78] The tone of these appeals could vary a great deal. *A Few Suggestions of the Wants of Sierra Leone*, a pamphlet written by Samuel Lewis in 1879 "for the information of a Member of Parliament," was typical of the moderate arguments. The peninsula, Lewis pointed out, was too small, with no industry, an insufficient agricultural base, and promising little in future productivity. Its fate was to rely on trade. The smallness of the colony made it impossible to carry out the original aims of the philanthropists: to civilize and regenerate the "Dark Continent" through the establishment of legitimate commerce and the development of its natural resources. Because the French were expanding into the British sphere of influence, moreover, and up-country wars continuously disrupted life and property, it was impossible to continue the informal activities of Britain and her subjects; the danger even existed that Sierra Leone would be left without command over any of the country through which the produce of the interior could be directed to the colony and its seaport. It was therefore essential that the British annex the hinterland and restore order.[79] Other trader-inspired

---

77. Fyfe, "European and Creole Influences," p. 121.

78. Letter to the editor, February 28, 1885; "My View of Things," June 13, 1885, *SLWN*; Fyfe, *History of Sierra Leone*, pp. 451-452.

79. See Samuel Lewis, *A Few Suggestions of the Wants of Sierra Leone* (Freetown, 1885).

writings, however, were much more shrill. "Vagabonds, thieves, and cut-throats who arrogate the name of chiefs ought to be taught that British interests cannot be injured with impunity," an editorial in the *Sierra Leone Weekly News* declared angrily.[80] "If things be allowed to take this same course," stated a letter to the editor in this same newspaper, "and no steps [are] taken in regard to the safety of British subjects, shall the property, the labour of years . . . be given up and destroyed in a day: Shall the lives of innocent British subjects be abandoned to savage butchery by the bands of barbarous ruffians whose thirst for blood and rapine can hardly be surpassed?"[81]

Gradually the colonial government did become involved up-country—both militarily, to halt the wars, and diplomatically to salvage some territory from the fast-encroaching French. Governor Samuel Rowe led armed expeditions to Moyamba and Rotifunk, southeast of the colony, in 1876 and 1878. The Yoni, who had been among the chief objects of Creole annoyance for their raids which disturbed the upper Mende country even as far as Songo Town inside the colony frontier, were defeated by a government military expedition in 1888. Another expedition "pacified" the southern country around the Mano River in 1890. The government sent out traveling commissioners to explore unknown country and sign treaties of friendship with chiefs along the way. Roads were cut and frontier policemen were left at key towns to insure the newly established *pax Britannica*.[82] In 1889 a preliminary boundary between the British and French spheres of influence was established. Soon afterward, it was permanently fixed. The British presence up-country, which in the past had been maintained informally through stipends to chiefs and the physical presence of Creole and European traders and missionaries, was formalized through the establishment of an administrative structure. In 1896, after concluding a final boundary settlement with the French, the British declared a protectorate over what remained of their sphere of influence in the hinterland of Sierra Leone.

Trouble began when the British authorities decided to impose a hut tax to cover the cost of administering the five new districts that were established up-country. Never anxious to spend money which could not be raised locally by the inhabitants for the maintenance of a territory, the colonial office insisted on a revenue-gathering device of some sort. Governor Frederic Cardew, who had had experience in Zululand and Natal, where a hut tax was being paid, decided on the particular form it would take.[83] The tax, which

80. Editorial, *SLWN*, May 16, 1885.
81. Letter to the editor, *SLWN*, May 16, 1885.
82. Fyfe, "European and Creole Influences," pp. 122-123.
83. The hut tax was planned as the major means of revenue gathering, but additional funds were also to come in through the sale of licenses to traders. In proposing a hut tax for the protectorate, and to justify the rates which were being asked, Governor Cardew

the chiefs were to collect from their people beginning in January 1898, was payable in cash or produce: five shillings a year for each hut with less than four rooms and ten shillings for larger habitations. Initially, the tax was to be collected only in three districts nearest the colony because they had been exposed to European and Creole contact the longest and, it was thought, would thus be more readily receptive to the idea.

The chiefs, however, regarded the hut tax as another incomprehensible action on the part of the Europeans. Clearly, the demands could not but have been puzzling to them. They had signed treaties of friendship with the Europeans and, suddenly, found themselves as subordinates under British rule, caught in a protectorate which they had neither foreseen nor wanted. And now they and their people, owners of the land, and the dwellings thereon, were being asked to make payments to the government on houses which by all rights were their own. It was not a situation which could be accepted without a struggle.

When war broke out in 1898 between the up-countrymen and the British it had two phases: one was concentrated almost entirely in the northern section of the protectorate, in the area inhabited largely by the Timne; the other centered in the south, in the Mende-Sherbro region. Each affected the Creoles in a different way.

In the north—in the Karene District—where hostilities first arose in February, a less than tactful attempt by District Commissioner Captain Wilfred Stanley Sharpe to collect the hut tax was the spark that ignited the fire. In Port Loko, the commercial center of the district, Sharpe had approached Creole traders to pay taxes for houses in which they lived but for which up-countrymen were landlords. The traders, who had been warned by the up-countrymen that they would be ejected and plundered if they did pay, refused. After a good deal of unpleasantness in which some traders were roughly handled by the district commissioner and his policemen, Sharpe turned on the town chiefs. He arrested five of them and sent them to Freetown for inciting their subjects to resist the law.[84]

Sharpe was convinced that the man who had influenced the people of Port Loko and the surrounding areas to thwart constituted authority and withhold

publicized the amount of taxes that people in other parts of Africa had to pay: Zululand: 14s. a hut/year; Natal: £1 (and more if the huts were situated on "private" land); Liberia: $1.00 for every male over 21 who did not own realty; for every owner of realty, without regard to sex or age, half of one percent of its assessed value with $1.00 minimum; for every male over 21, whether native or foreign, a navy tax of 50 cents. See *SLWN*, September 12, 1896.

84. See Great Britain, Parliament, *Parliamentary Papers*, vol. 60 (House of Commons, 1899) (*The Chalmers Report*, vols. 1 and 2, hereafter cited as *Chalmers Report*); "Varia," February 12, 1898; "The Port Loko Difficulty, No. 11," June 25, 1898, *SLT*; A. B. C. Merriman-Labor, *The Last Military Expedition in Sierra Leone* (Liverpool, 1899), p. 9.

the tax was Bai Bureh of Kasse—a chief who had proven himself a resolute warrior and leader as an ally of the British.[85] The district commissioner, therefore, proceeded to Kasse country with a number of Frontiers (the name given to the protectorate policemen) in order to arrest the troublemaker.

The fighting which ensued quickly took on characteristics of guerrilla warfare.[86] The Frontiers, who had been reinforced first by West India Regiment soldiers and, later, by the newly formed West African Regiment, were clearly better armed than the up-country "war boys" who opposed them. Nonetheless the "war boys," with *Chassepot* rifles acquired in French Guinea, flint-lock guns, and cane guns of their own manufacture which fired odd pieces of iron, could inflict impressive damage. With their unworldly banging noises, these guns bewildered new recruits and scattered undisciplined carriers; when used by knowledgeable fighters from behind stockades hidden in the bush, they proved dangerous weapons.

The fighting went on for months. Using their intimate knowledge of the bush to give them the advantage of surprise, relying on sturdily constructed stockades for defensive bunkers, and taking advantage of the intelligence and logistical support they received from their noncombatant countrymen, Bai Bureh's forces impressively battled the supply-laden British troops. More than six hundred government men were wounded and two hundred killed or listed as missing in the fighting.[87] But in the long run the weapons wielded by the up-country warriors could not stand up to the rapid-firing rifle and the Maxim gun. Systematically destroying town after town, the British troops whittled down Bai Bureh's defenses and neutralized his allies until his forces and his resistance disintegrated. Eventually convinced of the futility of pursuing his fight, Bai Bureh surrendered and was taken to Freetown as a prisoner.

Creole loyalties lay with the British, but their sympathies were obviously with Bai Bureh. Even though one Creole trader near Port Loko was chopped to pieces by the "war boys" for conveying information regarding the movement of Africans to the district commissioner, Bai Bureh humanely spared the lives of all Creole and European missionaries and traders up-country who were not directly involved in the fighting. The Sierra Leone press was impressed by his kindness. "Other chiefs would have long ago destroyed all the British subjects in his territory," stated a letter to the editor of the *Sierra*

85. Merriman-Labor, *Last Military Expedition*, p. 21; "News," *SLT*, February 26, 1898. For Bai Bureh, see LaRay Denzer and Michael Crowder, "Bai Bureh and the Sierra Leone Hut Tax War of 1898," in *Black Protest*, ed. Robert I. Rotberg and Ali Mazrui (London, 1970).

86. "News," *SLT*, March 5, 1898.

87. Merriman-Labor, *Last Military Expedition*, p. 20. The figure six hundred includes carriers who were wounded, but the figure two hundred does not include the many carriers who deserted.

Leone Weekly News, "but this, Bai Bureh refuses to do.... Call him a barbarian, a heathen, or a savage; but considering [his] good treatment to English subjects and missionaries, during these outrages, I say he is a charitable and humane ruler."[88]

Bureh also caught the imagination of many Creoles for his stand against the heavy-handed imposition of taxation—never a favorite institution among Sierra Leoneans. "The end is not far off," wrote a Creole who saw justice in the war chief's cause.

> Might is now in the ascendant, and must conquer Right. Bai Bureh must eventually succumb to the irresistible force, and inexhaustible resources of English might.... This man is not fighting against law or order, but against tyranny and oppression.... Bai Bureh, in his own words, said that he was quite sure that his insurrection will be the means of his death, and the destruction of his people and country by the white man: but that he felt himself old enough to die for Liberty, even if he does not get it.[89]

Similarly "An Ode for King Bai Bureh," which appeared in the *Sierra Leone Times* at the height of the troubles in the north, praised the chief in high-flown terms yet warned him to yield to his "betters" and obey the laws of Britain:

Awake O lute! and chant the present lay
Of Afric's proud arms, and Bureh's lofty sway
Twixt Lokkoh Port and K'rene lies a large and vasty waste,
Commonly called Kassi country, and Bai Bureh King survey.
Now Bai, says his lord to me, pay and live;
Per house in thy sway, as annual tribute
Of pence, twice thirty, both you and your men;
If not Bai, be sure, shall perish . . . .
This the savage man perceived;
And to the lord's heralds thus with accent mild began:
"I know your message—by contraint you came
Not you, but your imperious lord I blame.
But first and to your lord declare
(That haughty Knight—let whose command you bear)
Unmoved by death Bai Bureh shall remain
Though prostrate his sway shall bleed at every vein . . . ."
But proud Bai Bureh learn this well, though, thou art wrongly defied

88. Letter to the editor by Musa Alhakim, *SLWN*, April 23, 1898. Also see "One Thing and Another," *SLT*, April 9, 1898, April 23, 1898.
89. Letter to the editor by Musa Alhakim, *SLWN*, April 16, 1898.

The man with whom thou now contend is but thy lord by strength too high
In arms, minds, and other strength and wisdom bless'd
By brave examples will confirm the rest.
Yet beware! for dreadful is the wrath of kings.
Be still, insolent chief, and to thy betters yield
Unknown alike in council and in field. For to-day
To one sole monarch God commits the sway
Her's are the laws, and let all obey.[90]

The war in the south was different in all respects. It burst forth suddenly
late in April in the Imperi District and spread rapidly and widely as far as the
frontier between the protectorate and Liberia.[91] It involved Mende, Sherbro,
Loko, Vai, and even some Timne and Susu peoples. Probably because the
Mende were the largest group represented, however, the war became known
in the colony as the "Mende War" and, as this identification tended to stick
in the minds of Sierra Leoneans, it was the Mende who tended to receive the
major blame for the atrocities that occurred.

The first notice of a mass killing of Creoles appeared on April 30, 1898, in
the *Sierra Leone Weekly News.* The story was then circulated widely. Traders,
missionaries, government employees—in many cases with their wives and
children—were being killed, their bodies mutilated or hacked to pieces, some
pegged-out on heaps of ignited palm kernels and burned alive.[92] The Freetown press was perceptive and quick in differentiating between the character
of events in the north and south. The *Sierra Leone Weekly News* editorialized:

> The brutality evinced by the Mendi war-boys could not be said
> to have been inspired by anything Bai Bureh may have done.
> Without attempting to justify the attitude which as a friendly
> Chief, he has felt himself compelled to adopt towards the Govern-
> ment, the way in which he has hitherto conducted the campaign,
> has been in accordance with the principles of civilized warfare,
> and is most creditable to him. All the Sierra Leoneans and others
> within his district were unmolested. He confined his warfare to
> those who have actually taken up arms against him. He even went

90. "An Ode for King Bai Bureh by Ana," *SLT,* April 2, 9, 1898. Two other poems
praising Bai Bureh appeared in the Freetown press: "Bai Bureh," by Walter Edwin,
SLWN, June 17, 1911, and "Ode to Bai Bureh," by Peggy, in *Sierra Leone Guardian and
Foreign Mails,* March 8, 1918.

91. Merriman-Labor, *Last Military Expedition,* p. 26.

92. *SLT,* May 28, 1898; Lt. J. Stewart, "Diary Written on Active Service Commanding 'G' Co. 2nd Battalion, West India Regiment," entries of May 15 and May 18, 1898,
manuscript diary in the Fourah Bay College Library, Freetown; Merriman-Labor, *Last
Military Expedition,* pp. 26, 29.

so far as to send away under an escort some of the native
missionaries with one of whom he entrusted a message to the
Governor. The Mendi war-boys, inspired by the spirit of rapine
and murder, have destroyed life and property without the least
compunction and consideration. We are at a loss to conceive how
these marauders are to be brought to punishment as to ensure the
safety of Sierra Leone residents and others in the Protectorate for
the time to come.[93]

Why did Creole penetration up-country elicit such a drastic reaction on the
part of the Mende, Sherbro, and other peoples of the southern protectorate?
Although Creoles, for the most part, seemed to deal fairly and on a basis of
economic equality with up-countrymen, enough of them deviated from the
acceptable standard to draw animosity and resentment toward the group as a
whole. Many chiefs, aggressively by-passed by Creole traders who wanted to
deal directly with the producers, resented the high-handed manner of the
intruders from the colony. Cheating incidents, moreover, were not infrequent—incidents in which Creoles were certainly not the only culprits but
which, when they were to blame, would tend to be recalled by up-countrymen when Sierra Leoneans acted obtrusively and overbearingly.[94] Occasions
existed when Creole miscreants employed laborers and did not pay them in
full, when they inflicted corporal punishment on debtors or servants, when
they philandered with men's wives and sweethearts, and when they insulted
and decried the people among whom they lived. These were all injustices
committed by individuals, to be sure, but they blemished the entire Creole
community in the protectorate.[95]

Even more harmful than the deviations of individual Sierra Leone wrong-
doers, however, was the more-or-less general consensus among up-countrymen
that Creoles were "white men"—the government's *pikin* (children). Associated with Europeans in the minds of the protectorate inhabitants, the
Creoles could not divorce themselves from the disruption of the traditional
way of life which accompanied the general intrusion of the West into the
interior of Africa. Policies wrought by the British administration in Freetown
were often attributed to the traders and missionaries in the protectorate. In
Mende country, Africans blamed Sierra Leoneans for bringing taxes to their
country, saying that if the Creoles had not been there the government would

93. Editorial, *SLWN*, May 7, 1898.
94. See T. J. Alldridge's "Reports on Tricks of Trade as Practiced by Traders and
Natives in the Protectorate," included in Governor's Confidential Dispatch No. 77 to the
Secretary of State, December 12, 1898, in Sierra Leone Government Archives; *Chalmers
Report*, 2: 18, pars. 326-330, 2: 116, pars. 2245-2249, 2: 128, pars. 2446-2454.
95. *Chalmers Report*, 2: 92, pars. 1859-1862.

not have introduced the rates.[96] Up-countrymen also associated Creoles with the new interference with their domestic slavery, prohibition of the sale of gunpowder, ammunition, and spirits, and the establishment of an undisciplined police force bent on rapine and pillage.[97]

How many Creoles were killed in the southern protectorate will probably never be known. Most figures given were mere guesses. Estimates varied from a few hundred to over a thousand persons killed.[98] If it was practically impossible to determine exactly how many Creoles were up-country at any one time, it was even more difficult to discover every last Creole murdered in some remote bush area. Nor, for that matter, is it particularly important to know the exact casualty figures. The killings made a profound impression on Sierra Leoneans in the colony and the very uncertainty about the magnitude of the crime magnified the danger, making it all the more frightening and ominous. The Creoles' worst nightmares seemed to be materializing. A few Creoles sensed that the murder of their fellow countrymen in the protectorate was an act of retaliation on the part of people who had not been fairly treated in the past. According to one witness before the Chalmers Commission, which investigated the Hut Tax War after reports of the protectorate insurrection had become known, one frequently heard uttered on the streets of Freetown: "We did 'em bad, God punish we."[99] The majority of Sierra Leoneans, however, probably did not associate cause with effect. Up-countrymen had merely proven themselves to be what Creoles had long sensed them to be—savages bent on the destruction of all intruders.

Freetown and the outlying Creole villages were in commotion, especially during the week immediately following the news of the uprising and murders in the south.[100] Creoles in the colony were fearful that the up-countrymen would act as a fifth column and cooperate with their kin in the hinterland by setting houses afire in the dead of night. A few Sierra Leoneans went so far as to dismiss their servants, and, had it not been for police orders to protect

96. Ibid., p. 437, par. 7387.

97. Editorial, *SLT*, May 14, 1898.

98. *The London Times*, June 13, 1898, printed an estimate by a Reuters correspondent of a thousand persons killed; Merriman-Labor, *Last Military Expedition*, p. 29, calculated an even higher figure than this; the names of murdered persons which were published in the Freetown papers added up to a few hundred. Also see Fyfe, *History of Sierra Leone*, p. 589.

99. Evidence of John Taylor Smith, Bishop of Sierra Leone, *Chalmers Report*, 2: 514, par. 8179.

100. In keeping with their community traditions of self-help, Creoles who were members of the Freetown Municipal Council set up "The Refugees Relief Committee," whose job it was to give some pecuniary relief to refugees from the Protectorate War. Although the committee was well intentioned, its pecuniary relief was usually too small to satisfy the claimants. Some complaints about this appeared in the letters to the editor column of the *SLWN* beginning in May 1898.

up-countrymen in town, some Creoles might well have decided to strike the first blow.[101] After the murder of Creoles in "Mendeland" the Mende who lived in Freetown were especially threatened with imminent retaliation. "Mendi man no gud" became a common street expression in the capital.[102] Incidents between local Creole toughs and up-countrymen multiplied throughout 1898 and 1899, especially after the war in the protectorate was over and soldiers returned to Freetown. A small riot took place in June 1899.[103] Nonetheless, the influence of the city's leading citizens, in the days and months immediately following the massacres, was sufficiently pervasive to prevent skirmishes between Creoles and hinterland immigrants from assuming uncontrollable proportions.[104]

A few days after the outbreak of the war in the south, the mayor of Freetown called a public meeting at Wilberforce Memorial Hall "to consider what steps should be taken to protect the city against possible aboriginal risings within it." Two resolutions were passed and presented to the governor. The first asked the government for permission to form a permanent volunteer corps which would act in defense of the peninsula whenever the colonial and imperial troops usually stationed in Freetown were unavoidably withdrawn elsewhere. The second asked the government to relax the colonial ordinances (in line with the General Act of the Brussels Conference of 1890) regulating the importation of firearms and ammunition, so that Creoles could arm themselves for self-protection. The governor did not acquiesce in easing the firearms control ordinances, but he did permit the creation of a volunteer force—not a permanent organization, as the leading citizens of Freetown would have wanted, but one which would be disbanded at the termination of the up-country troubles. Chagrined, editor Cornelius May of the *Sierra Leone Weekly News* was sure that the governor's actions showed that he did not trust the allegiance and loyalty of the Creoles.[105]

The volunteer force was commanded by a European officer and manned by about 250 Creoles. It drilled daily at the Memorial Hall and patrolled the streets at night. The effectiveness of the volunteers was nevertheless questionable. Burglars were active in spite of the patrols—one of the auction marts was

---

101. "One Thing and Another," *SLT*, September 10, 1898; "Meeting in Regard to the Rising," Native Affairs no. 118, May 13, 1898, in Native Affairs Department Correspondence, Sierra Leone Government Archives; "Rambling Talks by Rambler," *SLWN*, February 17, 1934.

102. *Chalmers Report*, 2: 145, par. 2701, 2: 514, par. 8179.

103. Governor Nathan to Secretary of State, October 8, 1899; Native Affairs Letterbook, Confidential, from No. 12, April 28, 1898, to No. 9, June 26, 1899, in Native Affairs Department Correspondence.

104. "Some Jottings by J," see *SLWN*, May 7, 1898, June 17, 1899.

105. *SLWN*, May 7, 1898.

relieved of a considerable quantity of goods one night, and the thief managed to elude the vigilance of the guards seemingly without difficulty.[106]

Freetonians had been psychologically prepared for war ever since a panic had erupted at Hastings and Waterloo, two colony villages, a month before the outbreak in the south. At that time, according to a report in the *Sierra Leone Times,* "the alarm got spread . . . that a horde of war-boys belonging to either Bai Combah or Bai Bourreh, was about to make a raid on the place, and that the latter had declared that he was coming to wash his sword in the brook at Hastings. This news got wing about the middle of the Morning Service, and a panic ensued which baffle[d] all description. . . . In less than no time, the stations as far as Wellington had been aroused. Old men and women labored to escape the coming trouble, and the Waterlonians and people from the hamlets as far as Hastings made a rush for Freetown."[107]

Fired by rumor, any military activity in Freetown in the days immediately following the outbreak in the southern protectorate was sufficient to keep the population in a frenzy verging on hysteria. And such activity was plentiful. Soldiers appeared to be everywhere: companies of the West India Regiment arrived from Lagos and the West Indies as reinforcements and the West African Regiment was being formed and built up with materiel. The actions of the British in the colony, furthermore, were not always designed to inspire confidence among the populace. At one time the commissariat, stores, cash, and various other essentials were removed from their vulnerable positions in town and brought to the barracks where they could be more easily defended. The sight of such a removal, showing the public that the establishment upon whom they looked for protection was also frightened, might have led to a general panic among Freetonians had not a quick-thinking British officer immediately ordered that the items in question be retransferred to their original locations.

The harbor was full of ships, loading and unloading, fetching and moving troops. Both the H.M.S. *Fox* and *Blonde* stopped off in Freetown prior to their battle assignments in the Gallinas and at Bonthe. The H.M.S. *Alecto, Thrush,* and *Phoebe* also appeared in the harbor.[108] Nerves remained tense. A rumor quickly spread that the first-class cruiser *Blake,* carrying twelve guns and 630 men, was coming to Freetown to bomb it because, according to the local press, English journals erroneously accused the Creoles of being in rebellion and had written that the lives of English residents in the colony were in jeopardy.[109] The *Blake,* in fact, had been sent to Sierra Leone by the

106. "Varia," *SLT,* May 14, 1898; Merriman-Labor, *Last Military Expedition,* pp. 28-29.

107. *SLT,* April 9, 1898.

108. Merriman-Labor, *Last Military Expedition,* pp. 26-27.

109. "Varia," May 14, 1898; "One Thing and Another," May 21, 1898, *SLT.*

secretary of state for the colonies for no other reason than to protect Freetown and, with nothing to do, sailed home again not long after she arrived.[110] Creoles, however, were hard to convince of the *Blake*'s defensive assignment. Even after she had sailed away, Fitz-John bid her farewell derisively in his "One Thing and Another" column in the *Sierra Leone Times*. "It is a precious good thing that we have no barnacles in our harbour," he said, "or else there might have been some danger of the first class cruiser catching some; and it would not conduce the dignity of a first class cruiser to go about the Mediterranean with 'nigger' barnacles sticking on her."[111]

It was much easier to restore the peace after the Hut Tax War than to eradicate the enmity with which events scarred the already sore relationship between up-countrymen and Creoles. To be sure, the sympathy which many Creoles had for Bai Bureh in 1898, and which they continued to hold for decades afterwards, can be taken as evidence that hatred and distrust were not the only sentiments influencing their attitude toward hinterland Africans. In the early months of the war, in fact, before the murders in the southern protectorate had taken place, letters to Sierra Leone newspapers occasionally suggested that the racial links between Creoles and up-countrymen were potentially stronger than the antagonisms keeping them apart. Because Creoles were being slighted on racist grounds by the British during this period, they tended to be sympathetic with up-country peoples who seemed to be similarly aggrieved. One writer, for example, describing injustices perpetrated on the up-countrymen by the district commissioners, the frontier policemen, and the institution of the hut tax, concluded: "We lament the death of some of the gallant servants of Our Most Gracious Queen and Governor, as we lament the mowing down of our brethren by thousands by the superior weapons of European warfare."[112] Even after the atrocities had taken place, and over 230 persons accused of committing crimes up-country were tried, the *Sierra Leone Weekly News* published an article hoping that all possible fairness be shown to the individuals being charged and that all those who were condemnded and hanged by truly deserving of their fate.[113]

For the most part, however, the effects of the 1898 war were detrimental. In a sense, the Mende atrocities fulfilled the Creoles' darkest dreads about up-countrymen: they had truly acted like the barbarians that all up-country-men were purported to be. Mende became stereotyped by the Creoles in the most virulent terms. They were referred to as "looters," "those bloody

110. Great Britain, *Parliamentary Debates* (Commons), vol. 57, May 9, 1898, pp. 699-714; *SLT*, June 11, 1898.

111. *SLT*, June 11, 1898.

112. Letter to the editor by Musa Alhakim, *SLWN*, April 2, 1898.

113. "The Protectorate and the Hut Tax," by a Special Correspondent, *SLWN*, January 28, 1899.

people," "fighters and robbers of other people's properties," "that blood-thirsty tribe." Certainly, the massacre tended to legitimize the opinion of those Creoles who wanted to believe the absolute worst about up-countrymen and who had long predicted the eventual annihilation of the Sierra Leone community at the hands of the hinterland Africans.[114]

The Timne were rarely singled out and made the object of disparaging remarks, but neither did they fully escape the disdain-mixed-with-fear with which Creoles adjudged up-countrymen collectively. The majority of the Timne were Muslim—members of one of the world's "acceptable" religions—and, unlike the Mende, could not be called "heathens." The relative success of the Timne "war boys" against troops which were British-led and equipped, nevertheless heightened Creole insecurities about the "aborigine peril," and, in the irrational bogeyman Creoles constructed, they did not generally differ-entiate between "good" and "bad" up-countrymen.[115]

Although Creole traders slowly, and individually, returned up-country, the war for a time virtually closed off these avenues of intercourse which could have brought understanding, mutual benefit, and trust between colony and protectorate peoples—thus easing their social integration. The mere memory of the "Mende War" was, for many years, a hindrance to the evolution of amicable relationships and to the establishment of a feeling of colony-protectorate unity. But an equally deleterious obstacle developed from the attitude of the colonial government when the fighting had been concluded and peace restored.

Governor Cardew, whose admiration for Sierra Leoneans had soured rapidly when Creole officials were implicated in illegal activities during his administration, blamed the Creole press and traders for having instigated the rising.[116] "I am prepared to admit that the imposition of the house tax was

114. It was not easy for Creoles to forget past events even after they had decided to renew their missionary activity among the Mende in the years after 1898. Thus, when J. Abayomi Cole published his Mende primer in 1900, the *SLWN*, referring indirectly to the hut tax massacres, commented that this book would enable the Mende "to become useful citizens and to cultivate higher qualities than those which induce unnatural delight in sanguinary enterprises." See *SLWN*, June 15, 1901. A copy of the primer, *Hala goloi Mende yiahu, First Book in the Mende Language* (London, 1900), can be found at the School of Oriental and African Studies of the University of London. It was published originally at the encouragement of E. H. Elwin, principal of Fourah Bay College. Intended to supply the needs of missionaries and to serve as an elementary reader, it contained, among other items, the Lord's Prayer, the Ten Commandments, the Apostles Creed, and the Benediction.

115. See Merriman-Labor, *Last Military Expedition*, passim, for an example of how Creole attitudes toward the Mende and Timne differed. Also see "Some Jottings by J," *SLWN*, June 17, 1899, and the editorials in the *Sierra Leone Guardian and Foreign Mails*, November 21, 22, 1919.

116. See Fyfe, *History of Sierra Leone*, pp. 523-524, 532-534, 537-538, for ex-amples.

the exciting cause of the disturbances," he wrote to Chamberlain, the colonial secretary, "but I wish to qualify this by adding my conviction that if the community of Freetown, the press, and the traders had loyally supported the government in its policy, or even remained neutral, the tax would have been paid without disturbance. But the contrary, I regret to say, has been the case; the press has directly encouraged the natives not to pay the tax."[117]

In his testimony to the Chalmers Commission, Cardew elaborated on his charges against the Creole press: "Inasmuch as they [the newspapers] threw contempt on and vilified the Governor, as they showed marked sympathy for the insurgents and eulogized the rebel Chief Bai Bureh and held him up to admiration as a hero, their tendency has been to incite the natives of the Protectorate not to pay the house tax, and to encourage them in their resistance to the forces of the Government."[118]

The governor's accusation, made before time had cooled tempers and restored a semblance of objectivity, was overdrawn, jaundiced, and practically without foundation. It was illogical in the extreme to maintain—especially regarding the southern protectorate—that people would rise up and murder the persons who had supposedly urged them to revolt in the first place. Sierra Leone traders, to be certain, had attacked provisions in the protectorate ordinance which limited traffic in guns, gunpowder, and spirits and had opposed the hut tax because they feared it would disrupt trade in foodstuffs. The Manchester and Liverpool chambers of commerce, however, had voiced these objections as well.[119] Up-country, some Creoles did encourage Africans not to pay the tax by making it clear to them that there were no property taxes in the colony. This, of course, reinforced the feeling among up-countrymen that they were being dealt with unfairly.[120] But Creole action undoubtedly reflected their long-standing aversion to direct taxation of any kind and was not intended as agitation against the British government. Similarly, when a number of chiefs visited Freetown in 1897 for Queen Victoria's Diamond Jubilee celebration, a strong possibility did exist that anti-hut tax Creoles attempted to influence them during their stay in the colony. Since the chiefs already were petitioning against the tax, however, one wonders how decisive Creole influence could have been.[121] On the other hand, there seemed little doubt that a number of Creole traders and missionaries had worked to induce payment of the tax. Samuel Lewis, for example,

117. Governor Cardew to Secretary of State, May 28, 1898, quoted in *Chalmers Report*, 1: 60, par. 137.

118. Ibid., 2: 550-555, pars. 8612-8616.

119. Editorials, *SLWN*, July 17, 1897, August 28, 1897, September 18, 1897; Hargreaves, "Establishment of the Sierra Leone Protectorate," pp. 75, 80.

120. *Chalmers Report*, 2: 42, pars. 819-822.

121. Hargreaves, "Establishment of the Sierra Leone Protectorate," p. 67; J. D. Hargreaves, "Sir Samuel Lewis and the Legislative Council," *Sierra Leone Studies*, n.s., no. 1, (December 1953), p. 51; *Chalmers Report*, 2: 136-138, 141, pars. 2592-2603.

claimed that missionaries in the protectorate had preached sermons "advising the natives not to resist payment of the hut tax but to do it willingly."[122] Another Creole, J. A. King, stated that "we Sierra Leoneans were all regarded as being on the side of the Government [by up-countrymen] because we always advised the people to pay the tax and not resist."[123]

The press, having a less direct stake in matters than the traders, had never opposed the principle of taxation for the protectorate. Instead, Creole writers feared, quite justifiably, that the relatively high rate of taxation which was being asked would either bring on a revolt up-country or would drive the dissatisfied Africans to the French:

> What we thought should have been proposed was a nominal rate of a six-pence or a shilling on each compound to indicate the change that has come over the districts. . . . We have said before, and we now say it again, that the hinterland of Sierra Leone is not like Natal or Sululand [sic]. We have the French as our neighbors, who would any day gladly welcome a disaffected people within their own territory.[124]

A number of articles expressing criticism of the governor and his policies had appeared in the Freetown newspapers in the months before the war.[125] Nonetheless, any individual who interpreted such writings as incitements to rebellion would have had to be extremely sensitive or imaginative. The "Ode to Bai Bureh," which Governor Cardew cited as an example of Creole disloyalty, need only have been read in its entirety to reveal that its author, while impressed with the chief's stand and partial to his cause, discouraged him from continuing the battle because opposition to British might was without hope.[126] Cardew's allegations notwithstanding, the governor received relatively little direct criticism in the press. A few short news items did appear in the Sierra Leone Times, more humorous than mean, which hinted that many Creoles would have liked to see Cardew leave the colony. "A little bird whispered," one such item began jestingly, "that His Excellency has been appointed Governor of the Gold Coast."[127]

Even if some of the articles did in fact oppose government policies and occasionally presented their opposition in hyperbolic terms—a perfectly legal

122. Chalmers Report, 2: 162, pars. 2897-2899.

123. Ibid., p. 384, pars. 6519-6522.

124. Editorial, SLWN, September 18, 1897. For similar sentiments see editorial, SLWN, March 14, 1896; "One Thing and Another," SLT, April 30, 1898.

125. For instance see "One Thing and Another," SLT, October 10, 1896.

126. "An Ode to Bai Bureh," SLT, April 2, 9, 1898; Chalmers Report, 1: 61, par. 150.

127. SLT, March 19, 1898.

prerogative in the best tradition of British democracy and tabloid journalism—it still needed to be proven that these writings influenced up-country chiefs. The governor was sure "that the Sierra Leone papers had a wide circulation in the Protectorate, and that their contents were interpreted to a large number of natives through educated natives and Sierra Leonians [because] each Chief of any importance usually kept an educated native as clerk, who interpreted the papers to him."[128] Furthermore, Cardew maintained that the up-countrymen "have a great reverence for authority, especially of their Chiefs, whose rule, until the Protectorate came under our jurisdiction, was despotic in the extreme; to hear, therefore, the authority of the Government spoken of with derision and contempt cannot but have a most mischievous effect, and lead to actions subversive of that authority on the part of the natives."[129]

The editors of the two leading Freetown papers implicated by the governor, Cornelius May of the *Sierra Leone Weekly News* and J. A. Fitz-John of the *Sierra Leone Times*, rejected Cardew's allegations. Both claimed few, if any, subscribers in the hinterland among up-countrymen. Admitting that colony newspapers did reach a number of Creoles who lived in the protectorate, they emphasized the loss of immediacy in the lengthy transportation process. Most important, it required great naiveté, they maintained, for anyone to believe that up-countrymen had to wait until newspapers arrived and were read to them to find out what their own grievances should be. "Imagine Bai Bureh and his war boys," May wrote facetiously, "all unlettered men, sitting down, surrounded by hostilities, listening to a translation of what the Freetown Press has written of their exploits!"[130] Nor did knowledgeable Creoles generally accept the premise that every important protectorate chief kept an English-speaking clerk who would interpret, write letters, and read newspapers to them. According to the secretary for native affairs, J. C. E. Parkes, a Creole and perhaps somewhat defensive in this matter, only one Mende chief had a more or less permanent clerk while all other chiefs had temporary arrangements in which they asked traders to interpret and write for them whenever the occasion arose.[131]

The strength of the governor's accusation against the press rested on three

128. *Chalmers Report*, 2: 550, par. 8614.

129. Ibid., par. 8613. Other testimony about press involvement up-country more or less agreed with the governor that the chiefs were aware of Freetown press opinion. See ibid., p. 6, pars. 101-111, p. 16, pars. 294-296, p. 37, pars. 716-719. On the other hand, the manager of the trading firm and retail outlet Paterson-Zochonis, as well as Samuel Lewis and E. W. Blyden, felt that newspapers had little influence in shaping up-country events. See ibid., p. 24, par. 424, p. 139, pars. 2618-2623; *SLWN*, October 1, 1898.

130. Editorial, *SLWN*, July 23, 1898; *Chalmers Report*, 2: 516, par. 8191, 2: 522, par. 8297.

131. *Chalmers Report*, 1: 63, par. 145.

articles—two from the *Sierra Leone Times* of April 6, 1898, and one in the *Sierra Leone Weekly News* of April 16, 1898—none of which could have had much bearing on the initiation of hostilities.[132] As Sir David Chalmers, the royal commissioner, concluded in his report, the conditions which led to the war existed before the articles in question were printed.[133] Besides, the newspapers' policies about printing war news were judicious enough. Realizing that they did not have a reliable correspondent at the scene of the troubles, the editors published only those details about military movements and the progress of the war which came from official and reliable sources.[134] Editorials, of course, expressing opinion rather than hard fact, tended to be less objective than news stories. Even at the height of hostilities in the southern protectorate, however, the newspapers devoted a relatively small percentage of their column space to the "big story"—mainly because they did not have the information. Life went on much as before in the weeklies, and, besides the war, they concerned themselves with a variety of other events— the queen's birthday, Gladstone's death, the mayor of Freetown's Official Dinner. To blame the press for "rabble-rousing" at a time when military movements, rumors, and fear of attack kept the mood of the population at fever pitch revealed the British officials' great need for scapegoats.

Cardew's unjust accusations, although rejected by the Chalmers Commission inquiry, were made at a time when the Colonial Office was increasingly less inclined to give educated Africans the benefit of the doubt. Sierra Leoneans, therefore, were increasingly limited in their influence over protectorate affairs. Even though Major Matthew Nathan, who was acting governor while Cardew was in England on leave, could still rouse Creoles to great cheers by asking them, a year after the battles of 1898, to "take up the white man's burden" and to continue "raising" the people of the protectorate to a "higher state," the days were finished when the British counted on the Creoles as both the products and agents of a "civilizing mission."[135] Interestingly, when Nathan recited Kipling's "White Man's Burden" to the largely Creole audience, he diplomatically omitted the first stanza of the poem which spoke of "New caught and sullen peoples,/Half devil and half child."[136]

In the protectorate, the suspicion that the Creoles had instigated the rising branded Sierra Leoneans as potential troublemakers—a label up-country government officials seemed to equate with the mark of Cain. As British subjects and nonnatives in the protectorate, Creoles fell almost exclusively under the

132. Ibid., p. 60, par. 137.
133. Ibid., p. 63, pars. 145-147.
134. For instance see *SLWN*, April 23, 1898, for a policy statement on this matter.
135. Nathan's speech was given May 1899 at the semi-jubilee celebrations of the Wesleyan High School.
136. See *SLWN*, May 20, 1899, for a report on the acting governor's speech.

jurisdiction of the district officers and were vulnerable to their biases. Sierra Leoneans who went up-country as traders or missionaries, moreover, were kept isolated from the political, legal, and social institutions of the area in which they lived. They were compelled to remain foreigners—outsiders whose physical presence the up-countrymen usually tolerated but rarely understood and made welcome. And it was this continual lack of communication—both on the part of Creoles and protectorate Africans—which kept the gulf that had been formed by their long history of mistrust and cultural divarication open and difficult to span.

Chapter FOUR

"Black Skin, White Masks"?
Intellectual Reactions
to Disillusionment

> *We were aborigines, found upon our own soil, strangers to the white man, and certainly different from him if not in all, in many things. The position between himself and us was that of master and subject, ruler and ruled. We saw him in all the majesty of an alien civilization and we observed that as he either flitted past us, or dwelt in our midst, he had, invariably attending him, comfort, light, liberty, contentment. Did ever unsophisticated humanity dwell amid conditions stimulating admiration without seeking to conform itself to those conditions? Our forebears of 50 years ago, so near the primitive conditions of native life, and who sought to reproduce the European method of living which they admired were not to blame . . . . The white man came to them and was to them as a demi-god; his own civilization appeared to give him supremacy which he enjoyed; the black man also noticed that unless he "conformed" he could not be admitted into confidence, nor thought to be anything in the new European order.*
>
> Editorial, *Sierra Leone Weekly News*, August 6, 1910

> *His originality, name, language, dress, manners and customs were taken from him; and like a tropical fruit planted in a hot house, he became that ridiculous exotic, the black Englishman of Sierra Leone . . . .*
> "When Sierra Leone Ceases To Be British—Another Version by Czar,"
> *Sierra Leone Weekly News*, October 12, 1901

Defensive Africanization: Cultural

Some Sierra Leoneans, ever charitable toward Europeans, responded to the growing alienation from the British with anxiety and insecurity, blaming the turn of events not on external factors but on weaknesses in Creole society. Examining their own culture they agreed that something was amiss, that a

108

"lack of progress" had become the curse of their lives and that they were bordering on degeneracy.

> Whither . . . are we drifting? In Church, in State, in social life, whither? Painful as is the confession . . . we are drifting we know not whither, and the more we endeavour to blind our eyes to the fact by the substitution of artificial humbug and canting hypocrisy for reality and truth, the greater is the peril which threatens. The Church totters, the State grows worse and worse each day, and social life gasps daily for purer air. In these circumstances the outlook is alarming . . . .[1]

A belief that they were slowly dying out reinforced this growing Creole pessimism. Each time after the publication of the official census figures, in 1881, 1891, 1901, and 1911, the fear became especially pronounced. The statistics all seemed to point to a double decline among Sierra Leoneans—a decrease both in the total Creole population and in the ratio of Creoles to up-countrymen within the peninsula.[2] The editorial pages of Freetown newspapers in the last decades of the nineteenth and early twentieth centuries were frequently concerned with the question, "Why Do Creoles Die So Young?"

In fact, the census figures were misleading. The identification of ethnic groups for purposes of census classification was sometimes made on the basis of broad and inaccurate judgments, and persons who were lower class Creoles were often counted and listed as "Natives."[3] Statistics which seemed to indicate a low rate of fertility among Creoles were rendered inaccurate by the incomplete registration of births.[4] And the census figures did not clearly indicate that Sierra Leone had lost a substantial number of Creoles by emigration and not through death. Since the 1830s Sierra Leoneans had been leaving the colony either for temporary periods or as permanent emigrants. Some had simply gone up-country as traders and merchants. Others, who had become wealthy in Freetown, decided to return to the homes from which their ancestors had been taken as slaves. Departing Sierra Leone at various times throughout the century, they often became important actors in the history of Lagos, the Gold Coast, the Gambia, and numerous other places on the African continent.[5]

Creole explanations for their moral and numerical decline varied consider-

1. Editorial, *SLWN*, April 28, 1888; also see *The Watchman*, February 28, 1879.
2. In the decade 1891-1901 the population of the colony actually increased, but by a mere 306 persons.
3. Kuczynski, *Demographic Survey*, 1: 161, 163.
4. Ibid., pp. 12, 197-207, 278.
5. Ibid., p. 278; C. H. Fyfe, "Four Sierra Leone Recaptives," *Journal of African History* 2, no. 1 (1961): 77-86; Kopytoff, *Preface to Modern Nigeria*, passim.

ably in sophistication and depth of analysis. The old standard Victorian assumptions which blamed the ills of soul and body on "vicious indulgence," "intemperate habits," and "fast living" all seemed inadequate, especially since many of the people who were most affected could be counted among the colony's finest citizens.[6] One man attributed the situation to "inexorable decrees" by an "offended Creator" for "misused and abused advantages."[7] Others interpreted their state of being in terms of the survival of the fittest. Comparing their own felt lack of vitality, health, and strength with the vigor of up-countrymen, or even with that of their fathers and grandfathers, these Creoles believed themselves to be growing weaker, fading in mind and body, rapidly being surpassed by the vigorous Mende, Timne, and Limba.[8] Still others explained their situation as a vestige from their "slave past." "The slave mind," stated an editorial in the *Sierra Leone Weekly News*, "is one of the evil things which have come to us by inheritance from the inhuman traffic. . . . All the qualities of mind which are mighty [sic] to obstruct progress both of individuals and communities may be reasonably included in this evil property."[9] Some critics found in the early divisions among Sierra Leoneans explanations for the oft-repeated assertion that Creoles were selfish and unable to unite—factors which were also blamed for inhibiting the community's advancement.[10]

In order to soothe anxieties about their own situation and to assess in less deprecating terms why things had turned out the way they had, a number of Creoles took an altogether different tack. Feeling themselves to have been historically manipulated by a multitude of forces over which they had little control, these Sierra Leoneans turned an introspective eye on their own society, on its character and values, examining in particular the major premise on which their relationship to Britain had been based—the validity of the African assimilation of European ways.

Creoles given to this type of introspection had a great deal in common. The majority of them were at the peak, or very near the peak of the Creole

6. J. H. Spaine's lecture, "The Youths of Sierra Leone, Their Condition and Prospects," *The Independent*, July 22, 1875; editorial, "Early Mortality of Influential Natives of Sierra Leone," *West African Reporter*, June 3, 1882; Dulcie Nicolls, "Effects of Western Education," p. 45.

7. "The Passing Away of the Creole Element," *Colonial and Provincial Reporter*, January 17, 1914.

8. "One Thing and Another," *SLT*, June 24, 1893, August 28, 1897; letter to the editor by Abdul Mortales, January 9, 1898; editorial, January 4, 1902; editorial, June 22, 1912, *SLWN*; *Sierra Leone Guardian and Foreign Mails*, October 18, 1912.

9. Editorial, *SLWN*, March 4, 1911.

10. The term *yorubaism* was sometimes used to describe this inability to unite, probably in reference to the Yoruba civil wars. See *SLWN*, March 4, 1911; Luke, "Some Notes on the Creoles and Thier Land," pp. 61-62; Fyfe, *History of Sierra Leone*, p. 463; editorial, "The State of the Colony," *SLT*, February 17, 1900; *SLWN*, March 10, 1906.

class structure, star products of Britain's imperial mission in Sierra Leone, and in firm possession of European knowledge, techniques, and outlooks. As the persons most exposed to Europeanization, they were extremely sensitive and vulnerable to changes in European attitudes toward them. Culturally Europeanized but racially black African, they suffered a crisis of identity when rejected by the British on whom they modeled themselves.

The group was numerically small. But it included the most literate and vocal members of society, men with direct access to the Sierra Leone press and other vehicles of communication. Occupying the top rung of Creole society, they set fashions, shaped opinions, and exerted an influence far exceeding their numerical strength.

For the most part they were conservative in social outlook, advocating moral rather than political reforms in the way of life as they knew it. Caught up in the British idea of fair play, they were upset when their mentors deviated from the rules. But, when pressed, they were Victorian gentlemen looking for amelioration rather than revolution. Barricade fighting was alien to the tradition they had come to love and accept; to them, composing cleverly worded protest letters to the editor of the *Weekly News*, while sitting in an easy chair and sipping afternoon tea, seemed much more civilized and less foreign.

Edward Wilmot Blyden, although not a Creole himself, was one of their primary intellectual influences and spokesmen.[11] Early in life Blyden fashioned an ideology which combined a teleological belief in the perfectibility of man with a conviction about the uniqueness of races. Influenced by his Christian upbringing, his training as a minister, and his connection with the New York Colonization Society, he had no doubt that the millennium would ultimately come, but only after each race had fulfilled its divinely ordained destiny. "Each race is endowed with peculiar talents," he wrote in *Christian-*

11. Blyden, one of the most remarkable Africans of his time, was of Ibo ancestry, born on St. Thomas in the Virgin Islands in 1832. When he was refused admission to colleges in the United States, where he had been sent to study by an American missionary, he accepted an offer by the New York State Colonization Society to emigrate and to study in Liberia. Landing in Liberia in 1851, he began his long and active connection with West Africa. He spent the next twenty years of his life in that country practically without interruption. During this time he became an ordained and licensed Presbyterian minister, editor of the *Liberia Herald*, principal of Alexander High School in Monrovia, a professor, and, later, vice principal of Liberia College, secretary of state, minister plenipotentiary to the Court of St. James, and a three-time unsuccessful candidate for the presidency of the Republic. At the same time, largely through self-teaching, Blyden claimed to have mastered Latin, Greek, Hebrew, Arabic, Spanish, Dutch, French, and German. In the late 1870s, after acquiring powerful political enemies in Liberia, he spent more and more time in Sierra Leone. Eventually, although absent for extended stays in Europe, America, and other parts of Africa, Freetown and not Monrovia became his home until his death in 1912. For additional biographical informa-

ity, Islam and the Negro Race, "and watchful to the last degree is the great Creator over the individuality, the freedom and independence of each. In the music of the universe each shall give a different sound, but necessary to the grand symphony."[12] In Blyden's conception, differences between races did not mean that any one was inferior or superior, either physically, intellectually, or morally. Each was capable of equal, but not identical, development and progress. Europeans in this racially determined universe became God's rulers, God's soldiers, and God's policemen to keep order. In the divine plan, it was their role to work for the material and temporal advancement of humanity. Science and politics were their racial fortes; individualism was the basis of their society.[13] African blacks, on the other hand, possessed a different racial "personality" (Blyden termed it "Negro Personality"). They were members of a "spiritual" race, communal and cooperative rather than "egotistic and competitive" in social organization, and polygynous rather than monogamous in family life. Unlike the whites, their divine "gift" did not lie in political life but in spiritual advancement through church, school, farm, and workshop.[14] And, perhaps because they were by nature the less aggressive people, the qualities uniquely inherent in their race had to be nurtured, protected, and developed if they were to contribute their share to the total uplifting of mankind. As Blyden saw it, no man benefited from the dilution or destruction of the black African personality through the wholesale introduction and acceptance of European culture.

All these ideas, of course, had particular relevance for Creoles. Blyden shared the pessimism some Creoles held about their own society. He ex-

---

tion, see E. W. Blyden et al., *The People of Africa—A Series of Papers on Their Character, Condition, and Future Prospects* (New York, 1871), biographical note by H.M.S., pp. 1-3; obituary, *Journal of the African Society* 11 (1912): 362-364; *SLWN*, 10 February 1912; obituary, *Sierra Leone Guardian and Foreign Mails*, 16 February 1912; Hollis R. Lynch, *Edward Wilmot Blyden, Pan-Negro Patriot, 1832-1912* (London, 1967); Edith Holden, *Blyden of Liberia. An Account of the Life and Labors of Edward Wilmot Blyden, LL.D., As Recorded in Letters and in Print* (New York, 1967).

12. John R. Schott, "Edward Wilmot Blyden: First Pan Africanist?" (Paper presented at the Ninth Annual African Studies Association Meeting, Bloomington, Indiana, 1967), gives an interesting interpretation of the influences of Christianity and the ideology of the New York Colonization Society on Blyden's thought; E. W. Blyden, *Christianity, Islam and the Negro Race*, 2d ed. (London, 1889), pp. 317-318.

13. E. W. Blyden, *Proceedings at the Banquet in Honour of Edward Wilmot Blyden, LL.D., on the Occasion of his Retirement From His Official Labours in the Colony of Sierra Leone January 24th, 1907* (London, 1907), pp. 40-41; "Banquet in Honor of C. E. Wright," *SLWN*, November 28, 1903.

14. E. W. Blyden, *Africa and the Africans. Proceedings on the Occasion of a Banquet Given to E. W. Blyden by West Africans in London, August 15, 1903* (London, 1903), p. 44; E. W. Blyden, *African Life and Customs* (London, 1908), pp. 9-36; obituary, *Sierra Leone Guardian and Foreign Mails*, February 16, 1912.

plained the Creole lack of initiative and "African manhood," their superficial attainments, lack of progress, "artifical emotions," and their easily caricatured appearance, by blaming their European education and training:

> Sierra Leone . . . began as an exotic plant. Africans from across the sea, Nova Scotians and Maroons, denationalised, de-Africanised by exile—were brought and settled here with all the un-African notions they had imbibed among their foreign masters. . . . When they crossed the sea they brought their chains with them in the shape of uncongenial and incompatible religious and social institutions . . . . The Governors were obliged to govern through the governed, and the governed stood aloof from the natives and from everything African; thought themselves different from and superior to their surroundings; formed no connection with the indigenous inhabitants, but rather placed themselves in a hostile attitude—so they constituted themselves a social and political island, affecting habits and customs entirely out of keeping with their surroundings. . . . With the help of an inexperienced Government these *quasi* foreigners forced the helpless recaptives, when they arrived among them, to adopt their manners—their religion and their social arrangements. Sharing the fate of all things unnatural, these Nova Scotians and Maroons passed away, leaving the recaptives to follow their example . . . . This is the history of Sierra Leone in a nutshell. It has only two stages—infancy and decrepitude; never vigorous manhood.[15]

Since the races were divinely ordained to move along "parallel lines," and not "in the same groove," no amount of cultural interaction or tutelage would ever make Europeans from black Africans or black Africans from Europeans.[16] At best, those Africans who thought of themselves as Europeans were imitators; at worse they were "apes" and parasites, men without identity who had lost "the flavor of their race."[17] Speaking to the Freetown Unity Club, Blyden was explicit:

> Your first duty is to be *yourselves* . . . . You need to be told to keep constantly before yourselves the fact that you are African, not Europeans—black men, not white men—that you were created

15. "Banquet in Honor of C. E. Wright," *SLWN*, November 28, 1903. Also see Blyden to Earl Kimberley, 1873, in C.O. 267/324; Blyden, *Christianity, Islam and the Negro Race*, pp. 76-77, 254; Blyden, *Aims and Methods of a Liberal Education for Africans. Inaugural Address delivered by E. W. Blyden, LL.D., President of Liberia College, January 5, 1881* (Cambridge, Mass., 1882), pp. 6-11.

16. Blyden, *Christianity, Islam and the Negro Race*, pp. 317-318.

17. Ibid., pp. 43-44, 398-399; *SLWN*, April 11, 1891.

with the physical qualities which distinguish you for the glory of
the Creator, and for the happiness and perfection of humanity;
and that in your endeavors to make yourselves something else
you are not only spoiling your nature and turning aside from
your destiny, but you are robbing humanity of the part you
ought to contribute to its complete development and welfare, and
you become as salt, which has lost its savour—good for nothing,
but to be cast out and trodden down by others.[18]

Blyden had made a series of trips to the interior both in Liberia and Sierra
Leone, and he often met with Muslim traders from up-country with whom he
conversed in Arabic. To contrast with the coastal, educated, Europeanized
Africans—ironically, the group to which he himself belonged—Blyden offered
the people of the interior of Africa as prototypes possessing the true "Negro
Personality." He wrote:

In the European settlements on the coast, there are visible the
melancholy effects of the fatal contagion of a mimic or spurious
Europeanism. [Those] who have been to Europe, bring back and
diffuse among their people a reverence for some of their customs
of that country, of which the more cultivated are trying to get
rid. But, happily, the inhospitable and inexorable climate pre-
vents this pseudo-civilization, called "progress," from spreading
to the interior. The tribes still retain their simplicity and remain
unaffected.[19]

Undoubtedly, through his contacts, he should have had firsthand information
about the customs and ways of the hinterland. But his writings belie this. Not
particularly drawn to ethnographic study or description, Blyden built his
"interior Africans" into an abstraction—as removed from an African reality as
the noble savage of eighteenth-century Europe had been false to the character, appearance, and ways of the American Indians.

Even he, of course, considered the interior to be far from perfect. Like
other Europeanized Africans of his time, Blyden looked contemptuously on
"paganism, with all its horrors and abominations," which was practiced by
interior peoples.[20] He admitted that up-countrymen lived a "savage existence" in "quiescent and stagnant barbarism" but only because of the "cruel
conditions" of their environment.[21] Nonetheless, the good far outweighed
the bad. The people, Blyden felt, were quiet, unobtrusive, and conservative—

18. SLWN, June 20, 1891.

19. Blyden, Christianity, Islam and the Negro Race, p. 400.

20. Ibid., preface, pp. iii, iv.

21. Reprint of a letter from Blyden to the Christian Advocate in New York, the
official organ of the Methodist Episcopal Church in the United States, in SLWN, July 15,
1899.

possessing "virgin souls" which needed only direction and guidance to make them a center of widespread influence.[22] In the interior, he wrote, "every prospect pleases" and "man is not so vile."[23] Only by "judicious inter-marriages" and an emulation of the positive aspects of the "personality" of blacks from the interior could Creoles and other "degenerate" Africans who had succumbed to foreign influences and European habits be saved.[24]

Blyden's efforts to make West African blacks more conscious of their "true" racial identity and his challenge of their wholesale assimilation of European ways struck an exposed nerve among all Creoles concerned with the state of their own society. His uncomplimentary views about Europeanized Africans hit painfully hard, to be sure, but they were nonetheless the views of a fellow educated black and, as such, more easily received than if they had been made by a European. Moreover, no matter how harsh their implications for Creoles, his ideas were also extremely attractive: to believe in the distinctiveness and uniqueness of the black race and its destiny was an effective psychological salve against the pain inflicted by European insults and discrimination.

Influenced by Blyden, some Sierra Leoneans began to attribute the ills of their society to the perversion of their true racial personality by means of indiscriminate Europeanization. In their anxiety and depression they looked again at themselves—at their educational achievements, their social life and occupations, their dwellings and diet, their trousers, coats, top hats, and boots, their woolly hair parted in the European style—and were displeased to find a community of captive intellect, one that had grown up "aping the white man," blindly imitating manners and customs that were racially alien, and, in any case, unsuitable to the African environment.[25] A few expressed themselves in terms of Blyden's teleological vision—repudiating their emula-tion of European customs and manners as a falsification of a divinely ordained separation of races.[26] Others put their views in more secular terms:

22. Article reprinted from *The Charleston World*, in *SLWN*, January 8, 1890; "Bly-den in Lagos," *SLWN*, February 14, 1891.

23. *West African Reporter*, November 28, 1876.

24. Blyden, *Christianity, Islam and the Negro Race*, pp. 82, 234-235; Blyden speak-ing about Sierra Leone in Lagos, *SLWN*, September 20, 1884; "Address delivered at the celebration of the 20th Anniversary of the Educational Institute, L. J. Leopold, Prin-cipal," *SLWN*, September 20, 1903.

25. See, for example, James H. Spaine, "The Youths of Sierra Leone, Their Condi-tion and Prospects," *The Independent*, July 22, 1875; letter to the editor, *Methodist Herald*, December 10, 1884; letter to the editor by Latonday of Abeokuta, December 12, 1885; "First of a Series of Articles on 'The Degeneracy of the Civilized Blacks of West Africa,'" July 14, 1906; editorial, June 8, 1901, *SLWN*; "One Thing and An-other," *SLT*, August 28, November 20, 1897.

26. See "Notes by the Way," *SLWN*, July 28, 1888; also read the comments about the pageant which Blyden wrote for the festivities celebrating the centenary of the founding of Sierra Leone in *SLWN*, June 23, 1887; and *Memorial of the Jubilee of Her*

Nature must have her way. She is always insuperable. She will triumph over all our false aims and aspirations. Some say that we are now in a transition state, and that the process of all transitions is painful and sometimes destructive . . . . But, under our climatic and racial conditions, the transition only leads to death . . . . The fact is, that not only is there a want of adjustment between the two states of things, but an invincible incompatibility. The facts of European civilization will never fit in with the everlasting facts of African conditions. For the retention of certain social and domestic customs in African life the logic of experience is the strongest and surest justification. If Nature demands the continuation of the domestic and social customs of the natives as the price of the preservation of the race in this climate, the price must, of course, be paid or extinction will supervene.[27]

Still others, however, decided to break through the tyranny of foreign customs by a direct reversion to traits, manners, and identifications which they felt were inherently black African. William J. Davis, for example, who was senior master at the Wesleyan High School and the first Sierra Leonean to receive a B.A. from London University, changed his name to Orishatukah Faduma, a name which he derived from the Yoruba divinity Orisha and the oracle Ifa.[28] A letter to the editor of the *Sierra Leone Weekly News* written by Kufileh Tubohku—a man who himself had probably "Africanized" his name—explained Davis's action:

We have received an education and a civilization that have instilled into us an element of doubt as to our own capacity and destiny, that have implanted in us falsehoods about ourselves, which, instead of producing in us self-respect, efficiency, and self-reliance, with a sense of our own individuality—the outcome of a correct education—have rendered us self-detractors, self-depreciators, distrustful of our own possibilities, striving to escape from our own individuality if possible, contemptuous and doubtful of every native element, and indifferent to everything of our own originality . . . .
Those who censured Faduma for changing a name by which he had been known from his birth should remember that every one of our Liberated Negro Parents had a name given him in the land of his nativity by which he was called and known from his birth up to the time he arrived in the land of his exile. He had a

Majesty's Reign and the Centenary of Sierra Leone, 1887 (London, 1887), pp. 92-108.
    27. *SLWN*, January 12, 1901.
    28. Letter to the editor, *SLWN*, October 1, 1887; *Methodist Herald*, August 24, 1887; Parrinder, *West African Religion*, pp. 12, 26, 96.

name full of meaning . . . preserving a tribal or racial individuality. When transported through the baneful traffic of the Slave
Trade to this land, that name was exchanged for a foreign one . . .
void of meaning and insignificant to him. . . .

It is nought but a profound and crass ignorance that thinks a
man who would be civilized must forsake all that belongs and is
natural to him, in exchange for what is foreign and unnatural.[29]

A number of Creoles joined Faduma and "reformed" their names as well,
either shedding their "foreign" surname to adopt one with an African
"sound," or adding an African name to their European one. Thus A. E.
Metzger became Toboku-Metzger when he added his father's Yoruba name to
the name which the family had taken from his father's German missionary
pastor at Kissy.[30] O. T. George became O. T. Nana; Claude George, the man
who had written *The Rise of British West Africa*, became Esu Biyi; Isaac
Augustus Johnson changed to Algerine Kefallah Sankoh; and Africanus
Matthew Goodman became Eyahjemi Moondia.

Perhaps more important among these Sierra Leone Creoles than name
reform was the establishment of dress reform. A Dress Reform Society,
claiming E. W. Blyden, Reverend James Johnson, and Reverend J. R. Frederick as associates, was founded in 1887 by some of the most socially
prominent Creoles in the Colony. James Hasting Spaine, the colonial post-
master, was president, A. E. Toboku-Metzger was the secretary, Cornelius
May, editor of the *Methodist Herald* and later editor and owner of the *Sierra
Leone Weekly News*, was a founding member along with Orishatukah Faduma
and Enoch Faulkner, chief clerk at the colonial secretary's office and later
assistant colonial secretary.[31]

Creoles in the Dress Reform Society, in agreement with people such as the
Japanese, Chinese, and Indians, whose individual clothing styles underscored
what Blyden would have called "their separate racial identity," were convinced that Creoles' addiction to the "Religion of the Frock Coat and Tall
Hat" was yet another mark of their cultural subordination.[32] The society saw

29. Letter to the editor by Kufileh Tubohku, *SLWN*, October 1, 1887.

30. See Fyfe, *History of Sierra Leone*, p. 468.

31. Other founding members were: J. C. Sawyerr, N. F. Browne, C. E. Wright, J. B.
Mends, M. Benson-Nicol, J. W. M. Horton, E. Beccles Davies. Others who subsequently
joined were: J. C. May, publisher of the *Methodist Herald* and principal of the Wes-
leyan's Boy's High School; J. B. M'Carthy, a well-do-do merchant; J. Langley Grant;
T. Taylor; S. G. Roberts; R. Smith; T. Dundas; J. S. T. Davies; P. A. Bickersteth; S. O.
Lardner; E. C. Lisk. See supplement, *The Artisan*, December 31, 1887; *Methodist
Herald*, December 21, 1887.

32. Letter to the editor by C. W. Farquhar, *SLWN*, August 10, 1907, contains the
phrase "Religion of the Frock Coat and Tall Hat" to describe the Creole habit of wearing
European-style clothing.

the elimination of the most obvious badge of Europeanization—European dress—as the first, and most important, step in bringing about a gradual independence from all European customs.

> It should be presumption to state that the intended sphere of the Dress Reform Society is unlimited. It would set itself as time advances to grapple with other social and local questions. Its intention is to become the line of advance of all social improvements. . . . It is a society that could become more and more the rallying point for all who long for and are zealous for the independent national existence of Africa and the Negro.[33]

By means of dress reforms, moreover, they were hopeful that Creole degeneracy and early mortality would be counteracted. Convinced that their lives were ephemeral, their physiques inferior and less hardy, and their strength feeble, they associated their malaise with the European clothing that they had adopted.[34] A Creole columnist wrote in the *Sierra Leone Weekly News*:

> If we compare the state of our health with that of our friends in the Niger or elsewhere along the entire West African Coasts, we cannot but conclude that, on the whole, we in Sierra Leone are actually going out of order. Wherein then lies the difference? Not so much in climatic influences . . . for in the Niger, it is known to be twice as hot as we have it in Sierra Leone. The difference exists in the kind and quality of the clothes we put on. We please Civilization for the continuance of a practice as inconsistent with common sense, as it is injurious to the health.[35]

To counteract the perversion of their "racial personality" and to safeguard their health, the members of the Dress Reform Society adopted a new wardrobe. Instead of trousers with belt and braces, shirt, waistcoat, collar, and tie, they devised an "under-tunic" and gown, somewhat like a Turkish kaftan, to be worn over a pair of breeches reaching down to the knees, similar

33. *Methodist Herald*, December 21, 1887.

34. Ibid. The high, starched collars, ties, silk top hats, and heavy woolen suits worn by many men, the corsets or tight lacings, long dresses, and bonnets in style with the ladies had all been designed for colder weather and were not loose enough to allow for the free circulation of air needed in the tropics. See *SLWN*, May 19, 1888, for the reprint of a paper given to the Dress Reform Society by Surgeon J. J. Lamprey, Senior Medical Officer of the Army Medical Staff of the West Coast of Africa, on clothing to be worn in the tropics. Also see letter by J. J. Lamprey, *SLWN*, August 4, 1888; *SLWN*, February 9, 1889.

35. "My View of Things," *SLWN*, October 30, 1886. For similar opinions see "My View of Things," *SLWN*, January 16, 1885; letter to the editor, December 10, 1884; "Meeting of the Dress Reform Society," December 21, 1887, *Methodist Herald*.

to European knickerbockers but free at the bottom to admit the flow of air. Female fashions, however, were not altered at all. In the age of Victoria, reform bowed to discretion.

At no time did the members of the Dress Reform Society or the individuals who Africanized their name ever view their activities as steps to initiate direct cultural links between themselves and the African peoples in the immediate hinterland of Sierra Leone. The adopted names were generally in the language of the Creoles' forefathers—most usually in Yoruba—or, like the name "Africanus," were manufactured to sound African. They were not names generally found in Sierra Leone's up-country. The Dress Reform Society's wardrobe was an invention as well—somewhat like the short trousers and sleeveless country-cloth gowns of up-countrymen to be sure, but still different enough not to be confused with them. All this, of course, served a distinct psychological function. In defining elements of the black African personality as they saw fit—far enough removed from up-country realities so that no confusion would arise—Creole name and dress reformers were able both to have their cake and to eat it: they could believe that they were no longer wholesale imitators of the Europeans and were shaping their culture more in keeping with their "racial destiny," without, at the same time, fearing reversion to the ways of up-country "barbarian aborigines."

Dress reform was shorter-lived than name reform. The members of the Dress Reform Society wore their costumes to the relatively infrequent meetings which were held in 1887 and 1888. The strength of their convictions in a closed gathering weakened in public. Spaine, the president, argued that it was too expensive to replace overnight their European wardrobe by the newly adopted one.[36] But the basic reason for the failure of the society was that its members were too proud of their high status within Creole society to risk being laughed at and socially demoted for nonconformity, both by other Creoles and by the trend-setting Europeans.[37] Neither could the society's members answer the argument that Sierra Leoneans, unlike the people of Lagos or the Gold Coast who had not been removed from their traditional homes or had again returned to them, no longer had their own native costumes. Having been brought up and educated in the European manner, therefore, why should they not adopt European dress as well? Unable to counter this argument or to shrug off derision, the Dress Reform Society folded quickly, although the idea of dress reform resurfaced a number of times in Sierra Leone.[38]

36. *Methodist Herald*, December 21, 1887.
37. Ibid.
38. *The Artisan*, October 6, 1887, ridiculed name and dress reform in one of its articles; "The Degeneracy of the Civilized Blacks of West Africa," *SLWN*, July 21, 1906; Joseph Renner-Maxwell, *The Negro Question, or Hints for the Physical Improvement of the Negro Race, with Special Reference to West Africa* (London, 1892), p. 30.

Name changes, on the other hand, were obviously less visible and thus less prone to come under attack by people in the streets. Europeans seemed less amused by the decision of a few Creoles to Africanize their names than they were by the Creoles' choice of unusual Greek, Latin, or Biblical first names and by their seemingly pretentious inclination to add a hyphenated second name to their surname.[39] But even name changing did not escape derision completely, and the practice, while remaining a characteristic of Creole society long after the 1880s, became much less publicized.[40]

Defensive Africanization: History and Myth

Unable to escape the disparagement cast on their way of life, their past, and their achievements, it was essential for Creoles to regain their self-respect and to heal their battered race pride by restoring their heritage to a place of honor. In order to achieve this—to convince both themselves and their European detractors—they began to search back in history and, through a filter dictated by their own needs and expectations, sought evidence of great deeds and past glories.

The look back in history was not without obstructions. The direct ancestors of the Creoles had been torn from their traditional societies by the shattering experience of slavery. Although a number of them remembered the histories of their people from preslavery days, their links with the past had nevertheless been broken, and, with the passage of time, these memories tended to fade.[41] Thus the Creoles, as a conglomerate community originating from the intermarriage of settler Africans from a number of different ethnic groups, knew even less about the histories of their ancestors. Furthermore, since their formal education largely derived from European books and teachers, they had little opportunity to acquire this information outside the home. Knowing so little about the historical deeds of the people from whom they descended, Creoles could hardly be expected to rely exclusively on this material in order to impress skeptics. On occasion they did glorify their Settler and Liberated African ancestors—"those giants of our race," as a writer in the *Sierra Leone Weekly News* called them.[42] The same man wrote,

39. "Familiar Talks on Familiar Subjects," *SLWN*, September 25, 1915, discusses European attitudes to so-called "double-barrelled" names.

40. *The Artisan*, October 6, 1887; Fyfe, *History of Sierra Leone*, p. 468; *SLWN*, June 19, 1909, August 13, 1910, September 25, 1915, June 23, 1923. Many other examples of name changing exist as well.

41. See Philip D. Curtin, ed., *Africa Remembered: Narratives by West Africans from the Era of the Slave Trade* (Madison, Wis., 1967), pp. 317-333.

42. "Some Notables of Sierra Leone in the Past by DeeTee," *SLWN*, January 4, 1899.

How some of these men who like the ancient people of God, the Israelites, though kept in the house of bondage for hundreds of years, and made to serve their task-masters with rigour, yet on being enfranchised and liberated, became in a few years the equals of their benefactors and liberators, stood head and shoulders above the aboriginal inhabitants of this Peninsula, and laid the foundation for the social, religious, and political prosperity of the race, seems indeed miraculous . . . . The lives of these men would be recorded and their achievements chronicled in book-form. Had we these records, we would have no cause to deplore our non-progressiveness and lack of cohesion; for very shame we who pride ourselves in our improved civilization, would have been forced to emulate their deeds and add to their performance.[43]

Praise of this sort, however, was infrequent. Tainted by the indignities of their past slavery, these ancestors were not the ideal example of unqualified historical success.

Alternate sources for the kind of historical material the Creoles sought did, of course, exist outside their own immediate society. The histories of their neighbors in the interior of Africa could have presented them with deeds and stout heroes sufficient to belie European slander and to ensure the greatness of the black African past. They could have invoked the attainments of past West African empires like Ghana, Mali, and Songhai, or great African warriors and rulers like Sundiata and Mansa Musa. But this they did not do. Undoubtedly, given the cultural gulf that had grown up between themselves and the African ethnic groups of the interior, some Creoles were unsure that the people surrounding them even had a history, to say nothing of its being worthy of exaltation. Others, products of a Eurocentric educational system, knew relatively little African history. While many of them had indeed heard of men like Uthman dan Fodio, Sheikh Al-Hadj Omar, and other African leaders from the near and distant past, their knowledge was spotty and inaccurate. More contemporary accomplishments, like the British defeats by the Ashanti and Zulu and the French setbacks by Samori Toure, might be taken as indubitable proof of black African military prowess, but, at a time when European imperial expansion in Africa was at a high point, the honor and reputation of a race could hardly be made to depend on such isolated triumphs.[44]

43. *SLWN*, July 15, 1899.
44. "The Fall of Ashanti," a poem, *SLWN*, May 4, 1901; *SLWN*, January 28, 1899; Blyden, *Christianity, Islam and the Negro Race*, p. 10; speech by Blyden to the Freetown Unity Club, *SLWN*, June 20, 1891; Claude George, *The Rise of British West Africa* . . . (London, 1902-1903), pt. 5, app. Z, pp. 455-456.

Since they lacked the factual tools to reconstruct African history and to make it acceptable on its own terms, these Creoles had another alternative, one which would not only satisfy their own quest for honor but also be most likely to impress Europeans. European racial slurs were often made about black Africans in general—not just Creoles in particular. Creoles, therefore, responded as "black Africans"—as members of a large and wronged African community, rather than as individuals belonging to a particular group. Having been educated by Europeans, they used that education as an instrument of combat, to show that they not only possessed a great past but were in fact akin to the originators of the civilization cherished by the West. In this way a number of Creoles traced their cultural genealogy not to any contemporary group of Africans, nor their history to recent deeds or traditions, but back to what they believed to be the general black African past—back to the glories of Roman Africa, ancient Egypt, and the greatness of the biblical Middle East.[45]

Blyden's influence on some of these endeavors—exerted through his activities in Sierra Leone and through his many speeches and writings—is apparent. In his essay "The Negro in Ancient History" and in his travel account *From West Africa to Palestine*, his reconstruction of the glories of Negro antiquity anticipated the aims, concerns, and the methods of Creole writers like A. B. C. Merriman-Labor. In *From West Africa to Palestine*, Blyden described his visit to the great pyramids of Egypt. He saw these as the work of "the enterprising sons of Ham," the racial progenitors of his contemporary "Negro-Africans," men who had sent civilization into Greece and thus had been teachers of the ancient poets, historians, and mathematicians. Standing in the central hall of a pyramid, his fervent dream had been that Negro-Africans would retake their fame. And, in an aside to Europeans—as much if not more the intended audience for his writings than educated Africans—he hoped that they would accept the Negroes' participation in the great deeds of history.[46]

Even before Blyden, however, Dr. James Africanus Beale Horton had written of "Africa's Great Past" in his *West African Countries and Peoples*, a book which he revealingly subtitled "A Vindication of the African Race." The book was a direct response to a report of a select committee of the House of Commons which, in 1865, had studied British involvement in West Africa and had recommended imperial retrenchment everywhere "except,

45. "Education . . . as instruments of combat" is a phrase used by Georges Balandier, *Afrique Ambigue* (Paris, 1957), p. 280.

46. E. W. Blyden, *From West Africa to Palestine* (Freetown, 1873), pp. 104-110. Visiting the Sphinx, he commented: "Her [the Sphinx's] features are decidedly of the African or Negro type, with 'expanded nostrils.' Is not the Sphinx clear evidence," he therefore asked, "as to the peculiar type or race to which that king [of Egypt] belonged?" (p. 114).

probably, Sierra Leone," and the preparation of educated Africans for self-government.[47] Horton sought to counteract the detrimental evidence given to the committee by Creole-haters such as Richard Burton, and was particularly concerned with obliterating the infamous slurs cast on the entire community of educated West Africans, especially through the pseudo-scientific racism expounded by organizations like the British Anthropological Society.[48] In antiquity, Horton believed, Africa had been the nursery of science and literature. Both Greece and Rome had acquired these arts by means of the pilgrimages men like Solon, Plato, and Pythagoras had made to that continent in search of knowledge. Christianity, moreover, owed something of its development to Africa because men such as "Origen, Tertullian, Augustin, Clemens, Alexandrinus, and Cyril, who were fathers and writers of the Primitive Church, were tawny African bishops of Apostolic renown."[49]

Charles Marke, a Wesleyan native minister in Sierra Leone, paraphrased Horton's statements but embellished them when he stated that Africa was once adorned "with churches, colleges, and repositories of learning . . . and . . . was the seat of a most powerful government which contended with Rome for the sovereignty of the world."[50] J. Augustus Cole, who eventually Africanized his name to Abayomi Cole, lecturing before a crowded house at the Wesleyan Methodist Church in Richmond, Indiana, asserted that the ancient Egyptians were black Africans. Likewise, a Creole writer in *The Watchman and West African Record* reminded Sierra Leoneans: "Let it not be forgotten that we are the direct descendants of men that have built those stupendous Pyramids which have in all ages exacted wonder and admiration, and have baffled the most skillful of modern architects."[51]

Merriman-Labor, who had grown up at the height of British disdain for educated Africans, was satisfied in his *Epitome of a Series of Lectures on the Negro Race* that West African Negroes descended from Ethiopians because both "practice circumcision," "are in the same branch of language," and "are identical in physique, physiognomy, and colour." Ethiopians, in turn, "are descendants of Cush, the Son of Ham, the grandson of Noah, the ninth patriarch in descent from Adam, the father of all mankind. Therefore, in

47. Great Britain, Parliament, *Parliamentary Papers* (House of Commons, 1865), 5: 8513-19, 2045-46.

48. Known formally as "The Anthropological Society of London," this organization had Richard Burton as a vice president. Using "science," it sought to demonstrate the inferiority of nonwhites. See Fyfe, *History of Sierra Leone*, p. 335.

49. Horton, *West African Countries and Peoples*, p. 67.

50. Charles Marke, *Africa and the Africans* (Freetown, 1881), pp. 26-28.

51. *The Watchman and West African Record*, October 30, 1887. The *Methodist Herald*, April 27, 1887, reprinted an account of Cole's lecture from the *Richmond Daily Telegram*, March 19, 1887.

Adam through Cush ... is the origin of the Negro Race."[52] Having established this pedigree, Merriman-Labor then used it to link blacks to the great deeds which Europeans generally associated with "ancient civilizations." According to Genesis, which he pointed out to be divinely revealed and therefore unerring, the Cushites ("let us call them Ethiopians or ancient Negroes, just as we choose"[53]) achieved great distinctions. They founded Nineveh and other great cities and, under their leader Nimrod, built Babylon, the world's first kingdom. The ancient Negroes were, furthermore, chosen by God "to be the primitive leaders of the van of civilization and to teach mankind the first principles of good government." Before Nimrod, no governmental authority had existed except that of a father over his household. Under him, families and tribes were united into a commonwealth. These people, in turn, went on to teach "the elementary principles of government to the Egyptians, from whom Greece and ... Rome ... Europe and America, borrowed much that was profitable."[54]

After constructing a magnificent past for the Negro race, however, Creole intellectuals needed to rationalize its subsequent decline in Africa. God, according to Merriman-Labor, having employed blacks as the primitive leaders of the world, "knew what evils a continued leadership would entail." He thus took the "sun of civilization" away from them, in much the same way that He had taken it away from Moses and the Israelites, and allowed it to move westwards, first over Greece, then Rome, and ultimately over Britain. This idea combined religious determinism with the concept, old and persistent among European historians, of the "westward flow of civilization."[55] Cole fit the downfall of Negro greatness within the framework of a cyclical theory of history. "When a race has reached its zenith of physical intellectuality," he wrote, "and developed its highest civilization and can go no more in its own cycle, there is a tendency for it to progress to absolute evil. This has been the case with the Black Race who inhabited the ancient Continents—and no other race will escape it." Similarly, Horton discussed Negro decline in terms of the rise and fall of nations and the tendency for human affairs to undergo gradual and progressive deterioration.

In no case did Creole writers want to convey the impression that blacks, having declined from past greatness, were now doomed to perpetual stagnation. The contemporary state of affairs in Africa was seen as transitory—as a historical setback and not a permanent condition. "The race which is back-

52. A. B. C. Merriman-Labor, *An Epitome of a Series of Lectures on the Negro Race* (Freetown, 1900), pp. 11-12.

53. Ibid., p. 13.

54. Ibid., pp. 13-15.

55. Merriman-Labor, *Negro Race*, pp. 13-14. For a study of this idea see Loren Baritz, "The Idea of the West," *American Historical Review* 66 (April 1961): 618-640; Curtin, *Image of Africa*, pp. 249-250, 375-376.

Figure 8. A. B. C. Merriman-Labor. His *Britons Through Negro Spectacles* was banned in South Africa.

ward today," wrote Cole, "can be drawn by a new current of evolution and come again into prominence, when those in advance are descending." And, according to Horton, "those who have lived in utter barbarism, after a lapse of time become the standing nation." Since nations were subject to a cyclical law of history, West Africans could well hope that, in time, they would again "occupy a prominent position in the world's history, and . . . command a voice in the council of nations."[56]

As black Africans, most Creole writers felt that they would be able to view historical events relating to Africans from a different perspective than that employed by Europeans. Merriman-Labor's *An Epitome of a Series of Lectures on the Negro Race*, for example, was a child of its age—a reaction to the educational system then prevalent in British colonies which concentrated entirely on a Eurocentric curriculum and refused to acknowledge that Africans had a historical past worth studying.[57] "It is a matter for 'regret,' " wrote Merriman-Labor in the first chapter of this work, "that every intelligent schoolboy in our country knows much of the Caucasian Race, and at the same time little of the Negro section of mankind. Even the limited knowledge which he possesses of the Negro . . . is inaccurate and unmethodical; for it is acquired from books, the writers of which are not Negroes."[58] Because he was black, therefore, Merriman-Labor thought himself better qualified to write and lecture about his race than any person who approached the subject from a foreign point of view.

All too often, however, Creole intellectuals found themselves less distant from the framework of European thought than they were willing to admit. This was both the benefit and the burden of their Europeanized upbringing. Having believed their missionary teachers in the past—that European learning and technology were the keys to the kingdom of acceptance and modernity— they had readily absorbed European concepts and values and had become most adept at using materials from their Europeanized educational experience. For this reason, even what on the surface may have appeared as indigenous philosophy—like Blydenism—was in reality constructed from the intellectual bricks and mortar with which their Europeanized instruction had first acquainted them.

The Bible, for instance, was the book the Creoles employed most fre-

56. J. A. Cole, "The Place of the Negro in the World's Evolution," *SLWN*, October 30, 1926; Horton, *West African Countries and Peoples*, pp. 67-68; also see Robert July, "Africanus Horton and the Idea of Independence in West Africa," *Sierra Leone Studies*, n.s., no. 18 (January 1966), pp. 2-17.

57. See letter to the editor by Anoviphoee, *SLWN*, March 29, 1913, for a similar view pronounced in the second decade of the twentieth century; also see Sumner, *Education in Sierra Leone*, pp. 89-144.

58. Merriman-Labor, *Negro Race*, p. 7.

quently as a source of historical evidence. Blyden may have served to set the example. He relied heavily on the Old Testament to support his contentions about the black African past—and he did this in spite of the fact that he had urged African historians to collect "oral traditions" from among their own people so as not to be bound by the experiences and tools of a "foreign race."[59] Merriman-Labor interpreted the Bible as placing black Africans at the vanguard of civilization. Cole used the Old Testament to prove that blacks were destined to retain possession of Africa until the end of time.[60]

For the Creoles, the Bible was a book whose revealed authority many in Europe recognized and which could, therefore, counter the new testament of racism:

> That Negroes we are, we are proud to maintain
> Ashamed of complexion! unless if insane . . .
> The Bible instructs us one man God did make,
> To whom He gave Eve of his joy to partake;
> The two marred their joys and caused sin to exist;
> The consequence suffered, their purity ceased;
> To these, after fall, Cain and Abel were born
> But Cain slew his brother who'll no more return;
> But God in His mercy the sad parents cheered
> By giving another when Seth then appeared.
> From Adam through Seth righteous Noah did descend
> To whom were three sons on which sons we depend
> Pure friends to instruct, to the right way them lead;
> Remind them in earnest all sprang from one seed—
> From Shem, Ham, and Japheth good Noah's three sons.
> Strong weapons we've got, let's proceed on at once.
> From these three the white and the black and all men
> Descended we learn from God's book, why fear then?
> (The children of brothers first-cousins are called)
> Deny this you're godless, unfit for the world.
> "Be fruitful and multiply" God's words to man,
> Dispersion brought Ham to the African land;
> The Bible tells this, but it never doth say
> That Ham was become a baboon any way:
> Some ignorant men of the proud-colour tribe
> The notion that Negroes are monkeys imbibe;
> A pity it is we are sorry to know
> That some of our cousins themselves blind do show;

· 59. E. W. Blyden, *Proceedings at the Inauguration of Liberia College at Monrovia, January 23, 1862* (Monrovia, 1862), p. 28. Also see Blyden et al., *The People of Africa*, pp. 3-29.

60. *Methodist Herald*, April 27, 1887.

We only beg if *Anthropos* they are
To lift up their face and at us if they stare,
They surely will see we've the same upright form,
If Genesis read they will silent become.[61]

Even though Creoles held an unshaken belief in the Bible as revealed truth, their use of it in historical analysis was centuries behind general trends in European historiography. In Europe, historians had abandoned revealed truth as a basis for historical analysis since, possibly, Richard Simon (ca. 1675) and clearly by the time of Voltaire. By the nineteenth century, data from other disciplines—especially the work of physical anthropologists, ethnographers, classical economists, and biological scientists—were increasingly employed in historical explanations.[62] Though seemingly aware of the directions that European historical studies had taken, Creole writers nevertheless decisively rejected their approach. "Darwin," Merriman-Labor said, "is undoubtedly an excellent philosopher; but what is human philosophy to Divine revelation? Human philosophy may err, has often erred; but Divine revelation—the Bible—never!"[63]

The faith Creole intellectuals placed in the authority of the Bible was a result of their early Christian training. Religious instruction was an important part of the curriculum of the C.M.S. Grammar School, of the Wesleyan Boys' High School, and, of course, of Fourah Bay College, institutions which many of the most vocal Creoles had attended at one time or another. Before entering the grammar school in 1892, Merriman-Labor had been raised and educated by his maternal grandfather, John Merriman of Hastings, a deeply religious man who was prevented from entering the ministry when he lost his eyesight, but who was nevertheless called "Father Merriman" out of respect for his piety.[64] Horton began his education under the Reverend James Beale, and, before being sent to England to be trained in medicine, had attended Fourah Bay College, intending to become a Christian minister.[65]

More important still than the religious background of any individual writer was the character of the Christianity to which they all adhered and its all-pervading influence on the lives of the Creoles. The Christian faith, which had come to Freetown in the very beginning with the earliest settlers and the

61. Written by "S.A.C." from Fourah Bay College and printed in *SLWN*, November 17, 1888.

62. Curtin, *Image of Africa*, pp. 244, 388-389; Fritz Stern, *The Varieties of History* (New York, 1956), pp. 54-56.

63. Merriman-Labor, *Negro Race*, p. 13.

64. A. B. C. Merriman-Labor, *A Funeral Oration Delivered over the Grave of the late Father John Merriman* . . . (Freetown, 1900); *SLWN*, February 24, March 15, 1919; Fyfe, *History of Sierra Leone*, p. 526.

65. *Methodist Herald*, October 26, 1883.

missionaries, became more to the parents and grandparents of the Creoles than "just another religion." Their understanding of Christian dogma was probably no greater or less than that of the majority of their European contemporaries; the sincerity of their conversion to Christianity could only be measured on the basis of meaningless value judgments. Having been taught to identify Christianity with European civilization, however, they believed that an acceptance of that religion would reflect their own mastery of a way of life presented to them as better than any they had known before. Church services, for this reason, were well attended and long; and the congregation was thoroughly acquainted with the ritual and orders of procedure. Hymns were sung with much spirit, and they were seldom shortened by an omitted verse. The enthusiasm which had been characteristic of religion in the English evangelical movement merged with the predisposition for communal participation in worship, inherited from traditional African religion, and it remained characteristic of Creole Christianity. The Sabbath was kept holy, and special food and Sunday suits were reserved for its celebration. Sierra Leoneans had a general interest in questions of theology and a predilection for infinite debate on questions of eternity. If any book was to be found in a Creole home, it was certain to be the Bible; and the people took pride in being able to quote lengthy passages from memory. Like the missionaries who came to Sierra Leone in the early nineteenth century, even the most educated Creoles interpreted the Bible literally.

One other manifestation of the Creole tendency to stay within a European framework of thought is exemplified in their acceptance of the concept of the "true Negro." Merriman-Labor, for one, kept with the belief then popular in Europe (and which is still retained in the 1957 edition of C. G. Seligman's *Races of Africa*) which held that West Africa alone was the home of the "true Negroes," while other African peoples were mixtures of black and light-skinned invaders from outside the continent. Merriman-Labor defined "Negro Race" in narrow terms—as "the black descendants of a common ancestor"—and excluded "yellowish Copts . . . and Berbers" and "brown Kaffirs and Hottentots," because they were thought to lack the pure black skin color of the West Africans. Migration accounted for the settlement of Negroes in West Africa. Departing from Asia, the ancient Negroes traveled to Arabia and entered Africa over an isthmus now submerged. Some of the immigrants settled in Ethiopia while others "produced with the Egyptians the brown Kaffirs, Hottentots, and Hovaks [*sic*] of Madagascar." Still others—fishermen and hunters, captives and conquerors, seekers of congenial localities—emigrated from Ethiopia to other parts of the continent until they arrived in West Africa.[66]

In their reliance upon a framework of analysis learned from Europe and

66. Merriman-Labor, *Negro Race*, p. 13.

acceptable to Europeans, Creole thinkers ran the danger of being trapped by concepts which racists used to point up the inferiority of Negroes. By endorsing the notion of the "true Negro," for instance, Merriman-Labor was dangerously close to the proposition used by racist European historians to explain how, in a continent where Negro capabilities were thought to be so low, those "higher" cultural traits which did exist had been introduced by light-skinned outsiders from the East. But, caught up as they were between their acquiescence to the European model as the epitome of "civilization" and their psychological need to dignify the achievements of blacks in Africa, Creoles had few choices but to joust with these troublesome predicaments.

In accepting the premise that the Bible was a revealed authority, and therefore infallible historical evidence, Merriman-Labor and other Creole intellectuals had worked themselves into a logical dilemma. If, according to the Bible, Negroes were considered to be the descendants of Ham, logic demanded that Negroes accept the implications of Noah's malediction on the sons of Ham:

> And the sons of Noah that went forth of the ark, were Shem, and Ham, and Japheth: and Ham is the father of Canaan.
> These are the three sons of Noah: and of them was the whole earth overspread.
> And Noah began to be an husbandman, and he planted a vineyard:
> And he drank of the wine, and was drunken; and he was uncovered within his tent.
> And Ham, the father of Canaan, saw the nakedness of his father, and told his two brethren without.
> And Shem and Japheth took a garment, and laid it upon both their shoulders, and went backward, and covered the nakedness of their father; and their faces were backward, and they saw not their father's nakedness.
> And Noah awoke from his wine, and knew what his younger son had done unto him.
> And he said, Cursed be Canaan; a servant of servants shall he be unto his brethren.[67]

Noah's curse on Ham's descendants was often quoted by European writers to support their argument for the perpetual subordination of the Negro race.[68] Creole thinkers, however, were unwilling to question the authority of the Bible, yet loathe to accept the postulate of a divine malediction. They therefore played intellectual games with the Old Testament to disprove the curse on the sons of Ham while simultaneously destroying the assertion that

67. Gen. 9 : 18-25.
68. Curtin, *Image of Africa*, pp. 36-37, 403.

blacks were destined to be "hewers of wood and drawers of water." They took their lead from Dr. Alexander Crummel, a citizen of Liberia but frequent visitor to Sierra Leone. In 1883 Dr. Crummel published "An Examination of Genesis 9 : 25" in which he concluded:

1. That the curse of Noah was pronounced upon Canaan, *not* upon Ham.
2. That it *fell* upon Canaan, and was designed to fall upon him only.
3. That neither Ham, nor any of his [other] three sons, was involved in this curse.
4. That the Negro race have not [*sic*] descended from Canaan; were never involved in the curse pronounced upon him; and their peculiar sufferings, during the last three centuries, are not the result or evidence of any specific curse upon Ham.
5. That the fact of slavery in the Negro race is not peculiar to them as a people . . . . In God's providence, the Negro family have bitterly been called to suffer greatly, and doubtless for some high and important ends.
6. That the geographical designations of Scriptures are to be taken in good faith; and that when the "land of Canaan" is mentioned in the Bible, it was not intended to include the Gold Coast, the Gaboon, Goree or Congo.[69]

Merriman-Labor spent nine out of the thirty-two pages of his *Epitome of a Series of Lectures on the Negro Race* rationalizing the Biblical malediction. Like Dr. Crummel, he contended that Canaan alone was cursed. For this reason the descendants of Canaan, the Canaanites and Phoenicians, were servants to the rest of the world: the first as retainers to the congregation of Israel, and the latter as "navigators whose business it was to promote commerce and navigation, then practically the support of the ancient world." On the other hand, history was full of examples showing nations that descended from the other sons of Ham—Cush, Mizraim, and Phut—to be in frequent political and cultural ascendancy. The Egyptians, for instance, were "a people appropriately called the fathers of learning, when the entire world was in a state of semi-barbarism." The Ethiopians, descending from Ham's son Cush and direct ancestors of the West African Negroes, had also once numbered among the favored nations of the earth. Negroes, for this reason, had no connection to Noah's malediction.[70]

69. *West African Reporter*, December 1, 1883.

70. Merriman-Labor, *Negro Race*, pp. 21-23. James Bright Davies of the Colonial Treasury Department wrote "The Hamitic Race in Sacred History," another vindication of Negroes as the descendants of Ham. See *Independent*, October 14, November 11, 25, 1875.

Types of Response

Most Creoles, especially of the upper class, were at one time or another plagued by anxieties about their cultural identity. Blyden, the members of the Dress Reform Society, and the "name reformers" were neo-traditionalists. They rejected those aspects of Europeanization which they held unnecessary for progress in the modern world and, instead, sought to return to their idealized version of the traditions, values, and manners of black African society. Other Creole responses, however, ranged from indifference on the one end of the spectrum, through a more selective Europeanization, to an advocacy of total Europeanization and the complete destruction of even the most innocent vestiges of African culture.

"Europeanizers," Creoles advocating the total substitution of African cultural traits by European ones, sought to reject the past. They fervently wished to be accepted by whites as successful products of British mission work, as black men and women who had indeed become "civilized." They were proud of their imported material possessions, of their literary achievements, and of their representation in the clergy, the law, and medicine.[71] A poem, published in the *Methodist Herald* in 1887 by a Miss Thorpe, reflects their position well:

> Have we progressed? Just look at now and think of then,
> And ask the question once again
> Rememb'ring that our age is not yet five score,
> And that much may be done in years which are in store.
> Think how from men unlike in race,
> In tongue, in habits hardest to efface,
> Have sprung a people, faulty though they be,
> Such as to day around you all you see; . . .
>
> "European Models" some would say
> And thus pooh-pooh and turn their heads away,
> The growth of centuries, not of one,
> Is what you boast as having won.
> Oh! carping critics, ever croaking herd,
> Can nothing show you how absurd
> It is for mortals to expect to raise themselves
> Without some hand to guide,
> Some plan to follow, and some works beside
> To point where shoals or quicksand do abound,
> Where rocks, where channels may be found. . . .

71. Letter to the editor by "Achilles," March 7, 1885, September 5, 1885; T. B., "Our Mental Progress," November 2, 1889, *SLWN*.

We have but followed what we saw,
Because we recognize no other law,
But that which teaches that man learns from man
In every age wherever we may scan.
And you, ye critics who cry down,
All things not foreign in our town,
If there are errors to be seen,
Do you think our models always good and true have been?[72]

Many of the "Europeanizers"—believing that wars, kidnapping, slavery, and other calamities had destroyed their ancestors' powers of originality—justified assimilation to European ways as the only means to progress.[73] In every case, they were inexorably opposed to a withdrawal from Europeanization into a past whose validity they no longer accepted. "The circumstances under which the native manners and characteristic customs developed in the lands from whence our fathers came no longer obtain," stated an editorial in the *Sierra Leone Times* which well-illustrated the position of the "Europeanizers":

> We may not have attained to that acme of advancement possessed by those whom it is at once our pride and pleasure to belong to, but there can be no doubt that neither have we as a community, any thing in common with our ancestors of two centuries ago. We have adopted the European's dress, his language, his social, moral, political and domestic codes. We sail under the banner of England's potent and beneficent sovereign, and enjoy to the full as much freedom and advantage as any of her loyal subjects. Above all, we cling to those sacred truths which an army of sainted martyrs have, amidst innumerable difficulties, almost through a burning fiery climatic furnace, labored to plant in our midst. From, through, and by us, it may be, and is reasonably expected, that the aborigines still groping in that abyss from which our progenitors were happily rescued, would be brought towards the same path trodden by ourselves. Why then, the substance having gone, cling to the shadow, by the retention of those customs which land with no graceful effect upon the armour of civilization and education which we pride ourselves upon wearing . . . ?[74]

Joseph Renner-Maxwell, in his book *The Negro Question, or Hints for the*

72. *Methodist Herald*, January 12, 1887. The poem was recited by Miss Thorpe at an entertainment at the Wesleyan Educational Institution.

73. Editorial, *The Watchman*, February 28, 1879.

74. Editorial, *SLT*, June 23, 1894. Also see letter to the editor by Achilles, *SLWN*, September 5, 1885, propounding very similar sentiments.

Physical Improvement of the Negro Race, with Special Reference to West Africa, was an inordinate "Europeanizer," the most extreme example of this position. He was a Sierra Leonean of Yoruba ancestry whose father had been chaplain at Cape Coast. Attending Merton College, Oxford, where he took honors in jurisprudence in 1879 and his Bachelor of Civil Law degree in 1880, he was converted to Catholicism—a faith which strongly appealed to him because of what he considered to be its lack of racial prejudice.[75] After Oxford he first went to the Gold Coast to practice law and then to the Gambia to enter government service. Eventually, he rose to the position of chief magistrate of the Gambia in 1887.[76]

In his first book, *Advantages and Disadvantages of European Intercourse with the West Coast of Africa*, which was published in 1881, Renner-Maxwell had viewed the total Europeanization of black Africans as something which might be necessary in some cases but, for the most part, was neither essential nor preferable. "Where Western enlightenment can be imparted only by Western forms," he wrote,

> . . . then by all means have recourse to them; but do not let people for one moment fancy that except they eat European food, drink European drinks, speak European languages, and wear European dress, they are not worthy to be designated by the enviable appelation of Civilized Men. . . . It is not necessary that the traditions and ceremonies of civilization be in all places one and utterly alike, but may be changed according to diversities of countries, times, and men's manners, so that nothing be done to infringe its spirit.[77]

Renner-Maxwell later became convinced that selective Europeanization was folly and could not solve what he termed the "Negro Question." Instead, he became an impassioned advocate of miscegenation and married an English-woman, perhaps to offer proof of the viability of such a union. The thesis of his book, *The Negro Question*, was simple and perversely unique. He claimed that blacks were despised by Europeans not because they lacked intellect, nor because they were immoral or inhuman, but for no other reason than because they were ugly: "It is because he is ugly, because his woolly pate is not so becoming as the flaxen hair of the Anglo-Saxon, because the flat nose of the Negro is more like the nasal organ of the ape than is the aquiline nose of the

75. Renner-Maxwell, *The Negro Question*, pp. 134-147; Oxford University, *Oxford Honours, 1220-1894* (Oxford, 1894).

76. *SLWN*, April 25, 1891; obituary, *West Africa*, November 30, 1901; Fyfe, *History of Sierra Leone*, p. 406.

77. Joseph Renner-Maxwell, *Advantages and Disadvantages of European Intercourse with the West Coast of Africa* . . . (London, 1881), pp. 18-19.

Aryan races, because blubber lips are not as pretty as thin ones, because a black complexion is displeasing compared with a fair or olive one."[78]

Disagreeing with more orthodox Europeanizers, Renner-Maxwell was convinced that it was physically impossible for black Africans to pass themselves off as Europeans, an objective which could not "be brought about by anything short of a miracle." Influenced by the pseudoscientific racism which grew out of a misapplied Darwinism, he was persuaded that the Negro race would lose the struggle for survival. "The progress of civilization," he warned, "the struggle for existence, will not admit of the solution of questions of abstract right; if the white man wants room, the black, being the weaker and uglier, will have to make room for him."[79]

Even among up-country Africans, he believed, the standard of beauty was governed by lightness of skin color and the resemblance to European features, while intellectual, moral, and social qualities counted for nothing. Thus, he was sure that an illiterate white sailor, simply because of his race, would be much more respected both by Europeans and up-country Africans than would be the black chief of justice of Barbados, or a Blyden or Bishop Crowther. "It is much better that the Negro race should perish," Renner-Maxwell stated, "than it should abide forever amidst the decay of dynasties, the overthrow of nations, and the disappearance of other races, and continue, as now, the laughing stock of the world."[80]

Even though Renner-Maxwell was pessimistic, seeing little hope for blacks of his and his parents' generations, he was sure that for future generations the situation could begin to improve. "If a man finds his racial circumstances disadvantageous to his interests," he argued, "stunting to the development of his tone and manhood, and contemptible to his neighbours, he can at least ameliorate the condition of his progeny."[81] By marrying white women, black Africans would be instrumental in bringing forth a species of men that could be educated "to the highest pitch of perfection" while simultaneously eliminating Negroid features and skin color and the entire "Negro Question." Nor, he felt, should it be difficult to find white mates. England, Renner-Maxwell found, had thousands of prostitutes and poor women who would be contributing to "the progress of civilization" if they married "civilized Negroes" instead of plying their wares or prolonging their poverty.[82]

Owing to the scarcity of biographical information about Renner-Maxwell, it is difficult to establish why he moved from his earlier moderate position on African Europeanization to such a radical stance. His own Europeanization

78. Renner-Maxwell, *The Negro Question*, p. 10.
79. Ibid., p. 54.
80. Ibid., pp. 47-48, 103.
81. Ibid., pp. 65, 85-86.
82. Ibid., pp. 83-84, 104.

and the status it brought him paradoxically seemed both to please him and to make him insecure. Removed from Sierra Leone and relatively comfortable abroad, his educational attainments gave him an entrance to the white world and an awareness of its advantages. Surrounded by people who deprecated the past attainments and future potential of black Africans, however, he undoubtedly would have liked to become inconspicuous among Europeans. Seen in terms of his own frustrated desire to join Europeans culturally as well as racially, Renner-Maxwell's solution for the "Negro Problem" can more easily be understood.

Renner-Maxwell's influence on Sierra Leoneans was minimal. Neither he nor his work was well known in the colony. The *Sierra Leone Weekly News* did acknowledge him as "a Negro author of considerable ability," yet only made note of the *Negro Question* four years after it had been published in London and, even then, did not comment on the feasibility of his ideas.[83] A short debate about miscegenation emerged in that paper in 1898 when Edward Worsteine, a European merchant, suggested interracial marriage for "young gentlemen of the Caucasian races" who went to Africa, and Abdul Mortales, a Creole greatly affected by Blyden, opposed the notion as counter to God's special purpose in separating the races.[84] No evidence exists, however, that Renner-Maxwell's ideas about miscegenation gave birth to the debate. One suspects that his recommendations were perceived as so impractical as to be meaningless. For the majority of Creole men, racial intermarriage, if considered at all, was certainly nothing more than an academic question. As a general rule no unattached European women came to Sierra Leone, and only a handful of Creole men went to Europe with the specific intention of finding a wife. Although some Creole girls would on occasion form a liaison with a European male in Sierra Leone, the men were rarely willing to sanctify the union unless they had decided to make Africa their permanent home and were ready to bear social ostracism from the European community.

In sharp contrast to extremist Europeanizers like Renner-Maxwell, the selective Westernizers were pragmatists. A poem published in the *Sierra Leone Weekly News* in 1901, illustrates their position:

> Our fathers did their ancient work with zeal,
> His cardinal laws, God did to them reveal;
> Their every deed was done with honest will
> And shall we dare such honest deeds to kill:
> Their customs which doth make them justly proud,

83. *SLWN*, September 19, 1896.

84. Letter to the editor by Abdul Mortales, *SLWN*, January 22, 1898; Letter to the editor by E. Worsteine, *SLWN*, January 29, 1898.

>Are guided by old rules that are not bad;
>*Our duty is to bring to modern height,*
>*That which the fathers did by ancient light,*
>To give the honour due to Age is God's delight.[85]

Unlike Blyden, who viewed the Europeanization of black Africans as an aberration of a divine scheme for the separate development of the races, the selective Westernizers saw it as the only possible means to progress in a world dominated by Europe.[86] They agreed that not everything European was by definition good, and that "civilization" in the European manner did not necessitate the total destruction of all traditional African cultural practices. "The African was aroused," commented an editorial in the *Sierra Leone Weekly News*, "as the European also had been roused, from his slumber of ages and in a state of half somnolence was asked to pledge himself to dazzling but vain institutions."[87] They realized that Sierra Leoneans had strayed far from the original moorings of their forefathers as a result of misdirected education. But they were also aware that the antidote also lay in education— education "in the right direction," enabling them to modify the character of the Westernization they had received in order to suit their own particular exigencies. This education would give them an awareness of the incongruous elements in European culture they could exclude, and would also guide them in keeping those aspects of traditional African life that would enhance their development.

The position of the selective Westernizers regarding the relationship of Christianity to African traditional life was expressed perhaps most cogently by the Reverend James Johnson, who was born in Sierra Leone, educated at the C.M.S. Grammar School and Fourah Bay College, and who later became assistant bishop of Western Equatorial Africa.[88] In the article entitled "The Relation of Mission Work to Native Customs" submitted to the Pan-Anglican Congress of 1908, Johnson emphasized that Christianity was not intended to be the religion of any one particular race of people, but of the entire world. In every continent it wore a slightly different garb so as to blend with indigenous beliefs. Johnson believed that, so far as Africa was concerned, Christianity could spread without "denationalizing" and Europeanizing Africans. This did not mean that practices such as infanticide, ritual cannibalism, and witchcraft ordeals had to be tolerated. These were naturally repulsive, contrary to all justice, and were obviously legitimate objects of attack

85. Abiose, "Civilization—What Is It?," *SLWN*, March 9, 1901. Italics mine.

86. Editorial, *SLWN*, December 2, 1905.

87. Ibid.

88. *SLWN*, May 18, 1906; Kopytoff, *Preface to Modern Nigeria*, p. 289; Fyfe, *History of Sierra Leone*, p. 351.

and suppression. Body and facial tatooing, domestic slavery, home sepulchres—customs which were unenlightened but not entirely abhorrent—were to be left to die naturally through quiet ameliorative influence. But, Johnson warned, Christian missionaries should not meddle in name-giving, dress, and marriage customs of African peoples. African names, he pointed out, were not necessarily heathen, and African dress was merely a matter of convenience and taste which should not at all be taken to reflect on the enlightenment or lack of enlightenment of a particular individual. Likewise, since Jesus Christ did not prescribe any one particular marriage custom or ceremony, Johnson saw nothing wrong with native marriage practices and felt that they could continue in the traditional African manner. Furthermore, while he believed that monogamy should be an ultimate ideal, he was against excluding polygynists from the church.[89]

Johnson's views did not endear him to many of his fellow missionaries, nor to Creoles who viewed any apparent compromise in their Europeanization as a breach which would expose them to ridicule.[90] Nevertheless, his position toward selective Westernization—toward a syncretism of African and European practices—was probably the one shared by the majority of Creole society. It is, of course, impossible to document this or to give a numerical estimate of the proportion of the Creole population which fell into the position between that of the extreme Europeanizers and that of the hardly touched, those Sierra Leoneans who by choice, location, or lack of educational opportunity had escaped Westernization in almost all its forms. But there can be little doubt that in their everyday life most Creoles retained and mixed elements from traditional African culture with the ways of the West.

Creole Attitudes Toward Krio

A short historical survey of the Creole attitude toward their vernacular, Krio, should help elucidate the continuing split between those Sierra Leoneans

---

89. James Johnson, "The Relation of Mission Work to Native Customs," *Pan Anglican Papers, Being Problems for Consideration at the Pan-Anglican Congress, 1908. Political and Social Conditions of Missionary Work*, vol. 2 (London, 1908). In 1888 Bishop T. J. Sawyerr, bishop of the Diocess of the Native Pastorate, had also urged a new policy in respect to polygny if any progress was to be made toward evangelizing "heathens and Mohammedans" in Africa. The Bible, he stated, made no direct attack on this practice but, on the contrary, condoned it in many examples from the Old Testament. The C.M.S. Parent Committee, taken aghast by Sawyerr's statements, made him resign from the church finance committee. See T. J. Sawyerr, *Sierra Leone Native Church (Two Papers read at the Church Conference Freetown, 1888 held in Freetown, Sierra Leone, January 24th, 25th, 26th, 1888)* (Freetown, 1888), pp. 17-31; Fyfe, *History of Sierra Leone*, pp. 508-509.

90. J. F. Ade Ajayi, *Christian Missions in Nigeria, 1841-1891 . . .* (London, 1965), pp. 235-238; Kopytoff, *Preface to Modern Nigeria*, pp. 238-241.

hoping to show their modernity through the rejection of anything suggesting a "less civilized" African past, and those who, while perhaps just as eager to acquire the technology of the modern world, nonetheless wished to preserve elements of African culture not in contradiction with their modernizing position.

In the Sierra Leone *Daily Guardian* of October 24 and 25, 1939, Thomas Decker, a Creole who had been born in Calabar but who had settled in Sierra Leone to teach and to write, published a short "sketch in Creo" called *Boss Coker Befo St. Peter.*[91] Its first act takes place in a beer-hall where Boss Coker, "middle-aged and fattish and well-dressed and double-chinned," is involved in an argument in Krio in which he strenuously attacks the use of that language in Sierra Leone. Both his discussion and the act are interrupted by the sound of a siren signaling a blackout and enemy air raid. When the curtain again opens, we see Boss Coker attempting to get past "the gate of the pseudo-Christian's heaven" guarded by St. Peter. St. Peter greets Boss Coker in Krio but Coker answers in English, claiming contemptuously that he is not a "Creo boy" but "a native of Sierra Leone in West Africa" who "was strongly against the idle people who babbled about the Creo language." St. Peter agrees to give Boss Coker an English vocabulary test, saying that he would be allowed to enter heaven only if he passed. Meanwhile, men from England, France, Hausa, and Yoruba all pass by into heaven after speaking to St. Peter and being answered in their native languages. Boss Coker fails his test and is sent back to earth. As he departs, voices, presumably of angels, sing mockingly:

> Go down,
> Fanny Attara.
> Speak your modda-tongue,
> Fanny Attara.

"Boss Cokerism" may be seen to represent the attitude of those Sierra Leone Creoles who spoke Krio throughout most of their lives but who thought of it as an inferior form of English. In its most extreme manifestation, "Boss Cokerism" is good for a chuckle. One advocate, for example, found Krio to be of "poor metaphysical standard," "unsatisfactory ethically," and called for its abandonment. To this end he believed that persons who had studied up to the third standard should "be made amenable to Law if convicted of patois speaking."[92] Another, an eminent teacher, insisted that

91. See "Crusader for Krio," *West Africa*, August 14, 1965, for a portrait of Thomas Decker. Also see my article, "Creole Attitudes Toward Krio: An Historical Survey," *Sierra Leone Language Review*, no. 5 (1966), pp. 39-49, for a somewhat modified version of the following discussion.

92. "The Negro Problem," *SLWN*, July 22, 1911.

no "broken English" be spoken at his school. After haranguing his pupils on the subject and promising severe punishment to transgressors, he wound up his speech by saying, "Una no yeri?"[93]

From the beginning of the Sierra Leone settlement, English was the language of the colonial power. The majority of the new inhabitants, however, spoke a language akin to contemporary Krio. The basic form of this language had probably been shaped in the West Indies and the United States by the ancestors of the Maroons and other ex-slaves who eventually settled in Sierra Leone. The African elements of this language were strengthened when large numbers of Liberated Africans—predominantly Yoruba-speaking—arrived and were absorbed into the Sierra Leone community.[94] But, in so far as the missionaries and colonial servants were concerned, English was the language that mattered. In the early days of the colony it was taught with rather narrow goals in mind. Some teachers were satisfied so long as pupils knew enough English to read the Bible, to act as catechists, and to communicate in class and church. Others sought only to teach Africans to follow basic oral and written directions and to compose simple letters.[95] Some Sierra Leoneans, however, soon realized that they would have to speak English properly to achieve higher posts in mercantile houses and government. English became the language of upward social mobility. Those who found room near the top, who affected British styles and manners, and who spoke and wrote English fluently in spite of obstacles such as poor teaching and bad texts—in short, the Boss Cokers—associated Krio with those uneducated Africans from whom the elite had evolved but with whom they no longer wished to be associated.

The Boss Cokerites rationalized their position in a number of ways. To some, Krio hindered public speaking and formed "an obstacle to the study of the free and perfect expression of the mind in appropriate language."[96] Others simply found it "almost a language of invectives," too terse for rhetoric and, justifiably, since it was without a written literature, unable to

93. That is, "Do you understand?" See Reynolds, "Tete-a-Tete," *SLWN*, September 4, 1897.

94. See J. Berry, "The Origins of Krio Vocabulary," *Sierra Leone Studies*, n.s., no. 12 (December 1959), pp. 298-307; Frederick G. Cassidy, *Jamaica Talk* (London, 1961); E. D. Jones, "Mid-Nineteenth Century Evidences of a Sierra Leone Patois," *Sierra Leone Language Review*, no. 1 (1962), p. 19; John Eric Peterson, "Freetown: A Study of the Dynamics of Liberated African Society, 1807-1870" (Ph.D. diss., Northwestern University, 1963), pp. 342-343.

95. E. D. Jones, "The Teaching of English in Sierra Leone Colony Schools" (Thesis for the Diploma in Education, University of Durham, n.d.), p. 8.

96. Reynolds, "Tete-a-Tete," *SLWN*, September 4, 1897.

enhance a taste for reading.[97] In large part, Boss Cokerites were caught up in the cultural ethnocentrism which had been instilled in them by their European teachers. They equated Krio with a state of "semi-civilization" that no longer belonged in the Athens of West Africa. L. J. Leopold, the Creole principal of the Educational Institute, was bitter in his denunciation:

> The Sierra Leone patois is a kind of invertebrate *ominum gatherum* of all sorts, a veritable *ola podrida* [sic] collected from many different languages without regard to harmony or precision: it is largely defective and sadly wanting in many of the essentials and details that make up and dignify a language. It is a standing menace and a disgrace hindering not only educational development but also the growth of civilization in the colony.[98]

The rejection of Krio reflected the efforts Creoles made—if not always consciously—to proclaim themselves forever removed from the native manners and customs of their forebears. Like Eliza Doolittle in *Pygmalion*, who had to shed her Cockney accent to become a "lady," many Creoles felt that they would not be accepted as "truly civilized" if they spoke Krio to anyone but intimate friends and members of the family.

A counterpart to the "Boss Coker" attitude did exist. "In language," declared an article in *Saturday Ho! Monthly* of 1892, "we employ only the medium of communication peculiar to an alien race, and expect it to convey to all around us our tenderest feelings."[99] To offset the intrusion of this alien tongue, therefore, Krio was chosen as the preferable alternative. Its supporters admitted that Krio bore a resemblance to English but maintained that its ideas were entirely African. They explained that their forebears did not disembark in Sierra Leone as babies but as adults who could express themselves in their respective languages. Had they never come into contact with Europeans they would probably have adopted the predominant language among them or, there not being one, would have developed a composite language, which was, in fact, what happened. English words were included in this composite language but its structure and semantics were essentially African. "[Our ancestors] changed the old skin of their languages," explained an editorial in a Creole publication of 1885, "but the new skin they put on did not differ much from what necessity compelled them to discard: in appearance it might be mistaken for a *patois* of the English language, but in

---

97. O. T. Nana, "The Negro Problem," *SLWN*, July 22, 1911; George Nicol's letter in *Sawyerr's*, December 19, 1885.

98. *SLWN*, January 19, 1901.

99. Reprinted in *SLWN*, May 28, 1892.

its recesses, in its fundamental conceptions, are preserved in a large measure, the notions, proverbs, prejudices, ideas and sentiments of the native mind."[100]

The Boss Coker attitude and its counterpart surfaced regularly in arguments concerning the progress and policies of education in the colony. Throughout the latter half of the nineteenth and early twentieth centuries, higher education was designed not only to broaden the intellect but also to strengthen moral and religious convictions. The teaching of languages fell directly in line with these aims. Arabic and other scriptural languages were taught, not for their own sake, but because they prepared future missionaries to proselytize more effectively among Muslim peoples.[101] Similarly, the classical languages, being thought of as somehow more perfect than others, required greater discipline from the students. Discipline would develop "good character"—the Victorian hallmark of a gentleman. Krio, on the other hand, was generally not recognized as a legitimate language. Fourah Bay College, which could boast of long interest in the study of African languages, offered occasional lectures even before 1900 on Timne and Mende, as well as Arabic, but ignored the legitimacy of Krio.[102] One of its principals, the Reverend Frank Nevill, an Englishman, did get involved in the debate over Krio waged in a local journal during the years 1885-1886. Fearing that support of Krio in that periodical would arouse public sentiment in its favor to the detriment of "good" English, he attacked the Sierra Leone patois. He urged Creoles to "break off the slovenly and degrading customs which bind men to the imperfections of past generations" and to concentrate on the English language and literature whose authors "have striven in purity of diction to express the highest and noblest feelings of mankind."[103]

The predominant views of Creole educators favored Nevill.[104] Principal Leopold of the Educational Institute pointed out that he had been having some success in enforcing the English language as the only recognized basis and medium of communication in the colony. "We reasonably strive and labour *without reserve*," he wrote,

> ... to create, foster, and encourage a love for the English language pre-eminently above any other in our youths. ... This we

100. *Sawyerr's*, December 19, 1885. For similar opinions see S. H., "Letter to the Editor," in the same issue of *Sawyerr's*; E. T. Cole's "The Sierra Leone Vernacular," *SLWN*, November 3, 1888.

100. Arthur Carter, "Changes in the Curriculum in Secondary Schools in Sierra Leone, 1860-1960" (Thesis for the Diploma in Education, University of Durham, 1963), p. 5; Sumner, *Education in Sierra Leone*, pp. 3-42.

102. *SLWN*, January 13, 1900.

103. *Sawyerr's*, September 26, 1885; "City Notes," *SLWN*, January 26, 1901.

104. See "Letter to the Editor," February 28, 1885; "My View of Things," May 16, 1885, *SLWN*.

have found easy enough from results, and attainable in spite of the surprisingly growing tendency to perpetuate and encourage this parasitical nuisance, known everywhere as the *Sierra Leone patois*—this bane to a healthy growth in civilization, and this "bar sinister" to our progress in education—as a reliable means of communication.[105]

Other Creoles were convinced that the development of Sierra Leone would be retarded if English language training were sacrificed to the benefit of Krio. To their minds, Krio was insufficiently flexible and expressive, and did not contain the literature to meet modern demands.[106] They argued that since Creoles had English ready at hand—an optimistic belief at best—they would be foolish to raise Krio to the same level as the language that boasted of the literature of Shakespeare and Milton. "The attempt to turn an obscure vernacular into a national language when the nation is already in possession of one of the great languages of civilization," proclaimed a letter in the *Sierra Leone Weekly News* of 1913, "is not unlike in wisdom to the practice of burning bank notes in order to show contempt for the bank that issued them."[107]

Those Creoles who blamed the educational curriculum for its tendency to produce carbon-copy Europeans made a strong argument favoring the development of Krio as the language of literature and classroom. These ideological descendants of Edward Blyden criticized the books used in Sierra Leone schools for their lack of pertinence to Africa and for their failure to instill African readers with pride in themselves and their past. Reflecting the pseudoscientific racism prominent in the latter part of the nineteenth century, schoolbooks often taught that Africans were degraded heathens or foolish imitators of Europeans whose culture they could not possibly hope to grasp. Most of them dealt entirely with British history and culture, illuminating the narrative with European illustrations. Materials written by Africans, such as A. B. C. Sibthorpe's *Geography and History of Sierra Leone*, were not incorporated into the curriculum.[108]

The Reverend James Johnson, writing a long letter to the editor of the *Sierra Leone Weekly News* in 1908, suggested educational reforms. He urged the employment of African objects and subjects, books and biographies, so that students could identify with and take a greater interest in what was being

105. *SLWN*, January 19, 1901.

106. P. J. Taylor, "A Study of Some of the Reasons for the Poor Standard of English among Pupils in Sierra Leone and Efforts That Could Be Made for Improvement" (Thesis for the Diploma in Education, University of Durham, 1964/65), introd.

107. Anouyahvee, "Letter to the Editor," *SLWN*, March 22, 1913.

108. Carter, "Changes in the Curriculum," pp. 33-36; A. L. Tobuku-Metzger, *Historical Sketch of the Sierra Leone Grammar School, 1845-1935* (Freetown, 1935), pp. 18-19; J. S. Laurie, "Report on Sierra Leone Schools," in C.O. 267/298.

taught. Furthermore, if schools would teach their subject matter in the "Sierra Leone English"—which he called "the people's own natural and native language"—it would aid colony-born students in grasping concepts that had previously escaped them. Adopted properly, Krio would even help them to learn "England's English" because they would then appreciate it more readily and intelligently. Johnson admitted, however, that his suggestions would meet considerable resistance. He wrote:

> Unfortunately this language has not been considered elegant enough for either the schoolroom or the pulpit, though it is like every other language in the world, an outcome of the people's own situation; though it is the language that they readily understand and readily enjoy, and that which touches their hearts and influences them in a way that no other language has done or can do; though it has become to them what the Mendi, Timneh, Yoruba and Ibo and other African languages also are to the natives inhabiting these regions where these different languages are severally spoken; and so it has come to pass that the language in school and church is very different from that spoken generally in the streets and in every home in the colony.[109]

Although Reverend Johnson's suggestions were the subject of an editorial in the *Sierra Leone Weekly News*, the paper's invitation to the public for commentary received no attention.[110] From a practical point of view, therefore, Johnson's proposals had little effect. So long as Europeans drew up the curriculum for Sierra Leone schools and laid down educational policy there seemed little hope that they would ever be adopted.

The debate was revived in modified form in the changed political atmosphere of the 1930s. World War I, in which Africans had been active participants, had come and passed. It had been marked by much idealistic talk among the Allies about the self-determination of subject peoples. This talk had not been meant to apply to Africans but Africans, nevertheless, were not blind to its implications: nationalism and national identity gradually became important elements in the demands of many African leaders. When the Krio language debate was resumed, therefore, the arguments of its advocates were no longer entirely based on the idea that Krio was an "African language," better in tune with the "African personality." Instead, Krio was now claimed to be the national language of the Sierra Leone Creoles.

Thomas Decker was the first, and by far the most important, of these new defenders of the Krio language. He wrote with two goals in mind: to

109. *SLWN*, February 22, 1908.
110. Editorial, *SLWN*, February 22, 1908.

demonstrate that possession of a common language by Creoles gave validity to their claim to be a nation; and that Krio was a living language flexible enough for artistic expression.

Because their ancestors stemmed from many different areas and ethnic backgrounds in Africa and had no common heritage to equal that of such Sierra Leone peoples as the Timne or Mende, there always existed a strong tendency among Creoles to question their own identity. Even though their common colonial experiences eventually made for cohesion, the legacy of antagonism and distrust that had existed between the original Settler, Maroon, and Liberated African groups was partially preserved by their Creole descendants. Decker, therefore, championed the Krio language as a means to an end—as a symbol of group unity. "When we realize," he wrote in the *Daily Guardian*, "that . . . Sierra Leone Creoles are united by a common native language or vernacular or mother tongue; and when we remember that a nation is much more 'an aggregation of persons speaking the same or a cognate language' than anything else; it will be clearly seen that . . . Creoles are a distinct nation."[111] Whatever progress Creoles might hope to achieve as a nation, Decker argued, could only occur through their use of the vernacular. Creole leaders, he continued, could only begin to wake the masses to desired social, political, and educational reforms if they proclaimed their messages in Krio—a language Creoles learned as babes and spoke almost all of their lives. Moreover, if they took advantage of the fact that Krio was already the lingua franca of the protectorate, Creole leaders could forge unity between the two sections of Sierra Leone.[112]

Given the advantages he believed could be gained from a proper use and recognition of Krio, Decker grew extremely impatient with Boss Coker Creoles. In words reminiscent of Blyden, he wrote:

> We are African Negroes (very black ones in most cases) and yet we prefer to feel like Europeans and to do all that they do . . . . We prefer to read only IMPORTED literature, to see and hear IMPORTED music and dances, to be entertained with IM-PORTED plays and operas . . . . And, most exasperating still, we prefer to murder the English language (a foreign language which we pretentiously prefer to our own native language, "the patois") instead of reconciling ourselves with the sane idea that THE NATIVE LANGUAGE OF THE SIERRA LEONE CREOLE IS NONE OTHER THAN WHAT WE CALL THE PATOIS . . . .
>
> I am not out to preach any kind of impracticable and narrow nationalism. I am not out to tell you that a day will come when everybody will be ordered or advised to put on only AFRICAN

111. *Daily Guardian*, September 13, 1939; also see the issue of September 14, 1939.
112. *Daily Guardian*, October 23, 1939, July 1, 1940, February 15, 1947.

clothes, to eat only AFRICAN food, to sing, hear, dance and be entertained with only AFRICAN songs, music, dances and . . . to read only AFRICAN literature. . . .

I am out to preach . . . that the time's now overdue when we in Sierra Leone should begin to see the marked difference that there is between what is Native and African (and, therefore, natural and soul-satisfying) and what is Foreign (and, therefore, pretentious and somewhat unnatural).[113]

Decker also made an effort to set straight those Creoles who looked down upon their own language as a "pidgin" of English. He described West African pidgin English as "soul-less" in comparison to Krio because it was incapable of expressing the innermost hopes and feelings of a people. Unlike Krio, which, whether they admitted it or not, belonged to the Creoles, pidgin English belonged to no man and was used only when people of different ethnic groups and languages in British West Africa wished to communicate with each other. He offered numerous examples of the differences between the two.[114]

To illustrate the expressiveness and versatility of Krio, Decker attempted to put the language to a variety of uses. His sounding board was the *Daily Guardian*, a paper to which he contributed regular columns, eventually becoming its editor. He translated poetry, plays, Biblical passages, and wrote skits and articles in Krio. By his example, he hoped to demonstrate that the artistic potential of Sierra Leone could be expanded by the use of its own vernacular.[115] When the suggestion was made that the entire *Daily Guardian* be published in Krio, Decker changed the name of his column, "Relaxation Corner," to "Loosboddi Conna" and wrote it in Krio instead of English.[116]

Many Creoles were scandalized by Decker's passion for Krio. One contributor to the *Daily Guardian* interpreted the agitation for the recognition of the Creole vernacular as a plot to destroy the ability of Africans to speak English.[117] Another suggested that Krio be left to those that did not have the advantages of learning English properly.[118] And an editorial in the *Sierra Leone Weekly News* pointedly asked if the leaders in the community couldn't find more important things "to talk about than idle rubbish about 'Creeo.' "[119]

113. *Daily Guardian*, August 1, 1939.
114. See *Daily Guardian,* September 4, 1939, June 29, 1940, July 15, 1944, August 25, 1949.
115. See *Daily Guardian*, 1939-1940, for many examples.
116. Beginning in the *Daily Guardian*, October 16, 1939.
117. Crabbit, "The Krio or Creeo Language," *Daily Guardian*, October 18, 1939.
118. "School Notes No. 5," *Daily Guardian*, November 18, 1939.
119. *SLWN*, September 23, 1939.

The reaction could not have been unexpected. Decker's was the most serious attempt to change a leading Freetown newspaper from English to the vernacular. In the past Krio had appeared in the newspapers from time to time, included in stories, poetry, and even in the texts of advertisements.[120] Often, non-Creole contributors claimed to be using the Creole vernacular without, in fact, being able to differentiate between Krio and pidgin English. In every case, however, the use of a language other than English in the Sierra Leone press was ephemeral.

Viewed superficially, Decker's experiments with Krio in the *Daily Guardian* were unsuccessful. The owners of the newspaper were not ready to gamble as there was no guarantee that Creoles would buy a Krio publication in preference to an English one. And their fears had a basis in fact. Since no attempt had ever been made to standardize an orthography until Decker broached the subject in 1939, readers, even if favoring the use of the vernacular, found it difficult to follow Krio in its varying written forms.[121]

Once independence for the whole of Sierra Leone became a foreseeable event, the idea of promoting the vernacular of one particular ethnic group over that of another was neither desirable nor expedient. For the new leaders of an independent Sierra Leone, taking over the political structure intact from the colonial government, English served as a "neutral" language promoting the interests of national unity. Moreover, having been the recognized medium of communication for much of West Africa during the colonial period, English could ensure a smooth transition in the administration of government and facilitate international communication.

Since English was to be the recognized national language, this aspect of its conflict with Krio ceased to be relevant. More important, however, the attitudes of the Creole opponents of the vernacular underwent a change as well. As their upward social mobility no longer depended on their success in matching a standard set by Englishmen, they could look at the values of Krio more objectively. And it was in this respect that the efforts of men such as Decker were rewarded. Having shown Creoles the versatility of their language and its possibilities for literary expression, they had also eased the transition from the view that Krio was the language of the illiterate and lower classes to one which came to regard it as the language of home and family and the sentimental link with the past. With the achievement of independence, therefore, the debate over Krio was dead.

120. For examples see Jones, "Krio in Sierra Leone Journalism," pp. 24-31.
121. *Daily Guardian*, October 12, 1939.

Part III: A Changing Relationship

Chapter FIVE
New Hopes, Old Disappointments

"Wes pauda pan kondo." (Gunpowder is wasted on a lizard.)
Creole Proverb

From the 1880s until about 1910, Creole reactions to the increasingly racist tenor of British policies in Sierra Leone had been largely limited to the intellectual and cultural realm. They had sought, for the most part, to reconcile the ideal image of Creole-British relations with a frustrating new reality. Defensive in nature, disappointed in tone, the reactions had been internally directed—attempting to bring about reassuring adjustments in Creole, not British, outlooks and actions. At no time during this period had they directly challenged the new reality itself by asking the British to alter their colonial policies.

World War I marked the beginning of a different phase.

Superficially Sierra Leone changed relatively little during this period. Until strategic military considerations in the second decade of the twentieth century dictated otherwise, the colony's importance to Britain diminished, displaced by the wealthier and more obviously exploitable Gold Coast, Nigeria, and the various territories in East and Central Africa. Freetown, to be sure, had since 1893 become a municipality with mayor and aldermen. It had also acquired an African Direct Telegraph Company, which linked it with Europe, and a narrow-gauge railroad, which made overland transportation to the protectorate somewhat easier if not more comfortable. But roads re-

151

mained bad; most produce and merchandise continued to be transported by shank's mare, carried on men's and women's heads, not infrequently over long distances from the outlying villages to the Freetown markets. In 1916 a total of a mile and a half of good road existed in both colony and protectorate. Only during the war was this situation remedied for defense purposes, with the indirect consequence that by 1921 motor cars were able to supersede hammocks, rickshaws, and sedan chairs.

Freetown, in spite of the vitality of its inhabitants and the hustle and bustle of its daily life, managed to retain its uncanny ability to appear weatherbeaten and, on the surface, derelict.[1] At the turn of the century the city council had granted a monopoly to an English company to lay tramway tracks and to light the city electrically. Nevertheless, the contract remained unfulfilled, and it was not until 1927 that electric lights in the streets and houses finally displaced kerosene lamps. Water supplies continued to remain scarce and fires still raged regularly during the dry season.[2]

Throughout the war, Freetown acted as an important station for the British Royal Navy and the Atlantic Fleet. Not only did ships bring sailors and British army soldiers to the city in numbers larger than Freetonians had ever encountered, but enemy German prisoners, captured in the Cameroons or elsewhere, were interned at the Government Model School, at Mount Aureol, and at Fourah Bay College. Special constables were employed to watch for escapes and, along with military guards, patrolled various points

1. P. H. Marterey, "Freetown 1899-1938," *Sierra Leone Studies*, old ser., no. 21 (1939), pp. 81-87.

2. A. B. C. Merriman-Labor, *Handbook of Sierra Leone for 1901-1902* (Manchester, 1902), p. 29; *West Africa*, January 8, 1921, p. 1661, and May 28, 1921, quoting the *West African Mail and Trade Gazette; Colonial and Provincial Reporter*, January 17, 1920. After the great West Ward fire had destroyed dozens of homes the Freetown papers ran this ad:

The Fire Concert

Pity the Poor

A Variety Concert will be given at the Town Hall on the 5th of February by the "Native Comedy Company" . . . Several Ladies and Gentlemen, Europeans and Africans, of High Musical ability, etc., have consented to take part.

Special Train will run from Hill Station.

The Programme consists of an Act entitled "Codjoe the Black Comedian," The Fire Brigade on the scene, The Fire Son, Dialogues, Recitations, Humorous Coon and Rag-Time Songs, Pianoforte Solos, etc., all of Local and Foreign composition.

The proceeds will be donated towards the Mayor's Fund.

throughout the city. Well-known trading establishments owned by Germans, such as the Woerman Line African Trading Company, were closed.[3]

Less sophisticated inhabitants of the city, however, seemed less concerned with the war in Europe in 1914 than with rumors that "a horror of horrors called feety-goody" had been imported to Freetown from Gambia by an "evil disposed female."[4] The "feety-goody," it was believed, assumed "the shape of an insect which inflicted bites" that "in nine cases out of ten prove fatal after prolonged and excruciating torture." The only known defense against this monster was the color red, which it strangely detested. This was the reason, noted a writer in the *Sierra Leone Daily Guardian and Foreign Mails*, why so many women had suddenly taken to wearing red outfits in public and why the windows of so many Freetown residences sported red taffeta window curtains.[5]

Lady hawkers, crying "who de ask foh me?," "shine yuh mot," "sweet one de go, wahn na fain-o," and accompanied by the succulent smells of their fried meats, hot "cowfoot soup and yams," pancakes, and cassava bread, still crowded the streets each day during mealtimes, dressed in costumes which had scarcely changed for decades. Bra Weeks walked about selling stationery

Figure 9. A Sunday afternoon at the Wilberforce Maze, c. 1910-1911. (From the Smith albums.)

3. "The Review of the Year 1914," *Sierra Leone Guardian and Foreign Mails*, January 8, 1915; Cole, *Kossoh Town Boy*, pp. 112-113.
4. See *Sierra Leone Guardian and Foreign Mails*, January 30, 1914.
5. "A Credulous Age," *Sierra Leone Guardian and Foreign Mails*, July 3, 1914.

and religious tracts and was available for all funerals both as a participant, sympathetic mourner, and vendor of "shouts" leaflets. "Prophets" Brown, Fitzgerald, and Russell, itinerant preachers armed with collection plates, drew crowds to their respective street corners, forecasting hell and damnation, attacking "congosa" people (gossips) and slanderers, and urging their listeners not to depart without a small financial offering.[6]

For social life, the majority of the population had their dancing, feasting, and *awujoh*, their church events and Muslim festivals. The upper classes socialized at entertainments, teas, and "at homes"—all more separated racially than they had been throughout most of the nineteenth century—and on special occasions, such as Easter Monday, took the Mountain Railway to the Wilberforce Maze, where there was dancing ("both Foreign and Native"), as well as a merry-go-round and other outdoor amusements.[7]

World War I opened a Pandora's box of false hopes and misplaced optimism for Sierra Leone Creoles, as it had generally done for other colonial peoples. The Creoles' personal involvement in the war was relatively minor, but they could not help but observe that in Europe an era had ended: that confident, comfortable continent had been torn into battling camps, nation against nation, white killing white. African soldiers had departed from Freetown to

6. "Here and There by Fancy," *SLWN*, September 12, 1931, recalls street scenes in Freetown ca. 1910-1920.

7. R. Lumpkin, who was better known professionally as "Allimamy Bungie, the Sympathetic Undertaker," was particularly noted for the parties which he sponsored throughout this period. Before one especially memorable event, Bungie ran the following notice in the local newspapers—unintentionally revealing a great deal about Creole social life:

> Feast of R. Lumpkin (Alias Allimamy Bungie) General builder for the living and Dead . . . . Born 3d December, 5 a.m., 1870—47 years begs to inform his friends and numerous customers that he will be very pleased to accept presents from them up to the 15th instant—Chop and drinks preferable. Owing to the large sum of £180 indebted to him for coffins supplied, disables him to celebrate his birthday and to associate it with the feast to the public as usual. He will be very pleased if his debtors will extend their sympathetic feelings to him, by paying him at least about a quarter of that amount to strengthen him to make a Public (Awoojor) at the Recreation Grounds if permitted by the Authorities. . . .
>
> Bungie, Bungie, Bungie
> Our last friend, may he live for ever.

The advertisement ran in the *Sierra Leone Weekly News* throughout November 1917. Bungie's advertisements in the local papers, both for his business and for his social activities, were criticized by none other than Graham Greene in his *Journey Without Maps* (London, 1936), a perceptive but sour view of Freetown in the 1930s.

the fighting lines singing, "Goodbye Oh! We al go go die, we no go see Sa Lone again." They conducted themselves well, negated once more the apparent invincibility of Europeans, and began to think again of the potential power of the "dark races." For many Creoles the bearing of the black soldiers recalled past successes—the defeat of the Italians at Adowa, the military triumph of the Japanese over the Russians, and that symbolic struggle for racial supremacy in which Jack Johnson, black, had been victorious over Jim Jeffries, white, in the fight for the heavyweight boxing championship of the world.[8]

The Creole community was extremely anti-German during the war. The *Sierra Leone Weekly News* was full of German atrocity stories. Sierra Leoneans frequently reproclaimed their loyalty to the king and, taking pride in the title "My Ancient and Loyal Sierra Leone" which King George V had used in addressing a message to them, declared their willingness to cooperate and fight.[9] "Rambler," writing in the *Sierra Leone Weekly News*, hoped that Britain would see the necessity of encouraging military training for every man in the empire and, believing Creole boys to be born fighters, suggested the formation of a regiment called "The King's Own Creole Boys." Creole Muslims, joined by some representatives of Muslims from the protectorate, French Guinea, and Algeria, held a mass meeting to assert their loyalty to the king and to pass a unanimous resolution condemning Turkey's actions and alliance with Germany, the enemy of Great Britain, as unjustifiable by the Koran and the Hadis.[10]

Even before the war's conclusion, educated Creoles, who closely followed Freetown and British press reports of events on the battleground and in the European capitals, wondered what peace held in store for the West African colonies. The British dominions had already been promised a greater role in the future councils of empire, as a consequence of their activities in the war effort. The Freetown press uniformly expressed the desire that the war's completion would alter a situation in which the West African colonies were treated as poor relations. "The time has not merely arrived," contended an article in the *Sierra Leone Guardian and Foreign Mails*, "it is long past when what is known as the educated native population of our West African Colonies should be given a more direct voice in the Government under which they live, and thus, an influence on the laws made for them and their fellow

8. See "General News," *Sierra Leone Guardian and Foreign Mails*, October 23, 1914; "The Power of the Black," July 4, 1896; in praise of "Japan and African Mysteries," July 29, 1905; editorial reviewing events of 1905, January 6, 1906; for Johnson-Jeffries fight, July and August 1910, passim; for Blyden attacking the fight as a "struggle for racial supremacy," August 6, 1910, *SLWN*.

9. George V had sent this message to the people of Sierra Leone by way of his royal uncle, the Duke of Connaught. See *Colony and Provincial Reporter*, November 23, 1912.

10. *SLWN*, November 21, 1914.

citizens."[11] Was it in the interest of the British empire, "Africanus" asked in the *Sierra Leone Weekly News*, to continue the exclusion of Negroes from the upper classes of its civil and military service? Had the war not disclosed the advisability of according equal opportunities to all its children?[12]

And, if the fire of expectation was lit by the very real European need of African support during the war, it was stoked to a blaze by more intangible factors at the war's conclusion. In Russia a revolution had taken place which rejected Czarist imperialism and proclaimed the idea of egalitarianism and freedom from colonial domination. Such an event could not escape the notice of an attuned colonial world. Nor could Woodrow Wilson's and Lloyd George's lofty words about people's right of self-determination be stripped of their universal appeal and limited only to Europe. The world had grown smaller during the war, communications were better, news traveled rapidly, and shots fired in one continent reverberated quickly in another. Sierra Leone Creoles, like other contemporary educated Africans, soon grasped the revolutionary concepts and made them part of their own aspirations.[13]

The passing of time and the harvesting of experience also stripped Creoles of at least some of the crippling illusions from their past. Although they still hoped for fair play, no longer did they expect to be handed Utopia on a silver platter by right-thinking Englishmen. "If we cannot try to help ourselves," an editorial in the *Sierra Leone Guardian and Foreign Mails* asserted, "the lowest pit shall be our place in the world after the war. The average white man who is a minister has no uplifting Gospel for the Negro, and the merchant is worse in that regard. We have to work for our own salvation."[14] Coupled with this new awareness was a growing frustration stemming from economic dislocations associated with the war effort. Together, they brought on the first and most direct attempt by some Creoles to attain "salvation" outside the realm of cultural and intellectual reactions—a vehement and seemingly organized attack against the most vulnerable group in Sierra Leone, the immigrant Syrian trading community.

The Anti-Syrian Riots

With shipping and the arrival of cargo steamers more uncertain, flour and sugar became and stayed scarce until the last months of 1917, trade was dislocated, and public revenues contracted correspondingly. At first, prices rose surprisingly little. Government had quickly invoked precautionary regu-

11. *Sierra Leone Guardian and Foreign Mails*, July 21, 1916, reprinted from the *African World*.

12. "Africanus," *SLWN*, January 13, 1917.

13. See Rupert Emerson, *From Empire to Nation* (Boston, 1960), pp. 25-26; J. S. Coleman, *Nigeria* (Berkeley, 1965), pp. 187-188.

14. Editorial, *Sierra Leone Guardian and Foreign Mails*, October 26, 1917.

lations for the colony and, with the relatively abundant local supplies of food from the protectorate, prevented scarcities. Nonetheless, one eyewitness recalls that as soon as war was declared, the price of rice and foo-foo, which grew up-country and in the mountain villages of the colony and was not at all connected with decreases in imports, rose fourfold.[15]

In spite of government's precautions, food shortages began to be felt in the colony as early as mid-1915. Carriers for the Cameroons campaign were drafted from various chiefdoms in the protectorate, leaving some areas with a labor scarcity at planting time. The expeditionary force, furthermore, was provided with hundreds of bushels of rice, depriving chiefs of stored provisions which normally would have served the inhabitants over the hungry season. In what came to have ominous significance, there was a strong belief, even in the early months of the war, that Syrian traders in the protectorate had been buying up rice that was intended for the colony and hoarding it to drive up the price.[16]

The success of Syrians in Sierra Leone had long been an extremely sensitive issue with Creoles. The first Syrians had arrived in the colony in the 1890s, singly or in pairs, as common peddlers who went about Freetown carrying their few sale articles on a board which they strapped around the neck. Because their main stock was imitation coral beads made from celluloid, they were called "Corals." Many who came to Sierra Leone were Shi'ite Muslims who originated from the same or closely related communities in the Levant and who, when successful in business, sponsored others of their group to come to Africa. Their maxim, according to one observer, was "Never return to Lebanon with poverty; they have enough of it there."[17]

Syrians found up-country Africans, especially the chiefs, enthusiastic customers for the coral beads. Whereas in the past a single coral bead had cost £2 or £3, and as much as £50 for a string, imitations could be purchased for mere pence. With success breeding success, Syrians soon stocked other inexpensive items such as mirrors, pocket knives, and hair pomade. The profit margin on their sales was low but their overhead expenses were lower still. They lived communally, several families often crowding into rooms designed for no more than two or three persons, doing without even the slightest luxury such as soap, eating African foods, and wearing simple, inexpensive clothing. To the disgust and dismay of the Creoles, to whom many of these practices seemed unsanitary if not uncivilized, the Corals thus were able to

15. Cole, *Kossoh Town Boy,* p. 112.

16. "The Year 1914," January 8, 1915; editorials, July 28, 1916, September 8, 1916, August 24, 1917, *Sierra Leone Guardian and Foreign Mails.*

17. Fuad J. Khuri, "Kinship, Emigration, and Trade Partnership Among the Lebanese of West Africa," *Africa* 35, no. 4 (October 1965): 385-395; also see R. Bayly Winder, "The Lebanese in West Africa," *Comparative Studies in Society and History* 4, no. 3 (April 1962): 296-333.

save a good deal of their profit. By the first decade of the twentieth century, Syrian competition gradually began to eliminate Creoles from retail business in the colony and protectorate.

The Syrians were ultimately successful because they pooled their profits, much the same as the Liberated African ancestors of the Creoles had done in the nineteenth century, in order to buy wholesale goods in bulk and, therefore, at lower cost. Creoles, having grown away from the memories of common enslavement which had once unified Liberated African groups and stimulated economic communalism, were unable to meet the Syrian challenge by combining in turn. Nor were they able to return at this point in their history to the low living standards which had been commonly acceptable among Liberated Africans. Moreover, the children and grandchildren of Creole merchants preferred the higher status conferred by professions such as law and medicine to the less prestigious profits from trading and selling.

Syrian traders soon began to import directly through buying agents in England and continental Europe who were frequently their fellow nationals. In this way they were able to take advantage of inexpensive second quality and end-of-season goods, as well as job lots, and pass some of their savings on to their customers. The result was obvious: the Syrians bought textiles, haberdashery, and many other goods that Creole traders had once handled and were able to sell their items at a much lower cost than their Sierra Leone competitors.[18]

By 1914 the situation had become so serious that some Freetown newspapers talked about a "Syrian Peril" in an obvious attempt to link the Near Easterners with their Turkish coreligionists and to gain British official support for their expulsion from Sierra Leone. "Rambler" wondered why, now that war had been declared between Turkey and Great Britain, "our friend the Syrian ... subject to the same Sultan as the Turks, was still at large and undeserving of the lot of other enemies of Britain who were interned as state prisoners."[19]

In fact, according to Creoles, Syrians could do no right. When some Syrians became patrons of the Sierra Leone Y.M.C.A., sponsored the Grand Athletic Sports events, or gave to charity, Creoles saw these as Machiavellian gestures. About 25 percent of the money collected for the Red Cross in Sierra Leone during the first years of World War I, for example, was donated by Syrians. But most Creoles could not find credible their charitable intent. "What is their game?" asked a writer to the *Sierra Leone Weekly News*, "Who

18. See Alldridge, *A Transformed Colony*, pp. 81-83; *SLT*, January 5, 1895, February 25, 1895, January 18, 1896; *SLWN*, July 22, 1905, letter to the editor, July 29, 1905, "Notes and Comments," January 27, 1906; *London Times*, June 11, 1930.

19. "Rambling Talks," *SLWN*, November 14, 21, 1914; "Have We a Syrian Peril?," *Colonial and Provincial Reporter*, May 30, 1914.

are they bluffing? There must be a reason . . . . They are trying to buy themselves out not to be taken for what they really are—Turkish subjects, full of Turkish sympathies, therefore, aliens, enemies, and they should be treated as such."[20]

Tension between the Creole and Syrian communities was heightened by the great influenza epidemic of 1918—an event for which no one could be blamed had logic prevailed. But the unsettled and disruptive postwar atmosphere shaped Creole reactions. The epidemic began in August when vessels arriving from Europe, where the disease had been raging for some time, infected the port area. It spread through the colony and protectorate with deadly rapidity. It was estimated that at least 1,000 civilians—both African and European—died from the disease between August 23 and September 18. Because of scanty and incomplete reports and the depletion of medical and sanitary staffs during the war, it was not possible to get a true computation of the prevalence of the disease nor was it possible to stem its swell. In Freetown alone, however, approximately 70 percent of the population was afflicted and a similar proportion probably became ill in the protectorate. If one accepts the 1911 census figures, which put the population of Freetown at 34,000, the number of persons affected thus numbered a startling 24,000. And as the disease took its toll, Creoles increasingly accused the Syrians for having brought this wretchedness on Sierra Leone with their unsanitary living conditions.[21] The ironic parallel that immediately suggests itself, of course, is the European contention that Africans were lacking adequate sanitation—the rationale, at least in part, for segregation schemes like Hill Station.

The tension mounted. The armistice signed between the Allied representatives and German commanders at the end of 1918 brought the First World War to a close. But even in Sierra Leone the effects of the war were far from finished. The population of Freetown had been swelled by large numbers of up-countrymen who had been employed during the war to load coal and to work on ships in port. Their labor was no longer needed and, in the months before they were repatriated to the protectorate, they became Sierra Leone's

20. *SLWN*, June 15, 1918, "Random Jottings," July 28, 1917.
21. See Kuczynski, *Demographic Survey*, 1: 9-10, 244; Sierra Leone Census Report, 1911, pp. 5, 6, 21, 38, 1921, pp. 6, 20; Sierra Leone Colonial Reports, 1918, p. 14; Sierra Leone Medical Report, 1918, p. 55, in Sierra Leone Collection; *SLWN*, November 30, 1918. The following poem, "In Memoriam—Influenza Victims, 1919," by Claudius E. Knox-Hooke, appeared in the Freetown press in 1919; "Beneath those sweet and shady flowers/Ye victims of a plague do lie;/Contented low in Earth's great bowers/forever watered by our sigh./By means of Influenza plague/That straightened many of their beds,/And proved your efforts all but vague/In the attempts to raise your heads./No history of this land can tell/Of conflict parallel to this/That on so many hundreds fell/And caused their earthly toils to cease./Tumultous were the average deaths/When more than fifty souls a day/Collapsed, and quickly lost their breaths/To meet their Fathers where they lay."

flotsam of war, another potentially dangerous ingredient in the unstable situation created by the influenza epidemic and food shortages.

By the middle of 1919 the colony was in a state of incipient famine. Rice imports, which under normal circumstances would have been destined for Freetown's population, filtered out to the protectorate. There, outside the bounds of colony price controls, it was sold for sixty-four shillings or more per bushel instead of the government established price of twenty-eight shillings per bushel. The belief became ever more prevalent that Syrians were hoarding not only rice but also foo-foo and palm oil to drive prices up.[22]

Almost as if to offer themselves as evidence, three Syrians were prosecuted and fined in June of 1919 for selling rice in excess of the maximum price allowed by the government regulations.[23] The *Sierra Leone Weekly News* sensed the danger of the situation. "It is urgently necessary," an editorial stated, "that the Government should import a quantity of rice and corn and yams from abroad and sell to the people at reasonable prices. This will at once break the back of the present trouble, and introduce a bearable condition."[24]

But the government did nothing. In July 1919 Governor Wilkinson was on leave, and, in his absence, the senior assistant colonial secretary, Mr. Evelyn, became acting governor. Evelyn, an indecisive administrator, had not sought the job. Either because he was unaware of the seriousness of the situation or ignorant of the existence of thirty-one tons of rice in Freetown, plus an unspecified amount on ships in the harbor, the acting governor did not alleviate the shortage of grain in the colony.[25] Further, Evelyn failed to follow the Executive Council's authorization (April 14, 1919) to import an additional £5000 worth of rice on government account. He may, perhaps, have been too involved in the plans for Peace Day celebrations which were to take place on July 19 or, more likely, preoccupied by the strikes involving the daily wage staff of the Locomotive Branch of the Railway Department and of the Public Works Department.

The strike, not of great significance in itself, was the catalyst for an already tense situation. The striking workers felt they were being excluded from a war bonus that had been granted to all officials on annual salaries and to a number of classes of "daily wage men." Their strike was well-organized,

22. See *Sierra Leone Guardian and Foreign Mails*, July 28, 1919, September 8, 1919. Numerous other statements in the Sierra Leone press during this period give evidence of the widespread nature of this belief.

23. Enclosure in Governor Wilkinson's Confidential Dispatch to the Secretary of State, January 12, 1920, October 16, 1920, no. 40, in C.O. 267/585; Governor's Confidential Dispatch to the Secretary of State, C104/1919, July 31, 1919, Sierra Leone, no. 357, in Sierra Leone Government Archives.

24. *SLWN*, July 12, 1919.

25. "Sequel to the Anti-Syrian Riots—the Sierra Leone Chamber of Commerce and the Colonial Government," *Colonial and Provincial Reporter*, September 6, 1920.

with picketing, processions, and dispatch runners on bicycles—details, Governor Wilkinson later noted, familiar to England but not to Sierra Leone. Some violence and destruction of property took place and the acting governor, eager to avoid recurrences but not realizing that he already possessed the authority to issue a bonus and end the strike, told the strikers that he would have to apply to the secretary of state on their behalf.[26] The strikers, meanwhile, refused to go back to work, and some of them, in an atmosphere already taut with talk of Syrian chicanery, relieved their frustrations by blaming the Levantines for the unpaid bonus.

> Maria Mammy cry for Bonus,
> Ner Bonus kill am;
> We berh am Ten o'clock,
> Bonus, Bo-Bonus!
>
> Strike don cam for Bonus,
> We unite for Bonus;
> Creole Boy ner danger Boy,
> Bonus, Bo-Bonus! . . .
>
> Milner say pay Bonus,
> Barker say bit first;
> Maude say make Red-belleh shoot
> Bonus, Bo-Bonus!
>
> White man all get Bonus,
> Dem get pass Ten pounds;
> We want we small Bonus,
> Bonus, Bo-Bonus.
>
> Coral too get Bonus
> Dem dey go for Bonum [sic] ;
> Malay coral Bonus,
> Bonus, Bo-Bonus! . . .
>
> Last year we say ner Flu,
> This year we call am Strike;
> When all dem Coral go,
> Then Bonus, Sweet Bonus![27]

26. Wilkinson to secretary of state, January 29, 1920, *Sierra Leone Royal Gazette*.
27. "Maria Mammy cries for the bonus/The Bonus killed her;/We bury her at Ten o'clock,/Bonus, Bo-Bonus!/The Bonus strike has come/We unite for the Bonus;/Creole Boy is a dangerous Boy,/Bonus, Bo-Bonus! . . ./Milner said, pay the Bonus,/Barker said, bite first;/Maude said, let the soldiers shoot,/Bonus, Bo-Bonus!/All the white men received their Bonus,/They all received more than Ten pounds;/We just want a small Bonus,/Bonus, Bo-Bonus./The Corals [Syrians] also received a Bonus/They go for Bonum [sic] ;/Malay coral Bonus,/Bonus, Bo-Bonus! . . ./Last year we said about the Flu,/This year we call the Strike;/When all the Syrians go,/Then Bonus, Sweet Bonus!" Enclosure in Governor Wilkinson's Confidential Report to the Secretary of State on the

With the strike continuing, while the acting governor and a party of guests were sitting down to a leisurely game of bridge after dinner on the eve of the Peace Day celebrations, the anti-Syrian riots began.[28]

They began suddenly, while a torch-light procession advanced slowly along streets crowded with people milling about and singing patriotic songs. They lasted well into the morning—ironically Peace Day—and continued again the next morning. Up-country, in the Ronietta, Railway, Northern Sherbro, and Karene Districts, they took place almost a week later, just sufficient time, it was claimed, for those involved in Freetown to make their way to the protectorate and instigate disturbances.[29]

Attacks in the riot were directed against property rather than persons. A number of Syrians were beaten, but few of these received serious injuries. One man did die in the hospital as a result of the beating that he sustained. Another Syrian was accidentally shot by one of his countrymen. A Syrian woman, who gave premature birth to a child during the riots, also died in the hospital. Looting of Syrian stores, however, was widespread, and the riot's vindictiveness was evident by the fact that no European or Creole-owned stores were touched. Large quantities of cotton goods, rice, palm oil, and cash were taken. Many shops were completely gutted.

Because the attacks seemed to come simultaneously in different parts of town, moreover, indicating method along with madness, the acting governor and the commissioner of police believed that the riots had been well organized. One eye witness reported that a section of the mob was "led by a well-dressed Creole in white Panama hat and very shiny shoes." When the riots first started, these allegations may have had some foundation in fact. Creoles had certainly been most hurt by Syrian practices, and many were undoubtedly elated when their rivals received their comeuppance. Some Creoles, especially those who were unemployed, participated in the looting. A few may initially have directed rioters and, therefore, could deservedly be called "organizers." For those Creoles involved, the violence was a spontaneous expression of pent-up frustration discharged against the most convenient scapegoat in Sierra Leone—one which was foreign, numerically vulnerable, and could be held in contempt as somehow "less civilized." But Creoles who

---

Anti-Syrian Riots, January 29, 1920, in C.O. 267/585. Lord Milner was colonial secretary; E. G. Barker, acting general manager of the railway; and W. R. A. Maude, attorney general. The words of the Bonus Song were composed by W. Mends-Cole and were published by "The African Comedy Coy [sic]." The song was "sung during the Great Strike and Peace Celebrations, July 15th to 22nd 1919."

28. Governor Wilkinson, Confidential Report to the Secretary of State, October 16, 1920, in C.O. 267/585.

29. D.C., Karene District, to Colonial Secretary, enclosed in Governor's Confidential Dispatch to the Secretary of State, C104/1919, July 31, 1919; Commissioner of Police's Report to Colonial Secretary, enclosed in Governor's Confidential Dispatch to the Secretary of State, C104/1919, July 31, 1919, in Sierra Leone Government Archives.

participated were soon ably assisted, and even displaced, by the large number of up-countrymen who wandered about Freetown jobless and who were also ready to hold the Syrians accountable for their part in the scarcity and high price of goods. In spite of allegations about the simultaneous origins of the attacks, the riot quickly became the action of a mob.[30]

Three companies of the West India Regiment, aided by the police and by the Creole mayor of Freetown, S. J. Barlatt, and other Creole gentlemen who offered their services as special constables, restored order in Freetown. Two hundred and forty-five arrests were made. Up-country, the situation was never as severe, and, although many Syrian shops were looted, troops quickly re-established control. The large-scale insurrection the government expected—on the scale of the 1898 Hut Tax War—did not materialize.[31]

Syrians from the colony, and those who arrived from the protectorate—a total of 242—were all housed and supplied with rations in Wilberforce Memorial Hall, which the City Council had placed at the disposal of the government, and in two other buildings.[32] The government believed that they could best be protected there rather than in their own homes, and optimistically felt that all could return to their dwellings in a few days. But the temper reflected in the Sierra Leone press made it necessary for the Syrians to remain in protective custody for two months afterwards.[33]

The Creole press, which on occasion in the past had expressed a tolerant view of the Syrians, became uniformly anti-Syrian after the riots. In November 1918, seven months before the disturbance occurred, the *Sierra Leone Guardian and Foreign Mails* ran the following editorial:

> The Syrians are a rather peaceful people and very enterprising;
> and the God who always delights to bless peaceful and enterpris-
> ing people has blessed them . . . . We have greatly regretted the
> outcry which in some quarters has been persistently raised against
> our Syrian brethren. . . . We should not forget at all that the
> Syrian residents amongst us are a test of our character. God has
> sent them here that we may learn the importance of Enterprise,
> of Combination, of unity, of simple living from them. It is by

30. Commissioner of Police's Report to Colonial Secretary, enclosed in Governor's Confidential Dispatch to the Secretary of State, C104/1919, July 31, 1919, in Sierra Leone Government Archives. Also see "General News," July 26, 1919; "News," August 9, 1919, *SLWN*.

31. Commissioner of Police's Report to Colonial Secretary, enclosed in Governor's Confidential Dispatch to the Secretary of State, C104/1919, July 31, 1919, in Sierra Leone Government Archives; letter to the editor, *SLWN*, August 23, 1919.

32. A letter to the editor of the *SLWN*, August 9, 1919, showed concern that the congestion of the Syrians in these buildings might ultimately bring on the plague.

33. Governor's Confidential Dispatch to the Secretary of State, C104/1919, July 31, 1919, Sierra Leone no. 357, in Sierra Leone Government Archives; Wilkinson to Secretary of State, October 16, 1920, in C.O. 267/585.

these means and with honesty ... that these people have thriven.[34]

After the riots had taken place, however, the same paper asserted: "The Syrians have been unfeeling brutes who after making money in our country have planned to destroy us by creating unbearable conditions .... We learn with complete approval that a resolution to the effect that the Syrians are not wanted in the place was unanimously passed."[35] And: To guard against our being infected with another Syrian vermin it would not be out of place ... for the Government to pass an Ordinance to prevent further Syrian immigration.[36] *Aurora*, the newspaper the government considered to be most virulent, offered the following version of the advent of the Levantines in Sierra Leone:

> The Syrian came not in Cohorts gleaming in purple and gold. He was a *rara avis* in those days, a mere bird of passage. He came in twos and threes, a ragged mendicant, redolent of garlic and onions, supplicating the goodwill of our artless fathers.
>
> True it might be that there was something sinister in the look of the man, that through the fawning servility of those mobile features there gleamed fitfully an indescribable blend of the low cunning of the fox, the ferocity of the ferret, the voracious rapacity of the vulture, the relentless cruelty of the tiger, and the indecorous lechery of the he-goat; but our fathers were simple folk. The Syrian was a stranger and they took him in. He was hungry and they fed him ....[37]

And the *Sierra Leone Weekly News*, which Governor Wilkinson had called "the most moderate of the local newspapers" in one of his dispatches to the secretary of state,[38] printed a comment on *Aurora*'s venom belying the governor's judgment:

> Aurora! O! Aurora!
> What grand pen-pictures you did give
> Of the invasion of the thion [sic]
> Who vampire-like did thrive
> On the blood of the land.

34. Editorial, *Sierra Leone Guardian and Foreign Mails*, November 19, 1918.
35. Editorial, *Sierra Leone Guardian and Foreign Mails*, August 1, 1919.
36. Editorial, *Sierra Leone Guardian and Foreign Mails*, August 8, 1919.
37. *Aurora*, July 26, 1919, enclosed in Wilkinson to Secretary of State, November 13, 1920, in C.O. 267/588.
38. Wilkinson to Secretary of State, November 13, 1920, in C.O. 267/588.

From Syria's barren soil he came
To Afric's sunny land and free;
Sleeping land of classic fame,
To sell and buy and fatten
On the blood of the land.

The Grand Sierra Welcom'd him,
When to his valley fair he came
With Austrian goods cheap for sale,
And every profit he could make
On the blood of the land.

Royal mountain, guardian angel
Silent witness to our woes!
To thee we cry, to thee we call
All our plaints and all our woes
On the blood of the land.

Grass he tells us we will eat,
When on vengeance on rice did sit;
Leaves and brooms and all he cornered,
Farina, palm oil and Kola;
On the blood of the land.

Anon the people's fiat went:
"Destroy his house, his shop, his goods,
And every thing he has kept.
Touch not himself though he was throven
On the blood of the land."[39]

In the days and months thereafter, claiming that the riots had been "defensive" and not "offensive" actions "by people whose very life was rudely shaken to extinction by heartless traders who are aliens," many influential Creoles suggested the Syrians be made to leave the country.[40] The Freetown City Council sent an official dispatch and a memorial to the secretary of state for the colonies urging the expulsion of the Levantines. Their appeal was rejected. They drew scant satisfaction when the Legislative Council passed an ordinance to control the immigration of the subjects of foreign states which had recently been at war with Great Britain into the colony and protectorate.[41]

39. M'Makori, "The Syrians," *SLWN*, September 13, 1919.
40. "Thoughts on Recent Occurrences in Freetown," August 2, 1919; editorial, July 26, 1919, *SLWN*.
41. "Random Jottings," August 23, 1919; "General News," September 13, 1919, *SLWN*; Sierra Leone Legislative Council Debates, September 3, 1919, in Sierra Leone Government Archives. A. J. Shorunkeh-Sawyerr, a Creole member of the Legislative

The British government, in fact, seemed especially anxious to thwart the Creoles on this matter, contributing further to their sense of disappointment and frustration. In August of 1919 fifty-four persons were convicted in Supreme Court after having pleaded guilty in connection with the July riots and were sentenced to imprisonment for terms ranging from one-and-a-half to four-and-a-half years. At the trial, both the acting chief justice, Mr. C. S. King Farlow, and the acting attorney general, Mr. M. J. Macdonnel, shocked the Creole community by cavalierly dismissing the defense's contention that the rioters were impelled to action by hunger and that the Syrians were hoarding rice. They went on to salt the wound by suggesting that the up-country rioters were the mere tools of those Creoles who were envious of the commercial success of law-abiding, thrifty, and industrious Syrians.[42]

Using the special powers granted to the governor under the wartime "Defence of the Realm Act," the government proceeded to issue proclamation no. 28—the "Colonial Defence Regulations, 1919." With this law, the authorities not only sought to protect Syrians against further harm and to reinstate them into the colony and protectorate, but also desired to curb what they believed were the aroused passions of the Creoles. Thus the regulation required that colonial newspapers be registered with the government under a £250 bond, that penalties for the publication of seditious or libelous materials be extracted, that oral and written "incitements to violence" be forbidden, and that any conspiracy to exclude Syrians from renting Creole houses or to bring about economic pressures against them be prohibited.[43]

The *Sierra Leone Weekly News* certainly reflected the mood of the majority of Creoles in its testy retort to the proclamation. The imposition of the £250 bond on newspapers, blazed an editorial, was a vicious attempt to gag and destroy native journalism in Sierra Leone. The colonial government was an integral part of the government of Great Britain and not of Turkey. Had it forgotten that Sierra Leoneans had always been known as law-abiding people? Did not King George V call the land "My Ancient and Loyal Sierra Leone"? Had Sierra Leoneans not behaved satisfactorily during World War I? Furthermore, *The Weekly News* could assure the government that no respectable inhabitant of Freetown took part in the raid on the Syrians. On the

---

Council, and a man who had actively worked to bring the riots to an end, opposed the expulsion of the Syrians.

42. "News," *SLWN*, August 9, 1919.

43. Some talk had indeed taken place in Freetown to the effect that, in the likely case that the Syrians were not expelled from Sierra Leone, Creoles should refuse to rent houses to them for stores and dwelling places. Since the Syrians had not acquired landed property in Sierra Leone, such an action might truly have forced them to pack up and leave the country. See "Random Jottings," *SLWN*, August 23, 1919; also see *Extraordinary Royal Gazette*, September 13, 1919, for the full text of proclamation no. 28.

contrary, for twenty years and more it was the Creoles, "who are now being relentlessly pursued so as to be hunted down," who gave quarters to the Syrians and, in all sorts of ways, encouraged them to dwell among them. The proclamation, declared the editorial, was absolutely unnecessary.[44]

The consensus among Creoles was that the government had long contemplated imposing these regulations but was waiting for an excuse. The Syrian riots had provided it. And, although most colonial officials were fairly certain that members of the Creole upper class had not been involved in the planning or execution of the riots and had reported this opinion to the secretary of state, the government's punitive response served to convince Creoles that they were being treated unfairly, that they were distrusted, and that British "white men" would support even alien "white men" rather than coming to the defense of British subjects who happened to be "black."[45]

Not long after the riots, Gold Coast soldiers from Kumasi who had been called to Sierra Leone arrived in the colony. At the same time, West African Frontiers from Wilberforce barracks marched through the streets of Freetown and were posted about town—at the houses and shops from where the Syrians had been ousted, and near the places where the Levantines were being protectively housed. Again, the *Sierra Leone Weekly News* was indignant. Had these "raw heads and bloody bones" imported from the Gold Coast, asked a columnist, come to bring "lawless Sierra Leone into 'law abiding-ness' "? If so, then there was no need for the machine guns, for all was peaceful in both colony and protectorate.[46] "When will the authorities realise," asked a letter to the editor, "that the Sierra Leoneans are a deeply loyal people and that they have not the traits of disloyalty which exist in other portions of His Majesty's world-wide Empire?"[47]

The authorities ignored Creole indignation. A bill entitled "An Ordinance to Provide for the Payment of Compensation for Damage Done During

44. Editorial, *SLWN*, September 20, 1919.

45. See Wilkinson to Secretary of State, November 13, 1920, in C.O. 267/588; and Wilkinson, Confidential to Secretary of State, October 16, 1920, in C.O. 267/585, for opinions vindicating a substantial number of upper-class Creoles from participation in the riots. Also see "The Ugly Syrian Domination in West Africa," *SLWN*, June 12, 1920, for an accusation that the British were supporting the Syrians for racist reasons.

46. *SLWN*, September 27, 1919, October 4, 1919.

47. *SLWN*, October 4, 1919. A clue to the government's tactless action appears in one of Governor Wilkinson's confidential dispatches to the Colonial Office. "There is no doubt in my mind," he wrote, "that there is a focus of disloyalty in this Colony. This disloyalty, I have some reason to believe, is inspired from outside the Empire and has money and organization behind it." See Wilkinson, Confidential to Secretary of State, October 16, 1920, no. 59, in C.O. 267/585. This may reflect Wilkinson's misunderstanding of the aims and organization of the National Congress of British West Africa, which was supported by the majority of the upper-class Freetown Creole community and, by this time in 1920, had already met in Accra.

Certain Riots in the Colony and Protectorate" received its first reading in the Legislative Council in September 1919. An amount totaling £36,635 was sought in damages from Freetown ratepayers for the Syrians affected by the looting and destruction. Creoles were enraged. In the first place, they claimed, correctly, that no historical parallels for such actions existed in Sierra Leone. None of the Creole merchants and traders who had suffered great losses in the protectorate during the 1898 Hut Tax War had received compensation. Secondly, even if the Syrians were to receive damage payments, Creoles could not see why Freetonians had to pay for goods looted or destroyed up-country, nor did they understand why the compensation was to be debited from Freetown revenues rather than from the general colonial revenue. To charge the damages to the Freetown City Council implied that the Creoles of the city—the ratepayers—were the ones to blame for the riot. This they vehemently denied.[48]

The governor, for his part, felt it was more reasonable to extract damage payments through the City Council "than to throw the burden upon the general revenue which is contributed mainly by protectorate natives who were in no sense anti-Syrian." Further, while he did not want the compensation measure to be thought of as "punitive," he was sure that it would have the beneficial effect of creating a sense of collective responsibility. "No one would call this population riotous," Wilkinson wrote to Secretary of State Milner, "but a perusal of its newspapers makes it clear that the tongue in Sierra Leone can be a very unruly member indeed."[49] By any standards, the entire concept of riot compensation reeked of paternalism. No teacher could better have disciplined his naughty pupils: for Creoles, compensation represented yet another betrayal.

In the haggling that followed, government eventually backed down from some of its demands. Governor Wilkinson returned from his leave preceded by reports of a speech that he had made to the Liverpool Chamber of Commerce in which he laid partial blame for the outbreak of the riots on the government's own mishandling of rice distribution.[50] By the time Wilkinson left the colony at the end of 1921, the compensation ordinance had still not been enforced. The government of Sierra Leone compensated the Syrians, but the City Council had not reimbursed the government a penny.

Aurora expressed typical upper-class Creole vexation with Governor Wil-

48. Wilkinson to Secretary of State, November 13, 1920, in C.O. 267/588. Enclosed were the "Petition from the Citizens of Freetown"; Paul Drewitt, "The Syrian Problem," August 9, 1919; editorial on the proposed riot damages bill, September 11, 1919, *SLWN*; Freetown Municipality Ordinance, no. 4 of 1921, and amendment to this ordinance.

49. Wilkinson to Secretary of State, November 13, 1920, in C.O. 267/588.

50. See *West Africa*, September 13, 1919; "Sequel to the Anti-Syrian Riots," *The Colonial and Provincial Reporter*, November 6, 1920.

kinson's administration when it printed the following ditty upon his departure:

> Governor Wilkinson has gone;
> Sing glory, glory halleluyah,
> Sing glory, glory halleluyah:
> Sing glory, glory halleluyah,
> Gone, but not forgotten.
> "The evil that men do lives after them."[51]

Summing up Wilkinson's administration as "one continuous run of tension,
commotion, anxiety, controversy, depression, estrangement, culminating in a
state of bankruptcy, unemployment, and general dissatisfaction," they attributed this state of affairs to the governor's contempt for Africans, particularly educated ones, and asserted that his rule heightened color prejudice.[52]
Whether justifiable or not, these charges accurately reflected the tenor of the
Creole community in these years—angry and bitter.

Ransford Slater, Wilkinson's successor, held an inquiry which concluded
that it would be unfair to charge the Freetown ratepayers £36,635 because
they, like everyone else, were affected by the world-wide depression of trade
and because "an appreciable degree of indirect responsibility for the riots
admittedly devolved on Government." Instead, Slater recommended that the
Freetown City Council pay the government £500 a year for ten years, and
that the government fund this money so that the total of £5000 be spent on a
special work of municipal improvement in Freetown on the condition that
the government was satisfied "in the event of any further disturbances
occurring in Freetown, that the law-abiding inhabitants took *active* steps to
support law and order."[53] Slater's "compromise" allayed the pains but did
not remove the scars incised by the government's mismanagement. Subsequent adhesions would make clear that the breach between the British and
the Creoles was not soon to be healed.

The Congress Movement

Creole involvement in the National Congress of British West Africa (NCBWA),
the major West African movement of the first quarter of the twentieth
century, was the clearest indication of their postwar shift from cultural
introspection to political action. The NCBWA emerged from the same cauldron of post-World War I expectations that had engendered movements like

51. "Sling Shots," J. B. C., *Aurora*, October 29, 1921.

52. Editorial, *Aurora*, September 3, 1921.

53. Sierra Leone Legislative Council Debates, 1922-1923, November 20, 1922, pp.
101-104, in Sierra Leone Government Archives.

the first Pan African Congress, held in Paris in 1919 under the leadership of W. E. B. DuBois, and Marcus Garvey's United Negro Improvement Association in the United States. The idea for a conference of West Africans which would meet in time for its members to make recommendations concerning the disposition of ex-German African territories at the Peace Conference originated in the Gold Coast.[54] Sierra Leone Creoles were quickly attracted to the suggestion and early in 1918, at the insistence of J. H. Thomas and

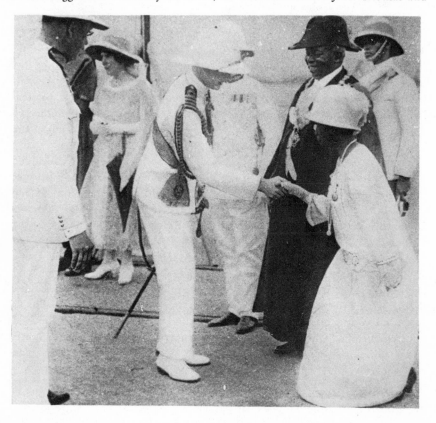

Figure 10. The Creole mayor of Freetown and editor of the *Sierra Leone Weekly News*, Cornelius May, and his wife greeting the Prince of Wales during his visit to Sierra Leone in 1925. One year later, after a controversial scandal which many claim to have been rigged by May's political enemies in alliance with unsympathetic colonial authorities, the Freetown Municipal Council was abolished and May imprisoned for embezzlement.

54. Coleman, *Nigeria*, p. 192, claims that Dr. Akinwande Savage, a Nigerian then residing in the Gold Coast, conceived the idea for a conference of West Africans as early as 1913 and, before returning to Nigeria, convinced influential Gold Coasters like Hutton-Mills and Casely Hayford of the soundness of this notion.

Cornelius May, formed a committee to take the first practical steps toward organizing such a conference.[55]

Even though Sierra Leoneans had reacted speedily, no conference took place before the Peace Conference, and, when a meeting was finally arranged for 1920, emphasis had necessarily shifted from concern with the ex-German colonies to the presentation of a general reform program to the colonial government. According to an article in *West Africa*, the conference was also meeting to initiate united action by the four British West African colonies at the imperial conference which Lord Milner, the secretary of state for the colonies, had announced for 1921.[56] An editorial in the *Sierra Leone Weekly News*, citing additional reasons why a conference was needed, considered the Allied victory in the war as the main impetus for united action on the part of West Africans. This victory, the editorial stated, "was an opportunity for protected people of the Empire to state their cases and lay claims to expanded and larger liberty which, due to their degree of enlightenment and in impeachable quality of their loyalty, they considered themselves entitled to."[57] Discrimination in the West African Medical Staff, the Syrian problem, the government's actions in the aftermath of the riots, and the general attitude of the Colonial Office to the economic welfare of Sierra Leoneans and to their "liberties as British subjects," were grievances which Sierra Leone Creoles especially hoped the conference would act upon.[58]

At the instigation of the well-known Accra barristers, J. E. Casely Hayford and T. Hutton-Mills, the first conference of the NCBWA was convened in the Gold Coast in March 1920. Its opening session was greeted by messages of congratulations from the governors of the British West African colonies and was attended by members of the Gold Coast administration.[59] Delegates from the European-educated African communities in Nigeria, the Gambia, Gold Coast, and Sierra Leone participated. The Sierra Leone committee, which had been planning the conference since 1918, elected Frederic William Dove, who was at this time residing at Accra, Leslie Macarthy, barrister-at-

55. "The Conference Movement," and letters to the editor, July 6, 1918; "A Golden Opportunity," November 30, 1918; "The Programme for the British West Africa Conference," December 7, 1918, *SLWN*; editorial, May 3, 1918; letter to the editor, "The Proposed West African Conference," December 14, 1918, *Sierra Leone Guardian and Foreign Mails*; Martin Kilson, "The National Congress of British West Africa, 1918-1935" in *Protest and Power in Black Africa*, ed. Robert I. Rotberg and Ali A. Mazrui (New York, 1970), pp. 571-588.

56. *West Africa*, May 29, 1920, p. 668.

57. Editorial, *SLWN*, March 13, 1920.

58. Ibid.

59. *West Africa*, May 29, 1920. These Europeans attended the opening session: C. H. Harper, colonial secretary and deputy governor; His Honor, Mr. Justice Porter; J. T. Furley, secretary for native affairs; Major Bettington, inspector of police.

law, and Dr. Herbert Bankole-Bright, to represent the colony at the proceedings.[60]

The delegates were reform-minded in the tradition of the British evangelical-philanthropists who had worked for the abolition of slavery in the nineteenth century.[61] They wanted to better the conditions under which West Africans were living—not through the withdrawal or the violent overthrow of the colonial authorities but by making reasoned appeals to the British public and government's sense of legality and fair play. Sierra Leone delegates, in particular, despite their difficulties with the Syrians, their displacement in trade, and their aggravated feelings toward the British, continued to keep their faith in the possibility of amelioration within the framework of the colonial system. For them, perhaps more than for any other West Africans represented in the movement, the alternatives were limited by circumstances, both perceived and real. Feeling hemmed in by up-countrymen in Sierra Leone, culturally distinct if not superior to them, the Creoles lacked the power base that might have enabled them to take a more combative line. Until this changed in the 1930s congress offered an opportunity for concerted action within a parameter defined by old assumptions: Britain's "most ancient and loyal" African subjects, aggrieved but faithful to the benefits and ideologies of a past missionary tradition, united with other "elite" West Africans to pressure their colonial masters into reform through gentlemanly debate.

The resolutions passed by the congress, which, drawn up into a memorandum, were brought to the secretary of state for the colonies in London by a special delegation, clearly reflected the moderate nature of the movement. Among other things, the congress asked for the following:

1. That education be improved and made compulsory throughout the British West African colonies and that a West African University be established. This revived an idea set forth more than half a century earlier by Dr. Africanus Horton and E. W. Blyden.

2. That immigration laws be introduced throughout West Africa to keep out "undesirable aliens" and that the possibility of repatriating Syrians from the West African colonies be considered. In this, the influence of the Sierra Leone delegation, particularly of Dove, who presented a paper on "Alien Problems" at the Accra meeting, was clearly discernible.

3. That sanitary reforms be carried out in the colonies and that discriminatory practices in the West African Medical Staff as well as fanciful "health segregation" schemes such as Hill Station be abolished.

60. *SLWN*, March 13, 1920.

61. LaRay E. Denzer, "The National Congress of British West Africa—Gold Coast Section" (M.A. thesis, Legon University, Ghana, 1965), pp. 2-3.

4. That all judicial appointments be opened to African practitioners, and an appellate court established.

5. That discrimination in the civil service cease, and all future appointments be made on the basis of examination.

6. That new constitutions be drawn up for the West African colonies which would change the make-up of the legislative councils so that one-half of its members could be elected by the people and the other half be nominated by the Crown.

7. That a house of assembly be created, composed of the elected members of the Legislative Council plus a number of financial advisors.

8. And, most interesting, that the congress wished "to maintain strictly and inviolate the connection of the British West African Dependencies with the British Empire" and to "record the attachment of the peoples of British West Africa to the British connection, and their unfeigned loyalty and devotion to the throne and person of His Majesty the King-Emperor."[62]

Judging from these resolutions, and in spite of the word "National" in the full name of the congress, the British need have had no fear that the congress was the harbinger of a "nationalist" wind which would sweep the West African colonies to independence. Nonetheless, many in Britain feared just that. Most of the delegates at the Accra meeting would undoubtedly have agreed with the explanation in Sierra Leone's *Colonial and Provincial Reporter* that the term "National," as it was used by the congress, was nothing more than a description of the racial unity of black Africans and an assertion that they were as capable as anyone to hold meetings and propose improvements to their own situation.[63] But the type of franchise for which the congress asked was generally misunderstood in Britain, and the occasional enjoinders by its supporters for an "African Empire" or "self-government" raised doubts about the sincerity of the organization's public declarations. Britain responded with coolness, and the congress was placed on the defensive.[64]

In London the congress delegation officially informed Reuters that the organization had never, directly or indirectly, asked for self-government, and

62. *Resolution of the Conference of Africans of British West Africa held at Accra, Gold Coast from 11th to 29th March, 1920*, National Congress of British West Africa (London, 1920); "National Congress of British West Africa. A Political Programme Placed Before the British Public," September 25, 1920, pp. 1242-1244; "The West African Conference," p. 502, *West Africa*.

63. "News and Notes," *Colonial and Provincial Reporter*, May 1, 1920. It was not until they were ready to adjourn in Accra that the conference members resolved to call their organization the National Congress of British West Africa—a step designed to perpetuate the movement and its work.

64. *Colonial and Provincial Reporter*, July 24, 1920; January 15, 1921, p. 1698; editorial about the ambiguity in the demands of congress delegates, *West Africa*.

Dove, in *West Africa*, was emphatic about the movement's moderate desires.[65] Nonetheless, *West Africa* summed up the suspicions which continued to be held by the informed British public about congress's aims:

> Either all that is wanted is improvement of the existing Legislative Councils—a perfectly arguable proposition—in which case there was no need to send a delegation here, at all events unless and until the Coast Governments had taken up an attitude of blank hostility; or what is wanted is full self-government, in which case it is out of the question to pretend that all legitimately interested sections in West Africa have had an opportunity of expressing their views.[66]

Congress delegates were sensitive to the allegation that they had not followed correct procedures in their demands for a new constitution. They were aware that, had there been any proposals for constitutional change or complaints within any *individual* colony, the governors should have been consulted first. Since the issue they raised, however, was the establishment of a new system of government for *all* British West African colonies, they felt the correct course was to petition the king directly. The king, following normal channels, would then refer the petition to the secretary of state for the colonies and, in turn, to the West African governors for advice.[67] But the accusation about which the congress delegates were even more sensitive—perhaps because here they were more vulnerable—was that they had no legitimate claim to represent anyone in their respective colonies except themselves.

Their "legitimacy" had bothered members of congress from the beginning. The conference president, Hutton-Mills, had confronted this problem in his keynote address to the Accra session. "Apart from the fact of the delegates to the conference being the *natural leaders* of the people of their several communities," he declared, "*they have in themselves the right* to appeal to His Majesty's Government for such constitutional reforms as in their judgement are necessary .... They carry with them the support of the people, who, whether educated or uneducated are sufficiently alive to the importance of this hour of seeking for the amelioration of British West African political conditions."[68] Soon afterwards, however, certain Gold Coast chiefs disavowed the congress as unrepresentative of the desires of the traditional "Native Institutions" in that colony, and congress delegates were hard pressed for concrete evidence of their right to speak on behalf of the mass of West Africans.[69]

65. Letter to the editor, January 8, 1921, p. 1661; February 5, 1921, *West Africa*.
66. Editorial, *West Africa*, January 22, 1921.
67. *West Africa*, December 11, 1920, p. 1549.
68. Quoted in *West Africa*, May 29, 1920, pp. 668-669. Italics mine.
69. For the text of Chief Ofori Atta's speech to the Gold Coast Legislative Council,

The problem was intensified by criticisms of the Nigerian delegates—Mr. Shyngle, a Gambian who was a practicing barrister in Lagos, and the Oluwa, one of the Lagos white-capped chiefs—two men who could not seriously be considered by anyone as spokesmen for the great number of communities in Nigeria extending from the coast to the fringes of the desert.[70] So, when Sir Hugh Clifford, then governor of Nigeria, made a scathing attack on the "self-selected and self-appointed congregation of educated African gentlemen who collectively style themselves the 'West African National Conference,'" congress delegates were ill-prepared to show fight.[71] The inability of the delegates to prove themselves representative leaders of their respective colonies stemmed precisely from the fact that they had relatively little popular backing for their mission. Some chiefs had been consulted in the Gold Coast, but rarely if at all in any of the other colonies. In the colony of Sierra Leone especially, where Creoles were still the most important element in the population but where protectorate Africans had become increasingly prominent, congress delegates made scant effort to discover the opinions or to get the support of non-Creole leaders.

Given the general antipathy educated Creoles had for up-countrymen, such consultation would have been somewhat out of character.[72] The Creoles, moreover, descending from colonists in Sierra Leone, differed from the majority of other West African delegates in that they lacked ethnic connections with interior peoples. The reality, however, was that all congress delegates stemmed from a small group of European-educated, largely urbanized, Christian Africans—persons from families which, for decades if not generations, had been considered among the "elite" of West Africa. They were the Europeanized aristocracy of their respective colonies—prone, perhaps, to a certain amount of *noblesse oblige*, but feeling no need to justify themselves to the less fortunate natives or to recruit them into their organizations. Little chance existed for the national congress to grow to the proportions of a mass movement like Garvey's United Negro Improvement Association.

When the London delegation of the national congress presented a petition and memorandum to the king based on the Accra resolutions, they were rejected by Lord Milner. Milner, as secretary of state for the colonies, had received information from the governors of Nigeria and the Gold Coast that the congress did not represent the "native communities on whose behalf it

---

see *West Africa*, February 5, 1921, p. 36, February 19, 1921, pp. 99-101, February 26, 1921, pp. 114-116.

70. Editorial, *West Africa*, January 22, 1921. Also see Coleman, *Nigeria*, pp. 192-194.

71. Quoted in Coleman, *Nigeria*, p. 193. For more on Clifford's attack see *West Africa*, January 22, 1921, pp. 1710-1712, January 29, 1921, p. 3.

72. "News and Notes," *Colonial and Provincial Reporter*, May 1, 1920; *West Africa*, September 15, 1920, p. 1241.

purports to speak; that its pretensions in this respect are expressly repudiated by the most authoritative exponents of native public opinion (including practically all the chiefs in the Gold Coast), and that the scheme put forward by the congress would in their opinion be inimical to the best interests of the community." The secretary of state had no reason to suppose, furthermore, that this situation would be different with respect to either Sierra Leone or the Gambia.[73]

In Sierra Leone, in fact, the Creole members of the national congress sought to prove otherwise. May, in his *Sierra Leone Weekly News*, hoped to overwhelm the Colonial Office with sheer assertiveness. "We insist," he wrote, "that the enlightened portion of West Africa is responsible for the unenlightened portion . . . . It is a right justified by the kinship of Race and Blood."[74] But this paternalistic approach was to no avail. When the delegates returned from London to the colony in April 1921, therefore, Sierra Leoneans tried a more spectacular approach. Two mass rallies were held in Wilberforce Memorial Hall to demonstrate that the congress did indeed represent the "native communities." A number of Freetown's tribal rulers, a few up-countrymen, as well as a paramount chief from the protectorate, were seated conspicuously alongside members of the congress to demonstrate their solidarity with the aims of the movement. And, even though it was difficult to reconcile this rather blatant token act of integration with the all-Creole character of previous local congress meetings, the delegates agreed that it was sufficiently exemplary to merit a special telegram to the colonial secretary.[75] The Freetown press, moreover, gushed with excitement. "What a terrible slap the other afternoon," read an impassioned statement in *Aurora*, "when the policy of divide and rule was smashed to atoms. The Creoles . . . the aborigines, and other factors joined in denouncing the heaped political rubbish bundled at headquarters [and] tied with the usual red tape."[76]

In the *Sierra Leone Weekly News*, S. C. John wrote this stinging ode:

> Let traitors sing their wild and deafening song;
> Malicious foes their poisoned arrows throw,
> And foreign wight [*sic*] uncalled for passion show;
> Let rulers white attempt us to divide
> So they'll remain basking full in their pride;

73. "Petition to King George V for the Reconstitution of the Several Legislative Councils and the Constitution of Houses of Assembly and Other Reforms. National Congress of British West Africa," reproduced in *West Africa*, November 6, 1920, pp. 1415-1416; *West Africa*, February 26, 1921, also reprinted a letter from the colonial office to Bankole-Bright, secretary of the congress delegation, rejecting the petition.

74. *SLWN*, March 12, 1921.

75. *Aurora*, April 16, 1921; *SLWN*, April 23, 1921.

76. "A Sierra Leonean's Diary," *Aurora*, April 23, 1921.

> Let pessimists the noble venture scorn,
> Of its success trumpet the sceptic's horn;
> In spite of these the Congress National
> For certainty shall steadily excell,
> And, soon or late, 'twill sing triumphal songs.[77]

Having lost the first battle, however, bravado was a poor substitute for success. In spite of all evidence showing that the educated African elite had clearly been rejected as the "civilizers" of Africa, this group—of whom the upper-class Creoles were the outstanding example—persisted in the illusion they were the favorite sons and heirs apparent of Great Britain. They refused to recognize that British policies now favored traditional chiefs within a system of indirect rule. More than in anything else, the failure of the congress lay in the inability of its members to confront this change directly and to design their tactics accordingly.

Early in 1923 the National Congress of British West Africa held a second session, this time in Freetown. Obviously handicapped by Milner's rebuff, it lacked the *esprit de corps* that had characterized the Accra meeting. Sierra Leone, the Gold Coast, and the Gambia sent representatives. Nigerian delegates were conspicuously absent.[78]

The opening of the session was heralded by special services in churches, chapels, and mosques throughout Freetown. Reverend J. C. O. During of Wesley Church preached a sermon based on Acts 25 : 2, "I appeal to Caesar" a particularly fitting choice for the occasion. Caseley Hayford's keynote speech and the resolutions the delegates subsequently passed showed that congress's demands had altered little from those which had been made in Accra and sent to London. Slightly more emphasis was now placed on the possible creation of a federation of the British West African colonies, with a governor general, much as it had been on various occasions in the nineteenth century when British possessions in West Africa had all been under the aegis of a governor general in Sierra Leone.[79] The acquisition of the franchise, however, was still the main plank of the congress's platform.

---

77. *SLWN*, April 30, 1921.

78. Casely Hayford, the vice president, presided over the session. Hutton-Mills, the president, was absent because of his wife's illness. Others present were: C. May, president of the Sierra Leone section; S. R. Wood, secretary of congress; A. E. Toboku-Metzger and J. B. Roberts, vice presidents of the Sierra Leone section; B. W. Davies, acting local treasurer in the absence of T. G. Refell; Dr. Bankole-Bright, general secretary of the Sierra Leone section; J. E. Leigh, J. S. Wright, J. O. E. Taylor, Professor O. Faduma, D. A. Samuels, F. A. Miller, A. J. Taylor, A. W. Lewis, and the two Gambian delegates, B. J. George and Reverend F. S. Oldfield.

79. See *West Africa*, February 24, 1923, p. 134, for Casely Hayford's speech; the issue of March 31, 1923, p. 314, for an official list of the resolutions passed at the second session; the issue of March 10, 1923, p. 213, for a summary of the daily activities

But while the demands remained more or less consistent, the atmosphere had changed considerably since Accra. Congress had experienced a slap; now it carried its tail firmly between its legs. A speech by S. J. Barlatt, twice mayor of Freetown, revealed this subtle change. God was behind the movement, Barlatt said, for he had permitted the changing conditions which had brought the delegates together. Self-consciousness was a divine gift which was awakened through contact with other races. Had Africans not received the blessings of Western civilization and Christian education, a movement like congress would have been impossible. "Ours is no Sinn Fein demand," he declared. "We are not asking for the supreme control of the affairs of our country, but for freedom to develop our God-appointed destiny within the British Empire. We plead for English justice and fair play to be meted out to all alike, for taxation with representation, for scope to those who show ability and character, and bar no colour to the high position of our land."[80]

What had been a search for amelioration in the moderate evangelical-philanthropist tradition back in the Gold Coast became even more sober and apprehensive in Sierra Leone. Worried by the "alarm and disquiet" caused by the national congress among "the ruling figures of the State," the delegates took pains to affirm and reaffirm that their movement was "neither seditious nor revolutionary."[81] They emphasized that the congress was working for the development of African character—for the social, intellectual, moral, and spiritual uplifting of the people—and in this lineup political advance seemed almost an afterthought. As products of a cricket-match mentality, the delegates stressed that they were playing the game fairly.

Two more full sessions of the National Congress of British West Africa were held after Freetown—one in the Gambia and another in Lagos in 1930. Each was a mere shadow of its predecessor. In Nigeria the organization never had much impact and its disappearance seemed hardly to matter; in the Gold Coast it faded after its chief protagonist, Casely Hayford, died.[82] Freetown continued to have a local branch of the national congress well into the 1940s. Even by the late 1920s, however, it had been transformed into what was largely a social club, with a ladies' auxiliary, sponsoring dances and entertainments.[83]

This was, perhaps, an undignified demise for a pioneer movement in

---

of the congress; *SLWN*, February 10, February 17, April 7, April 14, 1923. Also see "Review of the Year 1923," *SLWN*, January 20, 1924. A long poem, in three parts, praising congress appeared in the *SLWN* on February 17, 24, March 10, 1923.

80. *SLWN*, January 13, 1923.

81. Quoted in *West Africa*, February 24, 1923, p. 134.

82. See Coleman, *Nigeria*, pp. 194-195; Michael Crowder, *West Africa Under Colonial Rule* (Evanston, Ill., 1968), pp. 427-428, 461-463.

83. *Sierra Leone Guardian*, January 31, 1930.

African intercolonial cooperation. For the Creoles nonetheless, the failure of the National Congress of British West Africa, painful at first, marked a crossroad. The old leadership, ideas, and tactics had proven ineffectual. Creoles could retreat into the past and continue to seek nineteenth-century solutions to twentieth-century problems. They could try to maintain the illusion of themselves as Britain's chosen Africans, swallow their pride, and pretend that reality was but a temporary aberration. On the other hand, they could seek a completely new path—a more difficult one—which would begin to break down their long historical and attitudinal isolation from up-country-men and which would, ultimately, grant them the mass power base for a more successful confrontation with the British. It was in the 1930s that the choice would have to be made.

Chapter SIX

"Leppit Don Cam Na Ton": I. T. A. Wallace-Johnson and the West African Youth League

"We all na wan konko,
We all na wan konko."
("We are all within the same hut.")

A Krio call for unity in the 1930s

The decade of the thirties began in Sierra Leone on a downbeat—quietly, relatively uneventfully, calmly. On the surface the dominant political mood seemed placid, almost apathetic. The Creoles, stung by the series of traumatic reversals during the 1920s—the Syrian riot compensations, the rebuff to the national congress, the arrest and imprisonment of the mayor of Freetown, and the subsequent elimination of an elected City Council—were suffering a loss of confidence in their leaders and their tactics. They seemed to have turned inwards, away from their formerly prominent role in public affairs.

The apparent calm, however, was deceptive. The post-Depression years were among the most promising in Sierra Leone's economic history. Not only was the country fast developing into a center of mining—into the land of iron and diamonds—but Freetown's new designation as a key port for British imperial defense stimulated work projects aimed at improving strategically important marine and military facilities. These activities were accompanied by profound and frequently negative industrial and social changes in great areas of the colony and protectorate. Work-seekers rushed to Freetown and the mining areas in numbers far greater than jobs were open to receive them; promises of future benefits inadequately substituted for continuing poverty; newly arrived foreign technicians and soldiers frequently antagonized, if not downright insulted, Africans with whom they came into contact.

180

Not far beneath the surface, therefore, lay resentment and dissatisfaction, ready to be tapped and exploited by anyone offering leadership and a new hope. Eventually when this leadership did emerge, the decade that had begun so quietly was transformed into a period of tumultuous political, social, and intellectual activity. By the time World War II interrupted the dynamics of this activity, the character of the Creoles' relationship with the colonial government, with up-countrymen, and with each other had begun to undergo a fundamental reorientation.

The catalyst setting these crucial developments into motion was the appearance of one man—Isaac Theophilus Akunna Wallace-Johnson—and the inauguration of the West African Youth League, the first effective, large-scale political movement in the history of Sierra Leone.

Wallace-Johnson was born of poor Creole parents in 1895 in Wilberforce, Sierra Leone. His formal education, mainly in mission schools, was modest, and although he had already become a popular preacher, he was prevented from entering the ministry through his lack of proper educational qualifications. He tried surveying, farming, and teaching and worked with various commercial establishments. For a short time he clerked in A. Sawyerr's law office. In 1913 he entered the service of the colonial government.

His natural talents as an organizer and public speaker and his friendly and humorous manner with fellow workers quickly propelled him to a position of leadership. While employed in the Customs Department as a clerk, he was involved in the organization of the first trade union in Sierra Leone, among temporary customs officers. When he concerned himself with a strike in 1914, he was fired.

He entered the British Army in 1915 as a clerk in the Carrier Corps, serving in East Africa, the Cameroons, and the Middle East until 1920. Returning to Sierra Leone, he worked for various departments of the Freetown City Council, but resigned in 1926 to work in the merchant marine. He became a member of the United Kingdom National Seamen's Union and probably edited *The Seafarer*, an occasional journal of maritime labor news. Presently, he joined the staff of the *Lagos Daily Times* and moved back to West Africa.

Few details of Wallace-Johnson's odyssey during this period are known, but it was then that his future role as trade union organizer, militant journalist, nationalist political leader, and Pan-Africanist first began to take shape. In 1930, using an alias, E. Richards, he was the unofficial representative of the Sierra Leone Railroad Workers' Union to the First International Conference of Negro Workers in Hamburg, Germany, where he made a speech and was elected to the presidium. Fellow representatives included Jomo Kenyatta (then known as Johnstone Kenyatta), and George Padmore from the

West Indies. His activities brought him to the attention of the Comintern in Moscow, and, after organizing the African Workers' Union in Nigeria in 1931 (and acting as its general secretary), he and other black leaders were invited to Russia to attend the International Labour Defense Congress. He may at this time have enrolled briefly in the Peoples' University of the East in Moscow under his favorite pseudonym, W. Daniels. Later, he became an associate editor of the Communist publication, *Negro Worker*, contributing articles under several pseudonyms. All the while, he increasingly came under the scrutiny of British police agents.

After a brief stay in England, where he spoke under the auspices of the Negro Welfare Association, Wallace-Johnson returned to Freetown in February 1933. There he was disappointed that the "employed worker was not interested in the unemployed," while the unemployed struck him as "very care free." Discouraged, he left Freetown for Lagos and then for Accra.

In the Gold Coast he began to write for his friend Nnamdi Azikiwe's *African Morning Post* and to organize workers in the mining areas. Identified by the British as an "agitator" and "potential trouble maker," he was arrested in 1936, along with Azikiwe, for writing and publishing a seditious editorial "Has The African A God?" Convicted, he appealed and lost, and then appealed to the Judicial Committee of the Privy Council, the highest tribunal of British justice. Significantly, the action brought Wallace-Johnson to the attention of leading British left-wing intellectuals and politicians who saw in the imperial sedition laws, under which Wallace-Johnson had been convicted, an attempt by the authorities to restrict dissent throughout the British Empire.

During the same period Wallace-Johnson intensified his contact with George Padmore, Kenyatta, C. L. R. James, and others affiliated with the newly established International African Service Bureau, of which he held the post of general secretary.[1]

In April 1938 Wallace-Johnson returned to Freetown. He was to claim later that he had intended to make his stopover there, like previous ones since his departure in 1926, a short one. Allegedly his plan had been to return to England, pack his belongings, and then move to the United States, where he would not "bother about Africa any more as it was apparent that the people

1. *Lecture Delivered by Wallace-Johnson, Esq., to the Officers and Members of the Preston Literary Club, Freetown, on Friday, May 6, 1938, at 4:30 p.m.* (Freetown, 1938); transcript of an interview between I. T. A. Wallace-Johnson and John Cartwright, April 14, 1965 (I am grateful to John Cartwright for making this transcript available to me). Also see C.O. 267/3665/32208/1938; and Leo Spitzer and LaRay Denzer, "I. T. A. Wallace-Johnson and the West African Youth League,"*International Journal of African Historical Studies*, 6, no. 3 (1973): 413-452, no. 4 (1974): 565-601.

of Africa were not prepared to make a move."[2] His claim certainly had justification. His Gold Coast experience had ended badly, and he genuinely may have considered withdrawing from activist politics. But having tested the atmosphere in Sierra Leone briefly before his previous trip to England, he probably also knew that his homeland was ripe for political leadership and organization. Ironically, if his intent to disengage from anticolonial activities was indeed true, the British themselves created the incident which led to his reconsideration.

In view of Wallace-Johnson's previous activities, Sierra Leone colonial officials were looking for an excuse to nail him. When he landed in Freetown, therefore, customs agents seized two thousand copies of the *African Sentinel*, which he was bringing into Sierra Leone, as material likely to fall under the provisions of existing anti-sedition laws. "It is most undesirable that such *revolt* nonsense should be circulated among the population of Sierra Leone," the governor wrote to the secretary of state in support of the action.[3] Even though the Colonial Office eventually rejected the contention of sedition, the seizure of the newspaper was a grave error on the part of British officialdom in Sierra Leone.[4] The resulting publicity focused attention on Wallace-Johnson and presented him with an issue to exploit. Crowds rushed to the series of public meetings which were called on his behalf at the Wilberforce Memorial Hall.

Wallace-Johnson's oratory was brilliant; his targets well chosen; his audience receptive and enthusiastic. "In no other Colony in West Africa do I find the masses in such a miserable state of economic and social disabilities [*sic*]," he stated.

> Instead of progress, after a lapse of twelve years, I find conditions within the colony rapidly declining. . . . As a people, we have been too lethargic, drowsy and happy-go-lucky. . . . A very wide margin has been provided for the foreign exploiters—capitalists and imperialists alike—to drive the wedge of divide-and-rule within our social circle: and while we keep grasping at shadows, they (the foreign invaders) are busy rapidly draining out the natural resources of the land for their personal benefits, leaving us in poverty and want.[5]

2. Wallace-Johnson, *Lecture to Preston Literary Club*, p. 1; *SLWN*, April 30, 1938.

3. C.O. 267/665/32208/1938 also contains copy of seized issue (March/April 1938, vol. 1, no. 4), as does C.O. 267/670/32210/2, pt. 1 (1939). The issue includes an article by Jomo Kenyatta.

4. Minute by J. B. Sidebothom of the Colonial Office, in C.O. 267/665/32208/1938: "No action appears to be necessary. It seems to be generally agreed here that this article was not really seditious."

5. *SLWN*, April 30, 1938; *West Africa*, June 11, 1938.

He criticized the government for not permitting Africans to read what they wanted, mourned Sierra Leone's lack of economic and social progress after 150 years of British connection, attacked the African members of the Legislative Council for their conservatism, praised workers and damned their exploiters, appealed for the equality of African women, and urged the creation of a cooperative movement to fight for the rights and to defend the civil liberties of Sierra Leoneans of all ethnic backgrounds. "Now is the time and now is the hour," he declared,

> There is only one way out of our difficulties, and that is to organize and move. Although it has always been asserted by our so-called benefactors that we should take what we get and be satisfied, I maintain as Aggrey did, that we should not be satisfied with taking what we get or what has been given us but to use what we have been given to gain what we ought to have.[6]

Less than three weeks after his arrival, bolstered by a large, energetic following, Wallace-Johnson inaugurated the West African Youth League—Sierra Leone Branch.[7]

In the initial organization of the Youth League, Wallace-Johnson clearly succeeded far beyond his own expectations and, as the governor admitted to the secretary of state in a secret dispatch, far beyond that of the government as well.[8] The league organized mass meetings, founded trade unions, established a local newspaper, *The African Standard*, and contested elections. It arranged legal representation for members who were involved in litigation or prosecution. Membership, according to the league's manifesto, was open to all sections of the community, wage-earners and unemployed, rich and poor, the educated and uneducated, men and women, Muslims, Christians, pagans, Creoles, and up-countrymen. For the moment, its makeup banished the derisive nightmare, long accepted among many Sierra Leoneans, that they were unable to unite.[9]

Unlike earlier organizations, the Youth League spread beyond the colony boundaries, with branches throughout the protectorate, particularly in the mining and ore-dispatch areas.[10] At its peak during this period, the Youth

6. "An Appeal by Wallace-Johnson," *SLWN*, April 30, 1938.

7. Another organization, the West African Civil Liberties and National Defence League, was actually inaugurated some days before the Youth League and frequently termed by Wallace-Johnson and Youth Leaguers as the "parent organization." The "parent" was almost immediately overshadowed by its "offspring."

8. C.O. 267/665/32208/1938, 30 June 1938.

9. Speech delivered by Comrade Sydney M. D. Boyle at the WAYL's 26 June 1938 mass meeting at Wilberforce Memorial Hall, *SLWN*, July 9, 1938; *SLWN*, July 15, 1939.

10. A *SLWN* report (July 16, 1938) listed Youth League branches at Bonthe, Moyamba, Mano, Bo, and Buya.

League was large and dynamic—though probably not as large as the 25,000 colony and 17,000 protectorate dues-paying members Wallace-Johnson claimed. It was bonded together into an ardent fraternity by the word "Comrade," with which all members addressed each other, and by slogans which, for the first time in Sierra Leone history, called for unity among all the oppressed in the country, regardless of social, economic, or ethnic differences.[11]

Youth League meetings in Freetown during 1938 and 1939—held twice weekly, on Sundays and Thursdays—were immensely popular affairs, drawing crowds from every section of the city to Wilberforce Memorial Hall. Those who arrived there by 6:45 P.M. were usually fortunate if they found standing room at the back. By 7:15 there was no room in the hall, even the steps being impassable.[12]

The government initially minimized the immense popularity of the league, finding solace in the belief that "the press and the more prominent public men . . . have given the League the cold shoulder so far," and officials attributed the mass attendance at meetings to the "entertainment value" of the speeches and the lack of alternative distraction for the population.[13] Nonetheless, the government planted African police spies at the meetings, keeping careful track of speeches and participants.[14]

The novelty and "entertainment" Wallace-Johnson's Youth League brought to Sierra Leone would quickly have become stale, however, had its phenomenal appeal not been based on concrete, militant efforts to publicize and combat the economic, political, and social dissatisfaction which, by the late 1930s, affected the lives of the majority of the population. The repeated assertion by Sierra Leone officials that Wallace-Johnson was simply stirring up racial prejudice was, without doubt, untrue.[15]

11. E. W. Blyden, III, "Sierra Leone: The Pattern of Constitutional Change" (Ph.D. diss., Harvard University, 1959), pp. 169 ff.

12. *SLWN*, July 16, 1938.

13. Governor's Secret Dispatch to Secretary of State, p. 4, in C.O. 267/665/32208/1938.

14. See enclosure no. 19 in Sierra Leone Secret Dispatch, August 4, 1938, in C.O. 267/666/32216/1938. Interestingly enough, the policeman who spied on the meetings for the colonial officials was scarcely able to hide his support for Wallace-Johnson and the speeches in his reports. The governor dismissed this enthusiasm as "the notes made by a semi-literate police constable." See Governor to Secretary of State, August 4, 1938, p. 6, ibid.

15. See, for example, Report by Acting Commissioner of Police, June 20, 1938, in C.O. 267/665/32208/1938; and notes on Jardine's conversation with Dawe at the colonial office, in C.O. 267/671/32245/1939. Professor W. M. Macmillan, reporting on the economic and political situation in Sierra Leone after a visit to the colony and protectorate, found little racial antipathy. He was one of the few Europeans to take the trouble to attend a Youth League meeting. See Macmillan's observations in C.O. 267/671/32245/1939.

The reality was that Sierra Leone's recently discovered mining wealth and the new economic and strategic importance of Freetown were not translated into higher wages for the citizens of the colony and the protectorate, or, for that matter, into a perceptible decrease in unemployment. In fact, the economic boom was largely obscured for most ordinary Africans by a steady inflation in the cost of living. What Wallace-Johnson was able to exploit, therefore, was the popular sense of <u>frustration</u> with the imbalance between rising expectations and actual living conditions. Foreign investors were in control of the natural resources of the country, particularly in the mining areas, and working conditions and salaries for African workers were maintained at atrociously low levels, both in private employment and government. Employees in the Railway Department, for example, were paid as low as 2s. 6d. per diem, even if skilled. Policemen received around 2s. per diem, without additional allowances. Apprentice mechanics in the Public Works Department, with school training, were often salaried as low as 6d. per diem. Elementary school teachers were sometimes paid only 10d. per diem, received no transport or residence allowance, and were not given a pension. In the civil service, the government imported young Europeans, fresh out of school, at an initial salary of £400 per annum, and promised them an increment of £50 per annum after three years' service. In comparison, African chief clerks, often with thirty or more years of service, were rated at a salary of £264 to £372 per year, with a £12 annual increment.[16]

Private companies were, perhaps, even worse—their employment practices were characterized by long hours, low wages, indecent treatment, poor medical care, and unsuitable or nonexistent living accommodations. The United Africa Company, the largest trading company in the colony and protectorate, often worked employees 11 to 14 hours per day, paying them wages as low as 10s. per month or 4d. per diem. The Sierra Leone Development Corporation was a worse offender. In its principal mining center at Marampa, African mine workers faced the pit for wages ranging between 4d. per diem to a maximum of 1s. per diem. Living conditions in the mining compounds were terrible—congested, squalid, unsanitary, with practically no medical services available. Professor W. M. Macmillan, certainly not unsympathetic to British public and private investment, told Colonial Office officials after his visit to Sierra Leone that the Sierra Leone Development Corporation's works at Marampa and Pepel were "thoroughly unsatisfactory examples of the use of African labour by industrial enterprise."[17] Incidents in which African workers were subjected to flogging, stocking, and other forms of brutal treatment were common. The district commissioner of Port Loko substantiated complaints of mistreatment when he wrote:

16. C.O. 267/666/32216/1938; *SLWN*, February 5, 26, 1938.
17. Macmillan's observations in C.O. 267/671/32245/1939.

One thing which has repeatedly struck me not only at Pepel has been the attitude of contempt almost amounting to hatred with which certain Europeans regard the native labourer. Young Engineers are taught on their arrival that all Africans are lazy, dishonest and thoroughly bad and above all, that they are devoid of human feeling and self-respect. Ruthlessness and strict discipline are regarded as the essential qualities for handling native labour and any form of sympathy or consideration is condemned as the most culpable weakness.[18]

In reference to a strike which broke out at Pepel, the district commissioner wrote: "While I was at Pepel I discovered that there was a strong school of thought which suggested that the best method of dealing with the strike would be to arrest a number of strikers and have them tied up and soundly flogged."[19] As early as the end of December 1937, months before the return of Wallace-Johnson to Sierra Leone, the workers of the Sierra Leone Development Corporation at Pepel went out on strike.[20]

Wallace-Johnson therefore capitalized not on African "colour prejudice"[21] but on the popular sense of frustration arising from the disparities created by Sierra Leone's new economic dynamism and the generally static, even deteriorating, living conditions of the mass of inhabitants. His great talent lay in his ability to mold from this formless dissatisfaction a militant working-class consciousness. The Youth League, with its bi-weekly meetings and open forum, its comaraderie and rhetoric, was a means toward that end. But there were other means as well. Using his past experience in the labor movement, for example, Wallace-Johnson quickly and successfully organized some eight trade unions throughout the colony and protectorate.[22] In every case, the main object of the unions was to secure better wages and better conditions for their members through collective bargaining.

One of the greatest appeals of the West African Youth League, of course, was Wallace-Johnson himself. His rapport with his audience was immediate and complete. His working-class experience and lack of pretentiousness were immensely advantageous. "I am not anything above yourselves," he proclaimed to working-class Creoles and up-countrymen, "I am at par with you."[23] And in spite of his militancy, he was friendly and humorous, always

18. Enclosure no. 2 in Sierra Leone Confidential Dispatch, 12 March 1938, in C.O. 267/665/32199/1938.

19. Ibid.

20. C.O. 267/673/32254/8 (1939).

21. The words are those of the acting chief of police. C.O. 267/665/32208/1938.

22. The Public Works Workers' Union, The War Department Amalgamated Workers' Union, The Mabella Coaling Company Workers' Union, the King Tom Docks Workers' Union, The All Seamen's Union, The Bonthe Amalgamated Workers' Union, The Pepel and Marampa Miners Workers' Union, and The Motorists' Union.

23. Wallace-Johnson, *Lecture to Preston Literary Club*, p. 6.

ready with a good story. Even Governor Douglas Jardine, who disliked Wallace-Johnson immensely, conceded that his outstanding qualities were his "considerable personal magnetism for the masses, [and] some sense of humor." These qualities were, in the governor's opinion, equalled by his "unbounded conceit, and an unblushing disregard for the truth."[24]

As far back as 1918 the *Sierra Leone Guardian* had proclaimed the need for a "Social Reformer," a creative leader. "If he does not appear," the editorial had forecast, "then Sierra Leone is doomed."[25] That Wallace-Johnson clearly fulfilled this need in the minds of some is attested to by the doggerels, sincerely intended as poetry of praise, which appeared in the Freetown press and streets shortly after his arrival:

> Passing along the street one day,
> On a sun-lit morn in May,
> I heard some folks a-talking,
> Of the arrival of Wallace-Johnson.
>
> Wallace-Johnson has come to make us free,
> Born was he at Wilberforce Village,
> Born to free us from oppression,
> Born a King and yet unknown.
>
> The Youth League, Sierra Leone Branch,
> He did inaugurate,
> Thousands rallied round to join his Band,
> Great and small were all enrolled. . . .
>
> Come and join this Noble Band.
> Come along shout Comrade 1074,
> And so say Comrade Six double one
> And Comrade One Three Four.
>
> Comrade, what a noble name of Friendship,
> Class distinctions forevermore good-bye,
> Sierra Leone, Sierra Leoneans all unite,
> And co-operate for Liberty or Death.
>
> Listen to the strains of Comrade 387,
> And as we go marching along,
> Sing! Good-bye to exploitation,
> Sierra Leone, Sierra Leoneans all unite.

24. Governor to Secretary of State, November 28, 1938, in C.O. 267/666/32216/1938.

25. *Sierra Leone Guardian*, January 18, 1918.

May Heaven richly bless this Noble Band,
God of Host we praise Thy Name,
Mayst Thou succour and defend
Our Leader the Organising Secretary.[26]

fierce, passion
strijdlust

Wallace-Johnson's most attractive asset, however, was his truculence and his apparent willingness to thumb his nose at officialdom. The confiscation of the *African Sentinel* and the revelation that Wallace-Johnson was being kept under surveillance by the British immediately inflated his reputation among Sierra Leoneans. He enhanced his image by acting like a hero: cool, confident, bold.[27] Wallace-Johnson spoke facetiously of colonial officials and eminent statesmen whom Sierra Leoneans regarded with awe. In public speeches and private conversations, he nonchalantly referred to them by their first names, censuring them for their imperial policies "in diatribes and invectives the like of which had never before been heard in the Freetown society where decorum and *savoir faire* were the hall-marks of the leaders."[28]

26. Comrade no. 1074, "The Youth League, Sierra Leone Branch," *SLWN*, September 3, 1938. Other poems appeared as well. Aug. E. Venn, "Till Wallace Came," *SLWN*, September 10, 1938, is another example:

> No matter what the world may say,
> This fact no one can e'er gainsay.
> That Sa Lone was disorganized,
> Till Wallace came. . . .
>
> Our manhood lost, our homes destroyed,
> Our naked backs did bear the rod,
> With smiles we stooped unorganized,
> Till Wallace came. . . .
>
> Then up the heights where eagles soar,
> Came forth the awak'ning lions' roar:
> "Ye Sa Lone folks, start,—Organize!—"
> When Wallace came. . . .
>
> "Stand ready to destroy this thing!"—
> The critics yelled forth through their King,
> "Pour volleys irresistible!—"
> When Wallace came. . . .
>
> They've failed, and failure is their lot,
> And Wallace cares not for their rot
> For truth is light is good
> And light shines bright "cause Wallace came."

27. Mrs. Edna Elliot Horton, in whose living room the Youth League was officially founded and who was its assistant organizing secretary, considered Wallace-Johnson a brilliant leader and felt he was much feared by the government. His arrival in a town was preceded by the announcement "leppit don cam na ton" ("the leopard has arrived in town"). Horton-Spitzer interview, Freetown, January 14, 1966.

28. Blyden, "Sierra Leone," p. 172.

Furthermore, the fact that prestigious men in England—even members of Parliament—appeared to be associated with him and acted on his behalf added considerable stature to his reputation.[29]

Time and again, Wallace-Johnson managed to make the government appear foolish—much to the delight and amusement of the mass of Sierra Leoneans. Not long after the founding of the Youth League, he exposed details of the governor's confidential and secret dispatches to the Colonial Office in London and to subordinates in Sierra Leone. Some considered this an admirable action, to be enjoyed for the information it revealed as well as for the discomfort in which it placed the government. Others, the government in particular, were annoyed or even frightened when supposedly confidential information appeared in the local press or became topics of street corner conversation. There was little mystery as to how the information was obtained, and the government tried desperately to plug the leaks.[30] The Youth League had many supporters among members of the lower-ranked civil service—clerks or typists with access to confidential dispatches—some of whom gladly passed on information to Wallace-Johnson. In fact, one reason why Wallace-Johnson refused to reveal the Youth League's membership list to the government was precisely because it would have shown civil servants to be members of a political organization, an illegal act.

One purloined and published dispatch from Governor Jardine to the secretary of state proved particularly embarrassing, for it revealed the governor to have declared that an African workman and his wife could subsist on 15s. per month, and that little difficulty existed in securing labor at about 9d. per diem. To Wallace-Johnson and the Youth League, the governor's statement was clear proof of government compliance in the wage exploitation of Sierra Leoneans, and they set out to capitalize on the governor's indiscretion. Mass meetings took place, petitions were signed, telegrams sent: all demanded that the governor be recalled. A protest demonstration in which about seven thousand adults participated along with about half that number of children was organized by the Youth League affiliate, the West African Civil Liberties and National Defence League in Freetown, and, in a mass rally at the Recreation Ground, it passed a resolution urging the dismissal of the governor and "his exclusion from any Colony inhabited by peoples of African descent."[31]

29. See "Activities of Mr. Wallace-Johnson and the West African Youth League," in C.O. 267/666/32216/1938: "No doubt, however, his local prestige gains considerable support from the fact that he is able to get Questions answered by the Secretary of State in the House of Commons."

30. Horton-Spitzer interview, January 14, 1966.

31. See Governor to Secretary of State, 27 July 1938, in C.O. 267/665/32210/1938; "Leakage of Official Information," in C.O. 267/666/32216/1938; Wallace-Johnson, "On the Governor's Confidential Dispatch—A Preliminary Statement," SLWN, August 27, 1938; West Africa, October 29, 1938, p. 1499.

Governor Jardine then compounded his error by appointing a commission of enquiry to look into the unauthorized publication of government dispatches. Wallace-Johnson's testimony before the commission, an excellent example of his audacity and quick wit in the face of authority, tied up his hearing in semantic tangles.[32] To the delight of his followers, Wallace-Johnson was subsequently acquitted by the police magistrate, a Creole, of the charge that he did not answer questions fully and satisfactorily before the commission. The government declined to appeal. Such victories, of course, served to increase his popularity and, among some Sierra Leoneans, endowed him with almost supernatural powers.[33] The colonial government, however, was increasingly intolerant. Convinced that no African jury or magistrate could be trusted to convict Wallace-Johnson or any of his fellow Youth League members, British officials in Sierra Leone began to look for surer means to render this troublesome gadfly permanently harmless.

Government officials were not alone in finding the Youth League and its organizing secretary a threat as well as a nuisance. Both were at least as distasteful to the colony's "old line" Creole leadership which, as a group, had come under direct verbal attack by various Youth League members. Wallace-Johnson, entirely candid in his dislike for the Creole establishment which dominated African social and political life in the colony, had thrown down the gauntlet to them in an article he wrote for the *Sierra Leone Weekly News* soon after his return to Sierra Leone:

> As a people we need leaders in Sierra Leone. These must be sought out and given the opportunity to lead. There is obviously the belief among some of us that leadership is a sort of title reserved for a certain clan, group or family. For a certain class, caste, tribe or creed. For this reason, whenever we are asked to select leaders, we start to cast our searchlight upon the aristocratic, demagogic and so-called "High circles." It should be remembered that our struggle in Sierra Leone to-day is for economic and social emancipation and only those who are bearing on their shoulders the burden of the yoke, can truly and conscientiously lead the masses out of their difficulties.
>
> There are real and true leaders in Sierra Leone. We must find them out and bring them to the forefront with the determination to follow their lead by our words, deeds and actions.
> This we *must* do *now* and for always.[34]

32. See enclosure no. 1 in Sierra Leone Secret Dispatch, 28 November 1938, in C.O. 267/666/32216/1938, for a transcript of Wallace-Johnson's testimony.

33. Horton-Spitzer interview, January 14, 1966; *West Africa*, December 1938, p. 1707; C.O. 267/666/32216/1938.

34. *SLWN*, May 7, 1938.

A. Lisk-Carew, the first president of the Youth League, reiterated this challenge even more bluntly when, at his opening speech to a league mass meeting, he shouted "our leaders have failed to deliver the goods." He then proceeded to point out that the league was formed mainly to correct the failings of the old leadership, such as that of the African members of the Legislative Council and the principals of the once-active Sierra Leone branch of the National Congress of British West Africa.[35] The point was made over and over again: the Freetown "intelligentsia" had to be made aware that its leadership was not indispensable. The time for new, more radical, action had arrived. This position, of course, was not unique to Sierra Leone but was entirely consistent with the one Wallace-Johnson had taken earlier in opposition to the Gold Coast's establishment leadership.[36]

Ultimately, the struggle which emerged between new and old leadership—between a mass or elitist approach to the solution of Sierra Leone's problems—was played out in the columns of the local press, in bitter clashes between individual personalities, and in the realm of electoral politics.

The local press, always the preserve of the Creole establishment, had initially been tolerant but never overwhelmingly enthusiastic about either Wallace-Johnson or the Youth League. In the early days after his return to Sierra Leone, the newspapers frequently published articles by Wallace-Johnson and other Youth League members, and covered the activities of the new organization adequately and fairly. "Rambler," who wrote the popular column "Rambling Talks" in the *Sierra Leone Weekly News*, strongly supported the Youth League from the start and called it "a wonderful achievement for Sierra Leone."[37]

It was not long, however, before the relationship between the press and Wallace-Johnson began to sour—a development which was undoubtedly triggered by the organizing secretary's outspoken condemnation of the establishment leadership in the colony. The *Sierra Leone Daily Mail* printed a series of letters and articles in July 1938, each vehement in its criticism of Wallace-Johnson and the league. "Here we have for the most part INCIVILITY under the guise of bluntness," an anonymous writer declared, "Soap-Box Oratory which leads the rabble like UNTHINKING HORSES into battle, the untutored mind, abusive and insulting, the uncultured mind antagonistic to criticism, however honest, eloquent ribaldry misleading the rabble. . . . We want a Leader and not an Irascible Bobadil or a Migratory Monomaniac."[38]

35. Speech delivered at Wilberforce Memorial Hall, May 20, 1938. See *SLWN*, May 28, 1938.
36. See, for example, "Congress versus the Youth League," July 16, 1938; "The West African Youth League," August 20, 27, 1938, *SLWN*; Thomas Decker, "Looking Backwards and Forwards," *Daily Guardian*, December 1938 (Christmas issue).
37. "Rambling Talks," *SLWN*, June 18, 1938.
38. "The Youth League As I See It—by Speedo," *Daily Mail*, July 23, 1938.

The tone of the ill-tempered attack was maintained by another anonymous writer who attempted to discredit Wallace-Johnson in a letter to the editor of the *Daily Mail*. Questioning the authenticity of Wallace-Johnson's study in Moscow, and doubting his understanding of communism, the writer also labeled him a religious hypocrite and implied that he was a dishonest opportunist whose departure from England had been less than voluntary and who had already overstayed his welcome in Sierra Leone.[39]

The intensity of the attacks prompted Youth League members, after a mass meeting during which they registered a vote of confidence for their organizing secretary, to circulate a resolution to this effect to the newspapers, the governor, and to the secretary of state for the colonies. The attacks continued nevertheless and, particularly those by "Spectator," expressed vehement disapproval of the Youth League and its leadership.[40] "Spectator" sneered at the activities of the organization time and again and, in one column, admonished its Creole members to stop their agitation and remember to be grateful to Britain for freeing their ancestors from slavery.[41] "Rambler" wrote a scathing reply:

> This settlement was not founded by the British Government, as perhaps its coeval sister Australia was. It was founded by a few British philanthropists as a slight amend for the age long wrongs which their countrymen had done to Africans by originating the Transatlantic slave trade which wrenched hundreds of thousands of Temne, Mende, Sussu and other local tribes from their homeland to moil and toil in America and the West Indies for enriching British families. It was the sweat of the black man's brow which laid the foundation for the present day opulence of Britain and White America. What has England done for Sierra Leone in 150 years in comparison with what the Sierra Leone slaves did for England during their 400 years of forced labour in British plantation? Talk of gratitude? It is the other way about. . . . You cheated me of 400 years' income, traded with it, made a million percent profit and then flung a paltry 150 years' income back to me and expected me to put my hands behind my back and say "many, many thanks!" Can anything be more ridiculous? Who is to be grateful to the other? The cheat—or his victim? Not until the former makes full and complete reparation will there be any reasonable expectation of gratitude from the latter.[42]

39. "An Open Letter to Mr. Wallace-Johnson by Victor," *Daily Mail*, July 27, 1938.
40. See *SLWN*, August 27, 1938, March 17, 1939, April 1, 15, 22, 1939, July 8, 1939, for examples.
41. "My View of Things by Spectator," *SLWN*, July 2, 1938.
42. "Rambling Talks," *SLWN*, July 2, 1938.

Good catharsis, perhaps, but the exchange of diatribes had no practical value. Disillusioned with the *Sierra Leone Weekly News*'s anti-Youth League position, "Rambler" ceased writing his weekly column.[43] Finding himself ostracized by the local press, Wallace-Johnson had no recourse but to found his own newspaper. In January 1939 the *African Standard* appeared as the official organ of the Youth League. Unlike any previous newspaper in Sierra Leone, it was left-wing and lively, in the style of the *British Daily Herald*, the *New Leader*, or the *Tribune*. As was to be expected, members of the conservative establishment quickly rejected it, faulting it for not being "respectable" and for printing articles which were, if not seditious, certainly contentious. The great majority of Sierra Leoneans who belonged to the laboring class, however, adopted the paper as "we yone"—"our own"— relishing it as an effective means by which their grievances could be ventilated.

Instead of easing tensions the appearance of the *African Standard* brought added verbiage and vituperation to the battle between old and new leadership. Only rarely did humor replace self-righteousness as, for example, in the anti-Wallace-Johnson poem "The Gander of Willyfoss," whose anonymous author appropriately altered the "Gander of Glasgow" in a facetious, Krio, reference to Wallace-Johnson's Wilberforce birthplace:

> Then, vain as he was, how he shoed his poor spite
> To each bird of a nobler and loftier flight,
> Whose region of glory lay far out of sight
>   Of the blear-eyed Gander of Willyfoss,—
>   The great gaping Goose of the West.

> Have you'er seen a dance whose unfortunate lot
> Is to rail at the laurels of Southey or Scott
> You almost might swear that a hint he had got
>   From the envious Gander of Willyfoss,—
>   The pitiful Goose of the West.

> We do not insist on his manner and mien—
> For these we might find an excuse—
> But his gabble was gross, and his conduct obscene
> And he openly dwelt among creatures-unclean—
> A shameless and scandalous Goose![44]

43. On July 22, 1939, after a year's lay-off, "Rambler" began writing again. "My long silence," he said, "was not due . . . to any lessening of my interest in the affairs of my country and of the world, but was self-imposed because I could not see eye to eye with the Editor in a matter of policy." He claimed to have resumed writing because someone working for the *Daily Guardian* had usurped his pen-name and had begun to write a column under the name "Rambler."

44. "The Gander of Willyfoss by John Citizen," *SLWN*, May 27, 1939.

If anything, rumors that the *African Standard* was "out to kill" the *Weekly News* intensified the latter's outbursts against the Youth League. "In these days," an editorial declared, "we see the 'hoi polloi,' " including

> ... those who are called the Toiling Masses (women among them), head over heels shouting to the skies and determined ... to bring about certain Reforms by FORCE. No one among the thinking must lift up his voice in Protest. None must dare to say one word against a Ferment which it is plain can bring us no good but is already bringing us evil. Such a one must be shadowed, hooted, openly abused, threatened.[45]

For the *Sierra Leone Weekly News*, this kind of response was not entirely paranoid. Something was definitely going wrong with this long-lived paper, but it was not the fault of the *African Standard* or the Youth League. Once the leading and most influential newspaper in all of British West Africa, the *Weekly News* began to decline considerably in the late 1930s, both in the quality of its writing and, more important, in its relevance to changing times. While Africa stirred with excitement—Hitler demanding the restitution of the ex-German colonies, and a new nationalist spirit growing in British West Africa and even in "conservative" Sierra Leone—the main concern of the *Sierra Leone Weekly News* increasingly focused on religion in general and the church in particular. For its editors, what mattered most was the arrival or death of a leading churchman, the text of a Sunday sermon, and heavenly deliverance. In their columns they prescribed a messianic course of action—"have faith and go slowly"—at a time when the mass of the population was looking for accelerated results. An editorial published April 8, 1939, illustrates this tendency at its most pathetic—but other examples can be selected from most any issue of that paper in 1938-1939. In this instance, the editor complained that "certain elements in Freetown" had come to regard the *Weekly News* as "humbug." These same persons, he was convinced, also had come to deny Christ and His Church. "Are the people of Sierra Leone determined that by self-misdirection on their part, this Sierra Leone shall end in Utter Failure?" the editorial asked. "We tremble at the outlook and advise our people to return (1) To the God of their Fathers (2) To the Lord JESUS CHRIST (3) To the Church of Christ and lastly (4) To the Sierra Leone WEEKLY NEWS."[46]

Apart from the press battles, the confrontation between old and new leadership among Creoles, and between "radical" and "conservative" responses to the situation in Sierra Leone, was personalized in a bitter public

45. *SLWN*, May 13, 1939.
46. *SLWN*, April 8, 1939.

quarrel between Wallace-Johnson and Dr. Herbert Christian Bankole-Bright, one-time luminary of the National Congress of British West Africa and, since 1924, an elected member of the legislative Council. The clash was reminiscent of Wallace-Johnson's conflict with F. U. Nanka-Bruce in the Gold Coast, whose position among the African establishment political leaders was similar to that of Bankole-Bright. Bankole-Bright, descendant of an old and prominent Freetown family, was educated in the Wesleyan (Boys') High School and in British medical schools. Churchman, publisher, prolific writer, and effective public speaker, he had been a youthful critic of government policies both from within and without the Legislative Council and a vigorous irritant to the Colonial Office bureaucracy. While similar to Wallace-Johnson in political activism and daring, an irreconcilable difference nonetheless existed between them in terms of class background and outlook. Although both were Creoles, Bankole-Bright belonged to the upper stratum of Freetown society, to that propertied and wealthy class whose members had attended the "right" schools, visited the United Kingdom, and become successful professional or business people. Until the appearance of Wallace-Johnson and the Youth League, this elite had been at the center of political and social activity. Fearful of diluting its status by close identification with the less privileged classes, the elite had enthusiastically embraced the National Congress, with its limited membership and gentlemanly decorum. The Youth League and its "hoi polloi" was anathema.[47]

Less than six months after Wallace-Johnson's return, in November 1938, the Freetown City Council elections provided the context for the first major confrontation between him and Bankole-Bright. Neither stood for office, but both were active behind the scenes as campaign organizers and strategists. For the first time in Sierra Leone, the overwhelming advantages enjoyed by a mass organization like the Youth League became unmistakably clear.

Unlike in the Gold Coast, where Wallace-Johnson's following had been smaller and where it was more prudent for him to exchange support with already existing political groups, the situation in Sierra Leone was different. The practice in Sierra Leone politics had been for candidates to run as individuals, alone bearing the cost and burden of campaigning, with success or failure largely a product of personal popularity among a relatively small electorate. No political parties existed to unite persons seeking office behind a common platform or to provide them an opportunity to pool expenses. Wallace-Johnson changed all this. Pitching the appeal of the Youth League to the lower classes in the course of the City Council election campaign, he

47. For Bankole-Bright's earlier stand on judicial reform and his long fight for the abolition of the unpopular "trial by Assessors," see C.O. 267/602, 603, 604, 612, 614, 621, 622.

forged his organization into a political party along a British model, with a sponsored slate of candidates, a platform, and a campaign fund. Youth League election propaganda urged voters to create a united political front by electing all its candidates. Only through "concerted action," the league's manifesto proclaimed, could the "cause of the toiling masses" be represented and "constructive reform" be brought about. It denounced the practice of individual candidature as antiquated and unprogressive.[48]

The Youth League's success was devastating. Its four candidates, led by Constance Agatha Cummings-John, who became the first woman to hold elective office in British West Africa, demolished the opposition in every ward.[49] The writing was on the wall: from the perspective of Bankole-Bright and the Creole establishment, the common herd was now in command.

Nor were the victors charitable to the vanquished. During the campaign, anti-Youth League candidates and their backers had frequently spoken sarcastically of Wallace-Johnson, his lack of refinement, and the crudity of his supporters. Wallace-Johnson, it appears, blamed Bankole-Bright personally for the attacks. With vengeance—and somewhat raw humor—he reciprocated. Following the election, leaflets carrying "Obituary Notices," probably written by Wallace-Johnson himself, were sold by Youth League members.

OBITUARY.

It is with the most excellent delight that we announce the welcomed and timely demise of the Societies of City Fathers and Uncle Toms as represented in the fall of BRAHISM and the triumph of YOUTH at the Poll Stations of the City Council on Tuesday the 1st day of November, 1938, when representatives of the Ratepayers, and Liberatedities crouched on all-fours before YOUTH.

Death due to POLITICAL DIARRHOEA and the collapse of the White House Demoniacal Maniac whilst diligently oscillating the Political Pendulum of the Macroscopic Cocus suspected in the Big Cigars and the Body Politic.

Interment took place "sans ceremonie" at the Wilberforce Memorial Hall at 5 p.m., when the Registrar of Political Suicides made the following announcements:—

48. West African Youth League Manifesto, found in Blyden, "Sierra Leone," pp. 175-176.
49. West Africa, December 17, 1938.

YOUTH CANDIDATES.

CONSTANCE AGATHA CUMMINGS-JOHN	(Central Ward)	231	Votes
EDMUND ADOLPHUS COLLINGWOODE DAVIS	do	217	do
ERNEST DUNSTAN MORGAN	(West Ward)	110	do
OLUWOLE JAMES VON BRUMM TUBOKU-METZGER	(East Ward)	Unopposed	

REACTIONARIES

BRAH DUNSTAN	(Central Ward)	74	Votes
	Central Ratepayers Association		
BRAH NEWTON	do	63 Votes	do
BRAH BOISY	(West Ward)	100	do
	(West Ward Ratepayers Association)		

FUNERAL ODE.

Dunstan could not stand.
Newton's an old tin.
Boisy's merely noisy.
So! Banky's heart is broke!
May They Rest in Pieces!!![50]

It was a scurrilous attack, malicious, and, in its reference to the "White House Demonical Maniac," obvious enough in target to elicit a suit for criminal libel against Wallace-Johnson from Bankole-Bright. Wallace-Johnson boasted that no jury in Sierra Leone would dare to convict him and he was right. By this

50. Enclosure in Dispatch no. 27, January 14, 1939, in "Banky," of course, refers to Bankole-Bright. C.O. 267/671/32221/1939. Also see Governor to Secretary of State, November 28, 1938, in C.O. 267/666/32216/1938:

> Ding Dung Bell!
> Banky's in the well!
> Who put him in?
> A little YOUTH in teen!
> Who'll pull him out?
> No! never to be out.
> Oh what a jolly sight for Youth to see
> Big Banky in the well.
>   OKAY!!!

time, most members of the bar had become Youth League sympathizers and Dr. Bankole-Bright had to conduct his own case. Youth League supporters cheered their organizing secretary's victory, and Bankole-Bright recoiled, waiting for another opportunity.

British officials in Sierra Leone, frightened by Wallace-Johnson's ability to incite agitation and by the rapid expansion of the Youth League, heartily welcomed this dissension among Creoles.[51] Moreover, the government drew its greatest support during this period from a small minority of influential Africans who urged officials to take "strong action" and to limit political agitation. Their fear of mass participation in political affairs—with the implicit threat to their dominant position—was sufficiently strong that they even counseled curbing civil and political rights they had themselves fought hard and long to attain. So long as, in Governor Jardine's words, "the more respectable members of the public continue[d] to look askance at the League," and rallied to Britain for support and protection, it was possible to maintain order and the colonial status quo.[52]

In spite of the clamor in Freetown, particularly in Creole establishment and government circles, the West African Youth League was definitely not a revolutionary organization advocating the immediate cessation of Sierra Leone's colonial relationship with Britain. Given the high unemployment, low wages, and abominable conditions for workers, some type of economic agitation should have been expected and, judging from the enthusiastic support it drew from the masses, the Youth League's activities were long overdue. Its political objectives—greater representation in the Legislative Council, adequate representation in the Executive Council, an expanded political role for women, a universal franchise without property qualifications—were all within the best tradition of democratic reformism, palatable even to British Conservatives. Its nationalism, in this prewar period, was incipient, aiming to create a national consciousness among Sierra Leoneans from all ethnic backgrounds, colony and protectorate—a unity based on common grievances and objectives. At no time during this period did it advocate the direct take-over by Africans of all territory and power held by the British in Sierra Leone.[53] As I. J. F. Turbett, the Sierra Leone attorney

51. Governor to Secretary of State, November 28, 1938, in C.O. 267/666/32216/1938; *Daily Mail*, December 8, 1938.

52. Governor to Secretary of State, November 28, 1938, in C.O. 267/666/32216/1938.

53. See Otto Pflanze and Philip D. Curtin, "Varieties of Nationalism in Europe and Africa," *The Review of Politics* 28, no. 2 (April 1966): 124-153, for Curtin's definition of "African nationalism"; West African Youth League memo stating grievances, in C.O. 267/666/32216/1938. "Report by Acting Commissioner of Police," enclosure no. 2 in Sierra Leone Secret Dispatch, dated June 30, 1938, in C.O. 267/665/32208/1938,

general, admitted at a high-level Colonial Office discussion about Wallace-Johnson and the Youth League in February 1939, the Youth League's "avowed objectives were quite defensible."[54] Nevertheless, British colonial officials, particularly those actually in Sierra Leone, spared little in their efforts to curtail the organization and silence its leader. Perceiving a threat which did not yet exist in fact, they employed high-handed and undemocratic procedures, making cynical use of the threatening war with Germany to perpetuate the colonial status quo.

By the early part of 1939, Wallace-Johnson had become the *bête noire* of British officials in Sierra Leone. Their proximity to events and their position as targets of his and the Youth League's attacks rendered their perception of Wallace-Johnson more subjective, even paranoid, than that initially held by the Colonial Office in London. They saw him as "a most dangerous agitator and demagogue," a man "inimical to good government" who used the press and the public platform "to bring . . . white people into contempt among black people," a powerful individual with a large and enthusiastic following who had managed to purloin confidential government dispatches and, in the aftermath, had not only publicly embarrassed the governor but also made a government-appointed commission inquiry look foolish.[55] They also had come to fear his talents as a labor organizer and to appreciate his political acumen when he engineered the Youth League's total victory in the Freetown Municipal Council elections.

British officials had yet another reason to fear Wallace-Johnson. The Youth League's organizing secretary had been known to be connected with Communist organizations in England, and, after his return to Sierra Leone, the feeling persisted among British officials that his activities were being subsidized by "outside sources." Governor Jardine had little doubt that what he called "Creole agitation" was connected with similar unrest in the West Indies and "inspired and probably partially financed by London communists."[56] A. J. Dawe of the Colonial Office, on the other hand, thought that "the Communists may have been discouraged by dishonesty from financing

states: "He would alter the British Constitution by sending African representatives direct to the Imperial Parliament." I have found no other evidence to corroborate this.

54. Notes of a discussion held in Lord Dufferin's room on Monday, February 20, 1939, in C.O. 267/670/32210/2, pt. 1 (1939).

55. "I am entitled to say that there is a great feeling of uneasiness as to whom to trust where confidential matters are concerned. Such a state of things cannot but be harmful to the interests of the Civil Service, damaging to its efficiency and inimical to good government." Memorandum by Acting Attorney General (Sierra Leone) Charles Abbot, February 5, 1939, ibid.

56. He felt that an efficient police intelligence service was badly needed in Freetown and asked that Colonel Sir Vernon Kell of the War Office send one to Sierra Leone. See Jardine to Dawe, February 27, 1939 (written while on leave in England), in C.O. 267/670/32210/2, pt. 1 (1939).

him further"—a reference to Colonial Office information which asserted that Wallace-Johnson had left England suspected by his Communist associates of embezzling money from the *African Sentinel*. But Dawe also believed that the Youth League's organizing secretary would not reject offers of assistance from "other sources" if they were forthcoming.[57] Even when the government knew for certain that Wallace-Johnson was not financed by aliens bent on destroying the empire, they were loathe to part with the belief. "It may well be that he receives a subsidy from another source," wrote the acting attorney general of Sierra Leone in a characteristic report, "indeed I should be surprised if he did not. Whether he does or not, he is certainly rendering signal service to any power hostile to the Empire or to its system of government."[58]

The colonial officials were mistaken. The language of Wallace-Johnson's articles, especially referring to the exploitation of workers, did appear to follow the party line. So did the rhetoric of Youth League rallies—although here the language and spirit of Freetown's evangelical Christianity was usually dominant. But while Wallace-Johnson certainly remained Marxist in orientation, his break with the International African Service Bureau in London had set him free from compromising affiliations with international communism. The Communist party's decision to concentrate energies in Europe and Asia rather than Africa probably completed his breakaway.

The refortification of Freetown and its new role as a protected port with strategic importance for the British war mobilization effort ultimately created the milieu in which local officials could move against the Youth League's organizing secretary. Three closely related events triggered the decision—each relevant to Freetown's new status and, in combination, serious enough to convince the Colonial Office that some action against Wallace-Johnson was justified. The first was a strike declared by two trade unions, the War Department Workers and the Workers of the Sierra Leone Coaling Company, both of which shared offices and were affiliated to the Youth League and both of which were considered essential to the continuation of Sierra Leone's role in Britain's defense. These strikes, accompanied by some disorder and violence, necessitated the calling out of special police reserves and, on one occasion, resulted in twenty-five arrests and injuries to five policemen.

This was followed by the incident which British officials called "the tampering with His Majesty's Troops": the mutiny of the recently recruited African Gunners of the Royal Artillery under the leadership of a Creole named Emmanuel Cole. According to the charge, Cole had addressed the

57. Dawe to Colonel Sir Vernon Kell, War Office, March 6, 1939, ibid.
58. Abbott memorandum, February 5, 1959, ibid. Also see "General Comments on the Situation which Led to the Enactment of Sierra Leone Ordinances," enclosure B, in C.O. 267/673/32254/8 (1939).

Gunners and urged them to refuse to parade until British officers ceased pocketing an alleged seven and a half pence a day from the men's pay. At the ensuing court martial, the prosecution claimed that Cole had won over the soldiers by promising them the support of the Youth League. This allegation was supported by two receipts for the payment of dues to the Youth League which had been found when Emmanuel Cole's quarters were searched after his arrest. The defense argued that the Gunners' grievances had been old grievances, communicated to their superior officers long before the day of the alleged mutiny, and were completely independent of Wallace-Johnson and the Youth League. The soldiers desired boots for their feet and clothing similar to that given the police; they wanted higher pay and free food. Their protest was to no avail: they were found guilty and convicted with sentences ranging from eighty-four days of imprisonment with hard labor to fifteen years of penal servitude.[59] Not withstanding the circumstantial nature of the evidence, British officials in Sierra Leone were unshaken in their belief that Wallace-Johnson was behind all the trouble.[60] At the Colonial Office, various individuals were disturbed by the harshness of the conviction, but not sufficiently to interfere. One official succinctly summed up the position:

> There may, of course, be some factors of which I am unaware, but I am bound to say that the sentences rather horrify me. My information is that these African soldiers had been got at by Mr. Wallace-Johnson and thought that they could stage a little strike, and that the idea of mutiny never entered their heads. And, indeed, if one looks at the facts, it appears that what happened was that when told to go on parade they did not do so, but went and sat on the grass for about an hour, when after being talked to they paraded. However, it is, I suppose, none of our business.[61]

The final incident involved the *African Standard*'s publication of a series of articles which the British authorities in Sierra Leone understood to be designed to undermine the loyalty of the police force. One article, cited by the acting governor in a communication to the secretary of state, referred to the police as "a group of Africans held in the bonds of political and economic slavery . . . tools always in the hands of the authorities of all British col-

59. Detailed report re labour and military unrest (8.2.39), Acting Governor Blood to Secretary of State, Secret, in C.O. 267/670/32210/2, pt. 1 (1939); enclosure B, General Comments on the Situation . . . , in C.O. 267/673/32254/8 (1939); Abbott's memo, in C.O. 267/670/32210/2, pt. 1 (1939); SLWN, March 11, 1939.

60. Abbott memo, in C.O. 267/670/32210/2, pt. 1 (1939); enclosure B, in C.O. 267/673/32254/8 (1939), "Matters of Interest: The Youth League," March 1, 1939; "Sittings of the General Court Martial," April 1, 1939, in SLWN.

61. C.O. 267/671/32216/1 (1939).

onies."[62] Other articles, particularly those entitled "Under the Horrible Conditions Which Exist in the Police, Is It Impossible For Us To Strike?" and "Re The Horrible Conditions Existing in The Police Force," were considered equally seditious.[63] Since earlier Youth League activities and Wallace-Johnson speeches had unquestionably aimed at winning support among policemen by challenging them to improve their living conditions with shorter hours and better pay, this new attempt was seen as the final affront. The *African Standard*, it was known, was widely read in the force. In the acting governor's opinion, the newspaper's "subversive" nature "must adversely affect native readers." If the seditious material influenced both the army and police, was anything safe? Would the West African Frontier Force be next to be corrupted, as the Sierra Leone solicitor general maintained? Who would maintain law and order if trouble arose? Who would remain loyal in case of war?[64]

British officials in Sierra Leone were desperate. Wallace-Johnson, they believed, had successfully demonstrated great ingenuity in circumventing the law. With eighteen of the twenty-one lawyers in the colony active in the Youth League, moreover, the governor and his legal advisors were convinced that the entire jury system had been so thoroughly contaminated that it would prove impossible to impanel a jury which would convict any member of the Youth League for a criminal charge under existing law. Certain that Wallace-Johnson was a "menace not only to local interests but also to the Empire,"[65] they were also sure "that the Sierra Leone Creole is an excitable person who can be worked up by agitation to the point of dangerous rioting" and that "it was obviously extremely desirable to take measures to safeguard the position of a defended port . . . in a time when the international situation was evidently growing more and more threatening."[66]

While Governor Jardine was in England on leave for reasons of health in

62. *African Standard*, February 10, 1939.

63. *African Standard*, February 17, 24, March 10, 1939.

64. See C.O. 267/670/32210/2, pt. 1 (1939) for various copies of the *African Standard* submitted in evidence to support action against Wallace-Johnson. Also see Abbott to Attorney-General, June 28, 1939, in C.O. 267/672/32254/2 (1939), for draft charges drawn up by Charles Abbott (solicitor-general of Sierra Leone) against Wallace-Johnson, supported by forty-five clippings or extracts from the *African Standard* as evidence upon which certain of the charges were based. Abbott was particularly meticulous in collecting local newspapers, marking passages which he considered scurrilous in red. He found the *African Standard* "about as low an incursion into the realm of journalism as can well be imagined"—a paper designed "to bring His Majesty's Rule and His Majesty's European Subjects into hatred, ridicule, and contempt."

65. Acting Governor Blood to Secretary of State, Secret Dispatch, February 9, 1939, in C.O. 267/670/32210/2, pt. 1 (1939).

66. Minute *B*, in C.O. 267/673/32254/8 (1939); Abbott memo, pars. 9, 18, in C.O. 267/670/32210/2, pt. 1 (1939).

February 1939, the acting governor, H. R. R. Blood, and the acting attorney-general, Charles Abbott, initiated the offensive against Wallace-Johnson. For Blood, the action represented a departure from more moderate consideration of Wallace-Johnson and indicates how distorted Blood's circle of vision had become as a result of the strikes and disturbances which marred his tenure as acting governor.[67] In a long secret memorandum to the secretary of state for the colonies, he and Abbott urged the secretary's approval for the introduction of legislation which would provide for the deportation of Wallace-Johnson from Sierra Leone.[68]

In light of Freetown's strategic importance to Britain and the implied threat posed by Wallace-Johnson to the loyalty of the fighting forces and police, the Colonial Office studied the Blood-Abbott proposals with great seriousness. Memories of the 1919 anti-Syrian riots in Sierra Leone seemed still to linger, complete with the bias against Creoles as "rather an inflammable lot" and the fear that, unless government maintained a firm front, Sierra Leoneans could be harangued into rebelliousness.[69] It was, moreover, particularly disturbing to Colonial Office experts that no existing local law had served to stop the Youth League's organizing secretary from continuing his agitation.

The response from the Colonial Office was, nonetheless, carefully considered, designed to cover future contingencies as well as solve immediate problems. A few officials probably maintained some hope that the Youth League would, like the National Congress of British West Africa, soon die a natural death or, at the very least, be channeled into "more productive" directions.[70] They also believed that Sierra Leone's passionate affair with Wallace-Johnson would inevitably cool. Then, of course, there were political considerations. No precedent existed for prescribing a trial without jury in a dependency where a jury system was functional. Moreover, Wallace-Johnson, the secretary of state quickly realized, was not without sympathizers among members of the opposition Labour party in the British Parliament. They would surely object vigorously if any action were contemplated against him which departed radically from established judicial practices. He had, after all,

67. As Jardine's colonial secretary, Blood had seriously proposed that "the way to neutralize Wallace-Johnson's affect was to appoint him to the Legislative Council and not to try to repress him by severe measures." See C.O. 267/666/32216/1938.

68. Sierra Leone Colonial Secretary to Secretary of State, February 9, 1939, in C.O. 267/670/32210/2, pt. 1 (1939). Also in the same file see "An Ordinance to Provide for the Arrest, Detention and Deportation of Isaac Theophilus Akuna Wallace-Johnson" drawn up by Abbott, with blank spaces for dates and details which could be filled in at time of arrest.

69. Minute by Dawe, August 24, 1938, in C.O. 267/666/32216/1938.

70. Minute by R. Turnbull, January 4, 1939, ibid.: "in his absence the latter [Youth League] may die quite quickly, or, if he has acquired any decent lieutenants, the movement may conceivably settle into something more sober, lasting, and acceptable."

not been convicted of any crime in his native country and, Colonial Office personnel agreed, the case presented against him by Blood and Abbott was not yet sufficiently strong to warrant such an extreme step as deportation without trial.

Consequently, after intramural consultation and a discussion held in the office of the undersecretary of state, Lord Dufferin, attended by Sir Douglas Jardine (still on leave), Turbett, and by the full contingent of experts on West African matters and British colonial law, it was decided that it was impracticable to enact a special ordinance to exclude Wallace-Johnson from Sierra Leone. He was, like it or not, a native of that colony; it remained the task of that dependency to deal with him. As an alternative, however, Secretary of State Malcolm MacDonald suggested to the acting governor of Sierra Leone that, "in view of the potentialities for mischief in Mr. Wallace-Johnson's activities," he explore the possibility of strengthening the powers of the Sierra Leone government by the enactment of an ordinance along the lines of the United Kingdom Incitement to Disaffection Act of 1934. This would permit the government to deal effectively with any attempt to dissuade troops from performing their duties or maintaining their allegiance to Britain. Furthermore, the acting governor could consider enacting local legislation on the lines of a model ordinance sent out by the Colonial Office to all dependencies in 1934 to regulate the deportation of undesirable British subjects. The powers conferred by such an ordinance, while not permitting the deportation of Wallace-Johnson from his native land, would enable the government to secure his removal from Freetown and to restrict him under supervision of a British administrative officer to some other area, for example, a remote part of the protectorate.[71]

The Colonial Office also gave the Sierra Leone government permission to introduce legislation to control "undesirable publications"—an obvious thrust at the *African Standard*—and to strengthen existing laws against sedition.[72] In addition, recognizing the growing labor unrest in Sierra Leone and the potential danger from newly organized labor unions over which the government had no control, the secretary of state allowed Sierra Leone officials to regulate by law the formation of trade unions and to seek adequate powers to intervene in industrial disputes.[73]

Ultimately, therefore, while rejecting Blood and Abbott's blatant plan to

71. Secretary of State to Acting Governor in Sierra Leone, March 6, 1939; Discussion in Lord Dufferin's Room, February 20, 1939, in C.O. 267/670/32210/2, pt. 1 (1939).

72. Minute by O. G. R. Williams, in C.O. 267/671/32238/1939: "a moderate stiffening up of the Sierra Leone law might prove an effective check to newspapers under the influence of Mr. Wallace-Johnson." For additional material on the undesirable publications ordinance, see C.O. 267/672/32254/3 (1939); for the sedition ordinance, C.O. 267/673/32254/4 (1939).

73. Enclosure B, in C.O. 267/673/32254/8 (1939).

"re-establish peace and good Government in Sierra Leone" by deporting Wallace-Johnson, the Colonial Office was responsible for initiating a web of restrictive legislation which went far beyond the explicit requests of British officials in Sierra Leone in severely curtailing individual freedom. Six bills were more or less simultaneously introduced in Sierra Leone's Legislative Council as a result of the Colonial Office suggestions: (1) the undesirable British subjects control bill (frequently referred to simply as the "deportation bill"; (2) the sedition bill; (3) the undesirable publications bill; (4) the incitement to disaffection bill; (5) the trade union bill; and (6) the trade disputes (arbitration and inquiry) bill. Their introduction immediately led to the organization of strong protests in Sierra Leone and in Great Britain, as well as in other parts of the British Empire.

The protestors, largely unaware that Wallace-Johnson's activities had been the prime stimulus for the introduction of the bills, regarded all of them as an attack upon the civil liberties of the people of "Ancient and Loyal Sierra Leone"—obvious efforts by an unpopular government to take advantage of local political and economic unrest to stave off criticism and shelve reform. The Sierra Leone Bar Association, the Ratepayers Association of Freetown's three wards, the Rural Areas Assembly and Council, the clergy, Christian ministers and Muslim imams, the Committee of Citizens, the Sierra Leone branch of the League of Coloured Peoples, the West African Youth League, various women's groups, and even the members of the ubiquitous National Congress of British West Africa joined together to attack provisions of the bills. Workers and unemployed joined with business and professional persons to proclaim their displeasure.

In Great Britain, opponents called the legislation "monstrous," "drastic," "oppressive," "repressive," "fundamentally un-British," "openly Fascist," "totalitarian," "intolerable," "unconstitutional," "an attack on democratic liberties and a betrayal of the people's trust," "anti-working class," "a gross violation of rights," and "calculated to prevent the organization and expression of political opinion."[74]

Publicly, the secretary of state for the colonies brushed the criticisms aside. In private, however, the secretary appeared sensitive to the possible political consequences—particularly those which emanated from the Opposition in England. As a result, the Colonial Office suggested that the government of Sierra Leone remove two of the most unpopular provisions from the undesirable British subjects control bill. It was also probably a consequence of political considerations in Britain, rather than in Sierra Leone, which inhibited the colony's officials in moving directly to arrest Wallace-Johnson once the bills were passed and became law.[75]

74. See C.O. 267/672/23354/1 (1939) for a great deal of protest literature. Also see the *Sierra Leone Guardian* and *African Standard*, passim, May, June 1939.
75. C.O. 267/672/32254/1 (1939).

The main thrust of the opposition was directed against the deportation bill. Critics focused in on its vague definition of "undesirable person," on the possible danger of deportation of bona fide Sierra Leoneans owing to the difficulty of providing satisfactory evidence of nationality under its provisions, on the undesirability of making the judiciary a party to the carrying out of executive acts, on its insistence that an accused be heard in chambers rather than in open court, and on its denial of the writ of habeas corpus. Most significant, this bill was considered, more than any other, as an attack on the impartial administration of justice and on the fundamental foundations of personal liberty.[76]

When the deportation bill was first introduced into the Sierra Leone Legislative Council, public indignation reached such a peak that the governor considered it necessary to ask for a war ship to remain temporarily in Freetown. The Youth League organized a protest march to Government House, where the Legislative Council regularly met. Advising that children be kept home from school and that participants be attired in black or wear black armbands, the *African Standard* reported that fifteen to twenty thousand persons participated in the demonstration.[77] Singing the Negro spiritual

> Give me freedom, Give me freedom in our land,
> And before I'd be a slave
> I'd be buried in my grave,
> And go home to my Lord
> And be free,

the crowd staged a demonstration that was noisy but peaceful. It gave the British in the colony another opportunity to blame Wallace-Johnson for creating discontent, and it also stimulated Governor Jardine to analyze public hostility to the proposed legislation.[78] "The difficulty, as I see it," the governor wrote to Dawe at the Colonial Office,

> . . . is that the hostility is rooted in sentiment rather than in reason. Consciously or unconsciously, the tragic history of the servitude of their ancestors has made the Creoles irrationally tenacious of what they conceive to be their liberties. I really believe in their fundamental loyalty to the Crown and to the British *raj*; but the loyalty does not extend to the British representatives of the spot, whose every action is suspiciously watched with a view of detecting any possible infringement on their

76. Enclosure no. 1 in Sierra Leone Dispatch no. 504 of July 26, 1939, ibid.

77. *African Standard*, May 19, 1939.

78. Governor Jardine's account of the demonstration is also interesting. See Jardine to Dawe, 1.6.39, Report on the local political situation in C.O. 267/670/32210/2, pt. 1 (1939).

supposed liberties. To this end the acid test which they apply is whether any measure is in accord with the common law of England. If you cannot move a paid political agitator from Chatham to Manchester in England, then you should not have such powers in Sierra Leone and, if you make any attempt to make more power, you are being "suppressive, oppressive, and repressive," and it is a grave slur on the loyalty of the Sierra Leonean. It is a thousand pities as it makes it so very difficult to serve them; and I cannot help having a sneaking regard for them, except when they write me anonymous letters predicting my early and painful demise within a fortnight. " 'Bitten' (? beaten) to death" is the fate that one writer foresees for me. While they are about it, they might as well eat me too in the best African tradition.[79]

The protest march was to little avail. The Legislative Council, at the very sitting when the demonstration was taking place, passed the sedition and undesirable literature bills without division, without one dissenting voice, and without any material amendments. The other bills passed soon afterwards, and the deportation bill, delayed for a short period while tempers cooled, was eventually passed with some modifications, but with only three dissenting voices among the unofficial members of the council.[80]

The major reason for the rapid passage of all the bills was that in spite of opposition to them from among the general population, key establishment Africans supported the government during this crucial period. The editor of the *Sierra Leone Weekly News* seized on the introduction of the bills as an opportunity to score against Wallace-Johnson. Repeated editorials declared the bills were "EFFECTS which have flowed from CAUSES," implying, not too subtly, that Wallace-Johnson's "rabble rousing" in Youth League meetings and in the *African Standard* had driven the government to impose the new legislation.[81] If the root "cause" of trouble were removed, then the situation would, undoubtedly, return to peaceful normality. An editorial in the June 24 issue preached:

> The poor trading woman who after saying her prayer in the morning goes to the market place to look for her daily Bread and puts herself in no trouble with the Government will have nothing from the Government but Protection from harm. So with the work man who is a Mechanic; and so with all who are called the Toiling Masses. . . . It is the Evil Doer that has got to be afraid.

79. Ibid.

80. Governor to Secretary of State, July 6, 1939, in C.O. 267/672/32254/2 (1939); Early in July the bill was passed on the second reading.

81. See, for example, *SLWN*, May 27, June 3, 1939.

The Evil Doer that will not cease from Evil doing. Is there any such among us? Let him refrain from Evil doing, from incitements of people to injudicious and Fruitless strokes against Authority and our Land shall have peace as a Result.[82]

More important than the editorial help from the *Weekly News*, the government received strong support from the African members of the Legislative Council—particularly from its former critic, Dr. Bankole-Bright. Like that of the *Weekly News*, Bankole-Bright's stand illustrated the extent to which personal animosities among Sierra Leoneans influenced individual positions on political and social issues—even on issues as fundamental to African civil liberties as these 1939 ordinances.

In the Legislative Council debate which took place over the deportation bill on June 22, 1939, Bankole-Bright, then First Urban Member, spoke at length in defence of the legislation and, while never referring to Wallace-Johnson by name, attacked him as the "agitator" who "converted the loyalty of Sierra Leoneans into a seething cauldron of disloyalty and discontent." He implied that Wallace-Johnson's primary objective was "cheap money"—to milk the unsuspecting masses for cash with which he supported himself in style, buying a car and building a house, while delivering no benefit in return to the poor and destitute who followed him.[83]

Bankole-Bright's vindictiveness, however, did not end with his vote for the bills and his sniping against Wallace-Johnson in the council. In a private letter to the governor he completely reversed his long-held stand on judicial and electoral reform, urging that the jury system in the colony be scrapped and the franchise be suspended until "the baneful effects of the unconstitutional propaganda now in Freetown [are] eradicated from the minds of the people." "Since the formation of the West African Youth League in this Colony," he wrote, "there has been . . . an open defiance to law and order . . . seditious propaganda . . . publications of scurrilous and defamatory nature . . . the preaching of Bolshevik and communist doctrines." When cases were brought to a court of justice as a result of these activities, Bankole-Bright asserted, it had become quite obvious that juries refused to convict any Youth League member. Juries had been corrupted; mob law was predominant. If the mob became obsessed with the idea that it could riot and not fear punishment in court, violence would spread and the country would quickly run amok. It would be best, therefore, to allow criminal cases to be tried solely by a judge.

Dr. Bankole-Bright, furthermore, envisaged a catastrophe in the November

82. *SLWN*, June 24, 1939.

83. Sierra Leone Legislative Council Debates, June 22, 1939, in Sierra Leone Government Archives.

1939 elections to the Legislative Council. The "rowdy mob, a galaxy of irresponsibles driven to thoughtlessness by seditious propagandists of the Youth League and the frenzied display of a lawless man," would, undoubtedly, like in the City Council elections, sweep the polls with its own candidates. These men would then fetter the council's normal constitutional procedures. "In view of the intense International Situation, and in view of the Bolshevik and Communist Propaganda in the Colony," Bankole-Bright thus concluded, "I feel that the Franchise should be suspended." This, he believed, added to the government's own measures, would bring the people back to their senses, making them realize that government would not tolerate lawlessness but would maintain order. "I stand for an organic connection with the British Empire," he offered as further justification for his suggestion, "and anything that savours of disconnection must be repugnant to me."[84]

Bankole-Bright's vocal support of the government bills, his vote for their passage in the Legislative Council, and his vehemence against the Youth League and its organizing secretary doomed him politically in Sierra Leone for many years.[85] Having served on the Legislative Council for fifteen years, he made it known that he had no intention of seeking reelection in November 1939—publicly, because he "resented the thought" that he would be "representing the mob in Council"; privately, undoubtedly, because he realized that he would suffer an ignominious defeat. Even the semidefunct Sierra Leone Section of the National Congress of British West Africa, of which Bankole-Bright was vice president, was sufficiently piqued by his activities ("the outcome of a poisoned and revengeful mind") to call a meeting which passed a resolution asking him to resign his office in the organization.[86]

The intention of the governor of Sierra Leone originally had been to move against Wallace-Johnson as soon as the deportation bill passed, with the aim of gaining a restriction order which would remove him from Freetown to the protectorate. Governor Jardine had been assured by his legal advisors that this

84. Enclosure in Sierra Leone Confidential Dispatch to Secretary of State, July 6, 1939; letter from Bankole-Bright to Governor Jardine, June 27, 1939, in C.O. 267/673/32268.

85. Ironically, Bankole-Bright and Wallace-Johnson joined together in 1950 in the National Council of the Colony of Sierra Leone, a largely Creole organization opposed to a new constitution which was to give the protectorate dominance in a reconstituted Legislative Council. See John R. Cartwright, *Politics in Sierra Leone, 1947-1967* (Toronto, 1970), pp. 50-54.

86. Bankole-Bright to Governor Jardine, June 27, 1939 in C.O. 267/673/32268; enclosure no. 1 in Dispatch, Sierra Leone, no. 537, August 21, 1939, in C.O. 267/669/32157/1939. This resolution elicited the above letter from Bankole-Bright to Governor Jardine attacking the organization: "The Congress, in my opinion, as the Political Salt of Sierra Leone, has lost its savour; and if the salt has lost its savour wherewith shall it be seasoned, it is neither fit for the land nor yet for the dunghill."

was possible since they had accumulated "a vast mass of evidence" to show that Wallace-Johnson was an "undesirable person within the meaning of the Ordinance." The governor, however, then committed an error: he hesitated a little too long.

Jardine's reasons for hesitating were first expressed in a letter he wrote to A. J. Dawe at the Colonial Office. "I may be over scrupulous," he said,

> ... but I have never cared very much for taking so serious a step under the Ordinance on account of offences committed before the Ordinance became law or was even mooted locally. Do you think there is any good reason for this conscience prick; If Wallace-Johnson is going to stay here and be completely quiescent from the 1st June to the 1st August—which I can hardly believe—it seems to me all the more open to criticism to move against him for acts committed prior to his quiescence and the passing of the bill. I should very much like to know what you think about this.[87]

The Colonial Office was not helpful in dispelling the governor's anxieties. Criticisms in Britain about the Sierra Leone ordinances—particularly questions raised in Parliament by Labour Party M.P.s—had sensitized the secretary of state for the colonies to the fact that the actions of British officials in that colony would have to be explained and justified to people vocally concerned with the rights of the colonial working classes. British public opinion could not be totally disregarded.[88] The secretary of state, therefore, informed Governor Jardine that Wallace-Johnson could not be charged for acts committed before the operation of the ordinance—that in fact, no proceedings could be undertaken until Wallace-Johnson had perpetrated "two acts at least" after the ordinance became effective. The secretary telegraphed the governor:

> To ensure cooperation between us from the beginning, and to avoid possible embarrassment at a later stage, I consider that, it would be advisable for you to furnish me, by telegram if necessary, with particulars of the two acts selected before any proceedings under the Ordinance are commenced. This I am aware goes beyond what I said previously, but if and when action under the Ordinance is taken I am likely to be further questioned in Parliament and I shall be better prepared to deal with the matter there, and in a manner more helpful to you, if my information is up-to-date at each stage and if I am consulted from the beginning.[89]

87. Jardine to Dawe, June 1, 1939, C.O. 267/670/32210/2, pt. 1 (1939).
88. *West Africa*, June 17, 1939.
89. Private and personal telegram from Secretary of State to Governor, July 14,

Furthermore, the secretary of state was emphatic that any move against Wallace-Johnson would have to be based on charges which were "substantial in nature"—including only "really outstanding acts." He had been less than impressed by some of the clippings from the *African Standard* which British officials in Sierra Leone had collected and presented to the Colonial Office in the past as supportive evidence of Wallace-Johnson's evil-doing. The secretary thought, for example, that it would have been very difficult to support any charge against Wallace-Johnson on the basis of the clipping entitled "Irish Nationalists Plot to Blow up Buckingham Palace."[90]

Almost as if informed of the nature of the restrictions imposed by the colonial secretary on Sierra Leone officials, the activities of both the Youth League and its organizing secretary became more subdued after the passage of the ordinances, presenting no chance for the government to build up a case. In spite of their long, determined efforts to shackle Wallace-Johnson and the successful passage of legislation designed to accomplish this end, Wallace-Johnson remained at liberty.

But then came new opportunity. On September 1, 1939, after the close of a meeting of newspaper proprietors and editors at the colonial secretariat, Wallace-Johnson was arrested and charged with criminal libel. He was accused of libeling the Bonthe district commissioner, John Henry de Burgh Shaw. In an article in the *African Standard* entitled "Who Killed Fonnie?" Wallace-Johnson intimated that Shaw had given orders for, and been present at, the flogging of an African youth named Fonnie—a flogging which had brought about Fonnie's death.[91] The serious nature of the charge clearly broke the deadlock.

British officials in Sierra Leone, however, were not yet satisfied. Given the spectacular record of judicial triumphs by Youth League members, they could not be totally confident that Wallace-Johnson would indeed be convicted and imprisoned. The fact that he managed to win immediate release on bail did nothing to bolster the government's confidence. It was for this reason that colonial officials seized upon the declaration of war between the United Kingdom and Germany as a pretext for additional action against their *bête noire*—this time certain that he had no possibility of escaping. Using powers granted to colonial authorities under the newly instituted wartime emergency defense regulations, the governor ordered Wallace-Johnson's detention and internment. Under these emergency regulations, no judicial proceedings were

---

1939, in C.O. 267/672/32254/2 (1939).

90. Ibid. The secretary of state was responding to "Articles and Extracts from Articles from the *African Standard*" drawn up by Abbott, June 28, 1939, to support charges which he planned to make against Wallace-Johnson. In particular, see charge no. 19.

91. *SLWN*, September 2, 16, 1939; *Daily Mail*, September 2, 4, 1939.

necessary for the governor's actions, only the authorization of the secretary of state for the colonies. Neither was appeal possible—only a hearing before an advisory committee which, while able to consider objections to a detention order under the defense regulations, lacked the legal power to reverse a previous decision. In fact, since the regulations were "preventive" in nature, no crime need actually have been committed for them to be invoked. In the case of Wallace-Johnson, it sufficed to say that he was *intending* actions which would be prejudicial to the safety of the public and the defense of the colony.

Material evidence to support Wallace-Johnson's internment was clearly perfunctory. A police search of his premises, ordered by the governor a few days before the detention order was issued, turned up nothing surprising: unfinished articles and sections of articles written by Wallace-Johnson, Thomas Decker, and others active in the Youth League or sympathetic to its aims. Some of these had obviously been discarded before publication; others, intended for future inclusion, were neither more nor less "subversive" than the mass of similar documentation already in possession of the colonial authorities. Indeed, it is quite likely that the nature of the evidence did not particularly concern the governor: the new defense regulations had given him *carte blanche* to go after Wallace-Johnson. The collection of material evidence was designed to mollify Parliamentary defenders of left-wing colonial leaders, and to lend a semblance of legality to what otherwise would have appeared locally as a totally imperious decision. The secretary of state, for his part, had authorized Wallace-Johnson's internment *before* the Colonial Office had received copies of the seized materials.[92]

Ironically, even in spite of these precautions, Secretary of State for the Colonies Malcolm MacDonald was almost influenced to change his mind and order Wallace-Johnson's release. In Britain, criticism mounted quickly, notwithstanding the alleged incriminating documents the police had supposedly found. Many of the same individuals and organizations who had protested the introduction of the prewar ordinance complained to the Colonial Office or to Parliamentary representatives about this new travesty of justice. As a member of Parliament, the secretary of state for the colonies was sensitive to a variety of political pressures which affected British officials in Sierra Leone only secondhand, if at all. In Parliament, Wilfred Paling, for example, asked the secretary whether it was "proposed to detain Wallace-Johnson until he is convinced that this is a war for liberty?" Arthur Creech Jones, M.P., who would become secretary of state after the war, wrote directly to MacDonald asking to see the evidence against Wallace-Johnson and, on the secretary's

92. C.O. 267/670/32210/2, pt. 2 (1939). A Colonial Office minute, commenting on Wallace-Johnson's arrest reads: "This is most satisfactory."

invitation, came to the Colonial Office to discuss the case.[93] Most important, the Opposition in Commons had asked for and received a reconsideration of the wartime emergency powers defense regulations for Great Britain and, with Wallace-Johnson's internment clearly as their stimulant, began to pressure the secretary of state to reconsider the emergency colonial defense regulations as well.[94]

Even within the Colonial Office certain doubts persisted about the proper course of action in Wallace-Johnson's detention. The Sierra Leone experts in the Colonial Office were well aware that the case against the Youth League's organizing secretary was not strong. One official argued, moreover, that Wallace-Johnson had been mismanaged all along. He had, in a petition, guaranteed his future good behavior if released from detention, and they now wondered if this was not the proper time to "direct . . . his energies into more useful paths."[95]

The vacillation was short lived. Before the secretary was forced to commit himself, Wallace-Johnson was convicted in the Supreme Court of Sierra Leone on the charge of criminal libel in the "Who Killed Fonnie" case and sentenced to twelve months' imprisonment without hard labor.[96] British officials in Sierra Leone and the secretary of state must have been overwhelmingly relieved. It didn't matter that the conviction was accomplished without a jury, by a judge and three assessors. Nor did it matter that one assessor, P. H. Marteroy, was a Frenchman who had only recently become a naturalized British subject; that A. J. Momoh, the second assessor, was a government official; that L. H. Gibson, the third assessor, was an agent for Paterson-Zochonis Ltd.—a member of the commercial pool criticized by Wallace-Johnson in the *African Standard*.[97] What mattered was that Wallace-Johnson had been convicted under Sierra Leone law, not the more questionable emergency regulations. His internment could be resumed at the conclusion of his prison sentence, in more propitious circumstances.

Wallace-Johnson was detained initially in the internment camp for enemy

93. Dawe's minute, in C.O. 267/670/32210/2, pt. 2 (1939), in reference to the possibility that the "evidence" against Wallace-Johnson would be disclosed to Creech Jones, is extremely revealing of Colonial Office insecurities: "I am sure it is best not to promise any papers until we have seen what is in them."

94. Great Britain, *Parliamentary Debates* (Commons), House of Commons Office Report, vol. 352 (1939), col. 1914.

95. C.O. 267/670/32210/2, pt. 2 (1939). There were several minutes by the various Colonial Office officials on November 10, 11, 1939. The general consensus was that the Sierra Leone government had acted hastily and had not put together a very good case for Wallace-Johnson's detention.

96. Sierra Leone telegram 23.11.39, ibid.; *Daily Mail*, November 23, 1939; "Rex vs. I. T. Wallace-Johnson," *SLWN*, November 25, 1939.

97. *SLWN*, September 2, 1939.

aliens which was set up at the Government Model School. There, while subject to the same rules and regulations as enemy internees, he was nonetheless housed separately from alien prisoners—a separation which, according to reassurances from the officer in charge of the internment camp, reflected his status as a British subject and was not meant to be equivalent to solitary confinement.[98] He was transferred to the male prison yard of the Freetown Gaol after his criminal libel conviction and, after four months' imprisonment, was placed in solitary confinement at the Remand Prison for forty-five days—from April to June 1940.[99]

His health deteriorated considerably during this period until, eventually, he was transferred as a patient to the hospital ward of the prison where he spent the next eleven months. His sentence for libel had expired but the outcry against the emergency defense regulations had been made inconsequential by the seriousness of the ongoing war and the public's rally to Britain's defense. Wallace-Johnson was therefore moved to Bonthe, on Sherbro Island, for internment once again. A deputation of Sierra Leone trade union leaders did appeal to the secretary of state in September 1943 for Wallace-Johnson's release, asking that the government show faith in trade unionism by freeing the original organizer of the movement in Sierra Leone and emphasizing that Wallace-Johnson's talents were urgently needed. But colonial officials continued to maintain that Wallace-Johnson's restriction was essential to the interests of the war effort—that he had shown himself to be irresponsible in the past and would undoubtedly exploit the difficulties of the war situation if freed. Wallace-Johnson spent the remainder of the war on Sherbro Island, under the watchful eye of the British district commissioner, and was not released until the latter part of 1944.

Even though the Youth League continued to exist as an organization after the war, it was robbed of its dynamism and strength, reduced in membership, drained of its spirit. Sierra Leone was perhaps the only place in Africa where World War II effectively slowed, rather than increased, the pace of anticolonial nationalism. It provided the atmosphere wherein repression, invoked in defense of "national security," would breed virtually unchallenged. It called on dissenters to rally round the flag, to overlook measures which restricted civil liberties, to accept actions as expedient which, in more normal times,

98. "Copy of a Minute from Ag. Supt. of Prisons, Officer in Charge of the Internment Camp," and Secret Dispatch from O. G. R. Williams to Blood inquiring about the conditions of Wallace-Johnson's internment so that the secretary of state could be briefed for Parliamentary questions, in C.O. 267/670/32210/2, pt. 2 (1939).

99. See *Daily Mail*, June 19, 21, 1940, for details about Wallace-Johnson's lost appeal before the West African Appeals Court. Wallace-Johnson was later to remember this experience in a poem, "On Solitary Confinement," which was published in his collection of poetry from this period entitled *Prison in the Muse*, 3d ed., (Freetown, 1945).

they would have criticized and fought. The government, utilizing the powers granted by the emergency defense regulations, severed the Youth League's head from its body; invoking other 1939 ordinances it went after other officials of the League and the *African Standard* as well—George Cornwall, Nathaniel Thomas, Sydney Maurice Oluwole Boyle, George S. C. Willoughby—until eventually the movement was left virtually leaderless.[100] Without strong direction from the top, the Youth League began to fall apart. Internal tensions and rivalries, which had never been entirely absent from the mass organization but which had been kept successfully submerged by Wallace-Johnson, came to the surface. Important members resigned or switched their allegiance; less important members lost interest; many Creoles, true to their characterization by the British as the "ancient and loyal" Sierra Leoneans, felt compelled to fall into line with the war effort and curb their criticism of governmental injustice and private exploitation. Most important of all, the beginnings of a delicate cooperation under the aegis and direction of the Youth League between colony and protectorate—between Creoles and up-countrymen—all but ceased during the war. The government's continuous harrassment of the Youth League and its leaders, especially during the war when it had the power to proceed unhindered, not only managed to delay the formation of a mass nationalist political party but also of a true national consciousness among *all* the inhabitants of Sierra Leone. To overcome this setback would take many years and many unnecessary wounds.

100. *Daily Mail*, September 19, 20, 1940, and *African Standard*, March 30, 1942. Mrs. Horton, the league's assistant organizing secretary, was the only officer who, at one time or another during the war, was not imprisoned. Horton-Spitzer interview, January 14, 1966.

Conclusion: Toward Liberation

Although one may make only tentative generalizations on the basis of a single case study, the history of the Sierra Leone Creoles in the period between 1870 and 1945 does suggest the following hypothesis about the intellectual and political reactions of a colonized group to colonization:

In a colonial situation in which racial differences exist between ruler and ruled, the intellectual reactions to colonialism of the colonized group having the longest and greatest contact with the colonizers reflect concerns based on identity of class[1] and status rather than race—if the colonized group finds its opportunities for educational, economic, and social advancement relatively open. If these opportunities are curtailed as a direct or indirect effect of racism perceived by the colonized "elite," intellectual reactions turn to reflect racial concerns, such as questions of racial identity and racial "personality."

Political reactions by the colonized "elite" display a similar pattern. The initial reaction to colonialism is made on the basis of class identity. The reaction is "reformist," characterized by the search for legal amelioration within the system, contact with sympathetic individuals and organizations in the colonial metropolis, and a desire for a greater and more influential role in the political process for ascribed members of the group. With increased consciousness of racism and the application of racist policies to all colonized

1. See chapter 1, especially note 13.

peoples regardless of status, political reactions turn from class to mass politics based on racial unity.[2]

In the case of the Sierra Leone Creoles, the earliest response to colonialism, which predominated through the decade of the 1870s, was intellectual and cultural. This period can be characterized as an "Era of Good Feelings" because the Creoles, like many of their parents and grandparents who had been liberated from slavery, found the system of which they were a part acceptable by and large, and perceived the opportunities for upward mobility within it to be practically without limitation. The characteristic response during this era was assimilationist in the direction of Europeanization: a significant number of Creoles saw themselves as agents, if not partners, of the Europeans in the "civilization" of Africa. To this extent, the original Sierra Leone "experiment" as envisioned by British philanthropists and humanitarians was successful. Creoles viewed themselves as special, different from or even superior to Africans who had not experienced prolonged cultural contact with Europeans.

The dominance of the assimilationist reaction during this period, however, should not be taken to imply that Creoles totally rejected customs, practices, and outlooks which derived from their African heritage. As discussed in the sections dealing with the life-cycle and with Krio, the Creole culture which developed throughout the nineteenth century was inwardly syncretic, combining in a new and original brew both European and African cultural elements.[3] The significance of the assimilationist response lies in the fact that western-educated Creoles discriminated between both non-Creole Africans and Europeans on the basis of social class and status, *not race*. Their rapport and identification was with fellow "educated Africans"—in other parts of Africa, the West Indies, Europe, or America—and with Europeans from the lower-middle and middle classes.

2. The assertion has frequently been made that the Creole experience in Sierra Leone is so unique that it bears little relevance to historical developments in other parts of Africa or elsewhere. While all too little detailed comparative research has been done, several studies of specific Europeanized colonial elites suggest not only the comparability of the Creole case but also the general validity of the hypothesis derived from that experience. The work of Leo Kuper and others on South Africa, that of Jean Herskovits on the Saro in Yoruba and G. Wesley Johnson on the *originaires* in Senegal, and my own research in progress on Afro-Brazilian freedmen—all appear to present a solid foundation for future, explicitly comparative inquiry. See Leo Kuper, "African Nationalism in South Africa, 1910-1964," in *The Oxford History of South Africa*, ed. Monica Wilson and L. Thompson (Oxford, 1971), 2: 424-475; Kuper *An African Bourgeoisie* (New Haven, Conn., 1965); Kopytoff, *Preface to Modern Nigeria*; and G. Wesley Johnson, Jr., "The Senegalese Urban Elite, 1900-1945," in *Africa and the West*, ed. Philip Curtin (Madison, Wis., 1972) pp. 75-98, 139-187.

3. For a related discussion see Philip D. Curtin, "African Reactions in Perspective," in *Africa and the West*, ed. Curtin, pp. 231-244.

In the period characterized by "The Growth of Disillusionment," which stretched from the mid-1870s until the turn of the century, Creole responses made on the basis of class began to be blurred and distorted by the increasing prevalence of British racism. Those Creoles in closest contact with the West became aware that the possibilities for mobility and attainment within the system, once the predictable reward for talent and educational achievement, were diminishing. As a result, the intellectual response to colonialism was expressed by three distinct but closely related phenomena.

First, it became common during this period for Creoles to differentiate between Europeans, categorizing them according to their apparent racial empathy with black Africans. The English were thus measured against an idealized standard of behavior attributed to the original philanthropic founders of Sierra Leone, and referred to as a "Higher Class of English," "Benign Rulers," or "Big Men" if they fulfilled their expectations, and "lower Type of English" if they insulted Creoles or demonstrated racial arrogance either in their actions or writings.[4] These categorizations, it should be emphasized, were entirely independent of the actual class status of the European in question—clearly illustrated by the fact that Sir Richard Burton and Winwood Reade both qualified for the "lower Type of English" epithet.[5]

The second phenomenon associated with the Creole response during this period is described in chapter 4. Largely introspective and predominantly within a cultural realm, Creoles began to reexamine the values, outlooks, and practices which had come to characterize their society during the "Era of Good Feelings." Specifically, they began to question the basic premise on which Creole society had developed and was resting: African assimilation of European ways. This self-examination and search for cultural identity, triggered by the racism typifying British attitudes and actions toward Africans during the last quarter of the nineteenth century, resulted in the neotraditionalism espoused by the Blyden "school," the extreme Europeanization advocated by Renner-Maxwell, and the selective Westernization of men like Bishop Johnston. Each was an attempt to counterbalance the British attitudes which struck at the very nerve center of Creole culture—at the Creoles' pride in having successfully accommodated themselves, intellectually and socially, to contemporary British standards.

Finally, the Creoles' growing disillusionment led them to explore possible revisions of their relationship with up-countrymen, both in Sierra Leone Colony and what in 1896 came to be the protectorate. The Sierra Leone Creoles, unlike many other such western-educated African groups as the *originaires* in Senegal, the Saro in Yoruba, or the "school" people in South Africa, were for the most part unrelated through blood ties to Africans in

4. Based on Creole writings, particularly in the Freetown press, but also in essays and books. See my "The Sierra Leone Creoles, 1870-1900," in *Africa and the West*, ed. Curtin, esp. pp. 136-138.

5. Ibid., p. 136.

their own hinterland. Cultural differences which had already been apparent between the Creoles' newly liberated parents and grandparents and the people indigenous to Sierra Leone and its hinterland, were therefore accentuated even more with the growth and development of Creole society, and were not mediated by ties of kinship. As a minority settler community, moreover, the Creoles had acquired the belief that their position and survival as a people depended on the maintenance of separate identity and British support. They, like other people descending from settlers in a foreign land, tended to respond on a basis of fear and uncertainty—fear that they would be numerically and physically overrun by masses of "tribal war boys," and uncertainty about their ability to withstand even a peaceful challenge to their way of life through, what appeared to them, an ever growing influx of up-countrymen into Freetown and the colony (see chapter 3).

Creoles took the first steps in trying to bridge the gulf which had spread between themselves and up-countrymen. The initial effort was romantic in conceptualization: up-countrymen were described by Creole neotraditionalists as "simple and unspoiled," "virgin souls," and their "nobility" contrasted with the "degeneracy" of Creole society. This effort, modest as it was, nevertheless represented a radical departure from previous Creole responses. It replaced the identification and affiliation solely on the basis of class and cultural affinities with the beginning of an identification with other Africans on the basis of racial kinship.

When the 1898 Hut Tax War first broke out in the northern part of the Sierra Leone hinterland, an article in the Creole press sympathized with the interior peoples in their fight against the British, calling up-countrymen "bones of our bones, flesh of our flesh." Another lamented the news that British-led troops had "mow[ed] down our brethren" in battle.[6] Had this trend continued, intellectual reactions to colonialism could perhaps have been transformed into effective political action at a much earlier date in Sierra Leone's history than was to be the case. But the reason the transformation did not come about sooner was also a direct effect of the 1898 war. Creole opinions of up-countrymen reverted to their previous negativism, and perhaps even intensified, when Creole traders and missionaries, including women and children, were killed up-country in the Mende and Sherbro regions of the south.

When Creole reactions changed from the predominantly intellectual to the political sphere in the years between 1910 and the mid-1930s (discussed in chapter 5), activity was essentially confined to the Creole elite. The Sierra Leone section of the National Congress of British West Africa, the most

6. Letter to the editor by Musa Alhakim, *SLWN*, April 2, 1898; *SLWN*, February 5, 1898.

important political organization in the colony in the decade after World War I, suffered greatly from the lack of strength which mass, multiethnic, and multiclass support might have provided. Furthermore, despite repeated political rejections and economic setbacks the Creole elite seemed unwilling to try once again to overcome the historical, cultural, and social rift which kept them apart from up-countrymen. Thus debilitated and handicapped, the Creole upper class continued the politics of reformism and amelioration rather than of colonial liberation.

Only with the reappearance of Wallace-Johnson in Sierra Leone and the establishment of the West African Youth League beginning in 1938 (chapter 6) was this trend broken and a new alliance sought with non-Creole Africans from all classes and backgrounds. What distinguished this political effort from previous ones was that its leaders acted from the premise that the inequities of colonialism were universal, affecting all colonized peoples irrespective of cultural and social background. They particularly sought to raise the consciousness of the African working class—politically the least aware—while simultaneously forging unity between all African groups in Sierra Leone on the basis of racial kinship. In this respect colonial officials, especially the governor of Sierra Leone, who repeatedly accused Wallace-Johnson of fomenting racial animosity between Africans and Europeans during this period, were not entirely mistaken. Unlike the older Creole political leaders who, despite repeated indications to the contrary, refused totally to abandon hope for a return to the "Era of Good Feelings," the new leaders understood the fundamental reality of colonialism in Africa to be reflected in the fact that whites were the rulers and blacks the ruled.

These individuals were, to be sure, unsuccessful in sustaining their effort to unify the masses against colonial domination at this time. This was due less to any error in their assumptions or fault in their organizational skill than to the ability of colonial officials to subdue and discomfit the new leadership and to keep alive the cultural and social prejudice which, for many Sierra Leoneans, had not been buried beneath the surface deep or long enough to be easily obliterated. Aided by the outbreak of World War II, and the consequent rallying around-the-flag by most colonial subjects, the game of divide-and-rule was able to endure for another decade.

Appendices

Note on Sources

Bibliography

Index

Appendix A

AFRICAN POPULATION BY ORIGIN, COLONY OF SIERRA LEONE, 1881-1931[a]

Origin	1881	1891	1901	1911	1921	1931
Liberated Africans and their descendants (Creoles)	35,430	33,212[b]	33,518[c]	31,078	28,222	32,848
Mulattoes and persons of mixed blood				204	358	150
"Natives"(children of strange tribes born in Sierra Leone)	3,384	6,729	8,037 ⎫	42,587	55,230	62,548
Other Africans	21,068	33,807	33,430 ⎭			
West Indians	393	863	1,177	799	244	96
Total	60,275	74,611	76,162	74,668	84,054	95,642

[a]From Kuczynski, *Demographic Survey,* 1: 163, See Sierra Leone Census Reports, 1881, "Recapitulation"; 1891, "Recapitulation"; 1901, p. 30; 1911, p. 39; 1921, p. 40; 1931, pp. 73, 78, in Sierra Leone Collection.

[b]There was "a small number of persons of mixed blood estimated to be about 450" (Sierra Leone Census Report, 1891, p. 5, in Sierra Leone Collection), most of whom were probably included in the above figure.

[c]There was "a small number of persons of mixed blood" (ibid., 1901, p. 6), "most of whom would be classified as Creoles."

Appendix B

POPULATION OF COLONY OF SIERRA LEONE, 1871-1931[a]

Districts	1871	1881	1891	1901	1911	1921	1931
Total Freetown District[b]	25,930	32,572	40,326	45,772	44,952	55,569	68,821
Total peninsula[c]	38,936	53,862	58,448	67,782	68,115	79,561	90,168
Total colony[d]	38,936	60,546[e]	74,835[f]	76,655[g]	75,572[h]	85,163[i]	96,573[j]

[a]Kuczynski, *Demographic Survey,* 1: 26. He culls figures from Sierra Leone Census Reports, 1881, pp. 4, 6; 1891, pp. 3-4, 16, 22; 1901, pp. 3-5, 20; 1911, pp. 5-6, 21, 38; 1921, pp. 6, 20; 1931, pp. 22, 73, in Sierra Leone Collection.

[b]Includes Freetown, Kissy, Regent, and Wilberforce.

[c]Includes Freetown District, Western District, Eastern District, and in 1881 and 1891 Quiah, which in 1896 was included in the protectorate.

[d]Includes Bonthe, York Island, Tassoh Island, Kaikonkah, factories on Sierra Leone River, and in 1881, 1891, and 1901, Isles de Los, which were afterward ceded to France.

[e]Including 108 white "floating" population, (e.g., ships in harbor).

[f]Including 714 in vessels, etc., in port.

[g]Including 418 in vessels, etc., in port.

[h]Including 643 in vessels, etc., in port.

[i]Including 395 in vessels, etc., in port.

[j]Including 151 in vessels, etc., in port.

Note on Sources

Insofar as possible, this study is based on the Creoles' own accounts—on their literature, both oral and written. The Creoles published a large number of newspapers, books, and pamphlets containing some of the earliest comments written by Africans in English about their contact with the Western world. More than two dozen newspapers, for example, appeared in Sierra Leone in the last four decades of the nineteenth century. It was in these publications that the Creoles voiced their disappointments, their ambitions, and their grievances. At the same time, Creoles created a large body of oral literature in the form of songs, folk tales, and proverbs. This material, more difficult to interpret, is not as valuable for a reconstruction of historical facts as the "formal" oral traditions recited by professional bards, court remembrancers, and praise-poets in African societies less affected by the impact of Europe. They do, however, reveal a different dimension of the Creole world view, an invaluable complement to the written sources.

The type of literature used by various segments of Creole society reflected the relatively "tight-knit" nature of their community. Oral literature—Krio songs, tales, and proverbs—was not exclusively in the domain of the illiterate but, like the newspapers, was an important part of the experience of the entire spectrum of Creole society. Proverbs especially, being concise, indirect, and yet complex observations about social, political, and home life, were very much a part of the conversation of all Creoles—educated or not. The written literature of the upper stratum of Creole society was in English, both because English was the language of the Europeans who set the standards and because there was some stigma attached to the use of Krio. But neither stopped the

227

literature from reaching less literate or even illiterate Creoles. Freetown newspapers, for example, had much more influence in the community than their relatively small circulation figures would suggest. Being relatively expensive, newspapers were commonly passed among relatives and friends, and their contents read aloud. As many ruined publishers attested, lack of paid subscriptions, not readership, was the cause for the quick demise of Creole newspapers. "Four copies of the *Weekly News* and the *Sierra Leone Times*," wrote one columnist, "subscribed for by perhaps, four individuals serve the turn of all the mountain villages. From Kissy to Songo Town might muster say 20 more, and from Murray Town to Tombo a dozen. One single copy of the *Weekly News* has been known to serve the tune of a long and populous street in the centre of the city; and the original owner who is the subscriber, scarcely knew his paper when it was eventually returned to him."[1]

The greatest sources of oral materials are individuals. Proverbs are easiest to collect. Creoles quote proverbs frequently in the course of a normal conversation. Others can be found in sources such as the Sierra Leone *Daily Mail* which often printed Krio proverbs and their explanation during the 1930s. Krio folk tales are widespread, but tales and songs of historical interest are less easy to come by among Creoles than among those African societies that relied heavily on these kinds of oral traditions to recall the past. Because of the early and relatively widespread literacy among Creoles, no real need existed to memorize and retain this kind of material. Most popular songs or ditties containing social commentary which were not captured in print tended to disappear. The Sierra Leone Broadcasting System, however, has a collection of the more recent Creole folksongs and aphorisms on records and tapes.

The written materials are to be found scattered in a number of places—both private and public—throughout Freetown and Great Britain. The library at Fourah Bay College, for example, is now the principal repository of works about Sierra Leone in that country. The old colonial secretary's library was given to the college and now makes up a great part of the college library's "Sierra Leone Collection." This collection is extremely good for eighteenth- and nineteenth-century travel accounts, for literature about Sierra Leone written by Europeans, and for compilations of printed official sources dating from the period of the Sierra Leone Company to the present. The college library also holds a number of newspapers from the colonial and postindependence periods. The Sierra Leone Museum has a small library as well, in great part donated by Captain F. W. Butt-Thompson, who had an amateur historian's interest in Sierra Leone. Among other things, this library contains published and unpublished manuscripts by Butt-Thompson, a manuscript notebook of Creole songs, letters written by Archdeacon Crowther, and a number of books by Creoles that cannot be found in the Sierra Leone

1. "One Thing and Another," *SLT*, January 20, 1894.

Collection at Fourah Bay College. Most interesting of all, perhaps, the museum owns photograph albums from the turn of the century which are extremely useful in illustrating Freetown life as it used to be.

Outside Africa, the British Museum, the Royal Commonwealth Society, and the British Museum's Newspaper Library at Colindale together contain the most complete collection of writings by Sierra Leone Creoles. The volume of these writings is considerable. Colindale, for example, has holdings in over forty newspapers published, edited, and written by Creoles, spanning the period covered in my study and invaluable for an assessment of Creole thought and opinion. The libraries of the British Museum and the Royal Commonwealth Society (the former Royal Empire Society)—both because of the historical connection between Sierra Leone and Great Britain and because Sierra Leone climate was injurious to books in the days before air-conditioned libraries and archives—are now the only source for scores of books and pamphlets written by Creoles in the past century. The Royal Commonwealth Society and the old Colonial Office Library also own a number of photograph albums, postcards, and drawings from the last years of the nineteenth century. The Royal Commonwealth Society has the best and most complete subject catalogue on Sierra Leone of any library in the world. Its collection of periodical literature is also comprehensive—duplicating holdings in the British Museum to a certain extent, but much more accessible. The library of the School of Oriental and African Studies owns a number of Sierra Leone newspapers which are not available at Colindale, a microfilm copy of a rare pamphlet by E. W. Blyden, and Krio and Mende grammars written by Creoles in the 1890s and early 1900s. The London University Institute of Commonwealth Studies on Russell Square has a small collection of material on Sierra Leone, but emphasizing secondary sources. The archives of the Church Missionary Society and the Methodist Missionary Society, essential to any study of the early history of Sierra Leone, were less useful for my research owing to my primary emphasis on writings by Africans and concentration on a more modern period. The Public Records Office not only contains the correspondence between officials of the Colonial Office and of Sierra Leone, complementing the holdings of the Sierra Leone Archives, but also retains occasional newspaper articles, petitions, letters, and other writings by Creoles that the governors submitted to London. Rhodes House Library at Oxford is an important source of both published and manuscript material on Sierra Leone as well. Rhodes House owns the papers of the Anti-Slavery and Aborigines Protection Society, which contain interesting correspondence between members of these societies and Creoles who thought they were being wronged in some way by the British government. The Arthur Creech Jones Papers, important for a study of Wallace-Johnson and the Youth League, are also located there.

Bibliography

Public Documents

FREETOWN

Sierra Leone Collection. Fourah Bay College
  Sierra Leone Census Reports, 1881-1931
  Sierra Leone Colonial Reports
  Sierra Leone Medical Reports
Sierra Leone Government Archives. (See the mimeographed catalogue for the
  archives prepared by Mr. C. Fyfe which is available at the Library of
  Fourah Bay College, Freetown.)
  Local Letters Received. Books containing petitions, requests and miscel-
    laneous communications from residents of the colony and its hinter-
    land.
  Governors' Dispatches to the Secretary of State. (A complement to C.O.
    267 in the Public Record Office.)
  Native Affairs Department Correspondence.
  Sierra Leone Legislative Council Debates.

LONDON

Methodist Missionary Archives
  Boxes marked "Sierra Leone," "West Africa," and "Sierra Leone and
  Gambia" contain material from missionaries in Africa to the parent organ-
  ization in London. Included in this material can be found autobiographical

statements by Joseph Wright, Joseph Boston May, John Campbell, Charles Harding, and George Thompson and biographical information by J. May on Joseph Wright.

Public Record Office

C.O. 237 (1865-1921, passim). Correspondence, public and private, from Sierra Leone to the colonial secretary in London. Much of this correspondence can also be found, in duplicate form, in the Sierra Leone Government Archives.

C.O. 267 (1920-1939). Sierra Leone. Original Correspondence: Dispatches, Offices and Individuals.

C.O. 272. Miscellanea: Blue Books of Statistics.

C.O. 368. Register of Correspondence.

C.O. 484. Register of Out-letters.

C.O. 879 (1885-1909, passim). Confidential Prints.

OXFORD

Rhodes House Library

"Aborigines Rights Protection Society" papers and "Anti-Slavery Society" papers can be found here under MSS British Empire, S22. Volume G19 deals with Sierra Leone. Volumes G244, 245, 247, 248 contain letters dealing with discrimination in the West African Medical Service.

Arthur Creech Jones papers.

Published Sources

BOOKS

Ajayi, J. F. A. *Christian Missions in Nigeria, 1841-1891: The Making of a New Elite*. London, 1965.

Alldridge, T. J. *The Sherbro and Its Hinterland*. London, 1901.

————. *A Transformed Colony: Sierra Leone as it was, and as it is; its progress, peoples, native customs, and undeveloped wealth*. London, 1910.

Allen, W. F. *Slave Songs of the United States*. New York, 1867.

Balandier, Georges. *Afrique Ambigue*. Paris, 1957.

Banbury, G. A. L. *Sierra Leone, or The White Man's Grave*. London, 1881.

Banton, M. *West African City*. London, 1957.

Barker, W. H. *West African Folk Tales*. London, 1928.

Barnard, Henry. *National Education in Europe*. New York, 1954.

Best, J. R. *A History of the Sierra Leone Railway*. Freetown, 1949.

Blyden, E. W. *Africa and the Africans. Proceedings on the Occasion of a Banquet Given to E. W. Blyden by West Africans in London, August 15, 1903*. London, 1903.

————. *African Life and Customs*. London, 1908. (Reprinted from the *Sierra Leone Weekly News*.)

————. *The African Problem and Other Discourses Delivered in America in 1890*. London, 1890.

————. *Aims and Methods of a Liberal Education for Africans. Inaugural Address* . . . . Cambridge, Mass., 1882.

————. *Christianity, Islam and the Negro Race*. 2d ed. London, 1889.

————. *From West Africa to Palestine*. Freetown, 1873.

————. *The Jewish Question*. N.p., 1898. (Microfilm copy at School of Oriental and African Studies, London University.)

————. *The Negro in Ancient History—Mohammedanism in Western Africa*. London, 1874. (Two articles reprinted from *The Methodist Quarterly Review*.)

————. *The Origin and Purpose of African Colonization*. Washington, D.C., 1882. (The annual discourse delivered at the 66th anniversary of the American Colonization Society, 1883.)

————. *Proceedings at the Banquet in Honour of Edward Wilmot Blyden, LL.D., on the Occasion of his Retirement From His Official Labours in the Colony of Sierra Leone, January 24th, 1907*. London, 1907.

————. *Proceedings at the Inauguration of Liberia College at Monrovia, January 23, 1862*. Monrovia, 1862.

————. *West Africa Before Europe and other addresses delivered in England in 1901 and 1903*. London, 1905.

————. *The West African University. Correspondence between E. W. Blyden and His Excellency J. Pope-Hennessy*. Freetown, 1872.

———— et al. *The People of Africa—A Series of Papers on Their Character, Condition, and Future Prospects*. New York, 1871.

British Empire Exhibition, 1924. *Sierra Leone Exhibition Handbook*. London, 1924.

Burton, Richard F. *Wanderings in West Africa from Liverpool to Fernando Po. By a F.R.G.S.* 2 vols. London, 1863.

————, and J. L. Cameron. *To the Gold Coast for Gold*. London, 1883.

Butt-Thompson, Frederick Wm. *The First Generation of Sierra Leoneans*. Sierra Leone, 1952.

————. *Sierra Leone in History and Tradition*. London, 1926.

Buxton, T. *The African Slave Trade and Its Remedy*. London, 1840.

Cartwright, John R. *Politics in Sierra Leone, 1947-1967*. Toronto, 1970.

Cassidy, Frederick G. *Jamaica Talk*. London, 1961.

Church, Mary [pseud.] *Liberated Africans, In a Series of Letters from a Young Lady to her Sister in 1832-34*. London, 1835.

Clarke, J. I. *Sierra Leone in Maps*. London, 1966.

Clarke, Robert. *Sierra Leone Manners and Customs*. London, 1843.

Clarke, W. R. E. *The Morning Star of Africa*. London, 1960.

Cole, Christian Fred. *Reflections on the Zulu War and the Future of Africa*. N.p., 1883.

Cole, J. Abayomi. *Astrological Geomancy in Africa. A Lecture Delivered in London*. London, 1898.

————. *Hala goloi Mende yiahu, First Book in the Mende Language*. London, 1900.

————. *The Interior of Sierra Leone, West Africa; What Can It Teach Us?* Dayton, Ohio, 1887.

————. *The Needs of Africa and the Failures of a False Christianity*. N.p., 1887.

————. *A Revelation of the Secret Orders of West Africa*. Dayton, Ohio, 1886.

Cole, Robert Wellesley. *Kossoh Town Boy, An Autobiography of a Freetown Child*. Cambridge, 1960.

Coleman, J. S., and Rosberg, C. G. *Political Parties and National Integration in Tropical Africa*. Berkeley, Calif., 1964.

Conton, William. *The African*. London, 1960.

Crooks, J. J. *History of the Colony of Sierra Leone, Western Africa*. Dublin, 1903.

Crowder, Michael. *West Africa Under Colonial Rule*. Evanston, Ill., 1968.

Curtin, Philip D. *The Image of Africa: British Ideas and Actions, 1780-1850*. Madison, Wis., 1964.

————, ed. *Africa Remembered: Narratives by West Africans from the Era of the Slave Trade*. Madison, Wis., 1967.

Dallas, R. C. *The History of the Maroons, from Their Origin to the Establishment of Their Chief Tribe at Sierra Leone* . . . . 2 vols. London, 1803.

Davies, Jacob Stanley. *Selections from the Poetry of* . . . . Edited by Edward James Davis, Risca, Eng., 1960.

Davis, R. P. M. *A History of the Sierra Leone Battalion of the R.W.A.F.F.* Freetown, 1932.

Desbordes, J. G. *L'Immigration Libano-Syrienne en Afrique Occidentale Française*. Poitiers, 1938.

Easmon, Raymond Sariff. *Dear Parent and Ogre. A Play*. London, 1964.

Elias, T. O. *Ghana and Sierra Leone: The development of their laws and constitutions*. London, 1962.

Ellis, A[lfred] B[urdon]. *West African Sketches*. London, 1881.

Eminent Sierra Leoneans (in the nineteenth century). Freetown, 1961.

Fergusson, W. *A Letter to Thomas Fowell Buxton, Esq*. London, 1839.

Forde, Daryll. *The Yoruba-Speaking Peoples of South-Western Nigeria*. London, 1951.

Foster, Raymond Samuel. *The Sierra Leone Church, An Independent Anglican Church*. London, 1961.

Fyfe, Christopher H. *Africanus Horton, West African Scientist and Patriot.* New York, 1972.

————. *A History of Sierra Leone.* Oxford, 1962.

————. *Sierra Leone Inheritance.* London, 1964.

George, Claude [or Esu Biyi]. *The Rise of British West Africa, Comprising the Early History of the Colony of Sierra Leone, the Gambia, Lagos, Gold Coast, etc., with a Brief History of the Climate, the Growth of Education, Commerce and Religion, and a Comprehensive History of the Bananas and Bance Islands, and Sketches of the Constitution.* 5 pts. London, 1902-1903.

Gervis, Leslie William Charles Pearce. *Sierra Leone Story.* London, 1956.

Goddard, Thomas N. *The Handbook of Sierra Leone.* London, 1924-1925.

Gorvie, Max. *Old and New in Sierra Leone.* Africa's Own Library, no. 9. London, 1945.

Great Britain, *Parliamentary Papers.* Vol. 37 (Report of Colonel Ord, the Commissioner Appointed to Inquire into the Condition of the British Settlements on the West Coast of Africa); Vol. 60 (Chalmers Report: Vol. 1: The Report, Governor Cardew's official reply, and a summation by the Secretary of State Chamberlain; Vol. 2: Testimony). London, 1865, 1899.

Greene, Graham. *Journey without Maps.* London, 1936.

Gwynn, S. *The Life of Mary Kingsley.* London, 1932.

Hailey, Lord M. *Native Administration in the British African Territories.* 5 pts. Pt. 3, *West Africa: Nigeria, Gold Coast, Sierra Leone, Gambia.* London, 1951.

Hargreaves, J. D. *A Life of Sir Samuel Lewis.* London, 1958.

Hastings Descendants' Association. *Pamphlet in Honor of the Opening of the Centenary Hall, 1952.* Freetown, 1952. Pt. 1, *Centenary Celebration Committee, 1915-1922.* Pt. 2, *Descendants Association—1915.*

Hayford, J. E. Casely. *Ethiopia Unbound.* London, 1911.

————. *William Waddy Harris, the West African Reformer: The Man and His Message.* London, 1915.

Hayford, Mark Casely. *Mary H. Kingsley: From an African Standpoint.* London, 1901.

Herskovits, M. J. *The Myth and the Negro Past.* 2d ed. Boston, 1958.

————. *Trinidad Village.* New York, 1947.

Hilliard, F. H. *Short History of Education in West Africa.* London, 1957.

Hirst, A. E., and Kamara, Issa. *Benga.* London, 1958. (A sketch of the life of Bai Bureh.)

Holden, Edith. *Blyden of Liberia. An Account of the Life and Labors of Edward Wilmot Blyden, LL.D., As Recorded in Letters and in Print.* New York, 1967.

Hooke, Fred W. *Life-Story of a Negro Knight, Sir Samuel Lewis.* Freetown, 1915.

Horton, J. A. B. *The Diseases of Tropical Climates and Their Treatment. With Hints for the Preservation of Health in the Tropics.* London, 1874.

———. *The Medical Topography of the West Coast of Africa.* London, 1859.

———. *The Physical and Medical Climate and Meteorology of the West Coast of Africa.* Edinburgh, 1867.

———. *West African Countries and Peoples, British and Native. With the requirements necessary for establishing that self government recommended by the Committee of the House of Commons, 1865; and a Vindication of the African Race.* London, 1868.

Idowu, E. Bolaji. *Olodumare: God in Yoruba Belief.* London, 1962.

Ingham, E. G. *Sierra Leone After a Hundred Years.* London, 1894.

Johnson, James. *The Relation of Mission Work to Native Customs.* London, 1908.

———. *Yoruba Heathenism.* Exeter, 1899.

Johnson, Samuel. *The History of the Yorubas, from the Earliest Times to the Beginning of the British Protectorate.* London, 1921.

Johnson, Thomas S. (Bishop). *Story of a Mission.* London, 1953.

Johnson, W. A. B. *A Memoir of the Rev. W. A. B. Johnson, 1816-1823.* London, 1852.

July, Robert W. *The Origins of Modern African Thought—Its Development in West Africa during the Nineteenth and Twentieth Centuries.* New York, 1967.

Kennan, R. H. *Freetown 1800 to 1870 from a Sanitarian Point of View.* Dublin, 1910.

Kilson, Martin L. *Political Change in a West African State: A Study of the Modernization Process in Sierra Leone.* Cambridge, Mass., 1966.

Kingsley, Mary. *West African Studies.* London, 1901.

Kopytoff, Jean Herskovits. *A Preface to Modern Nigeria: The "Sierra Leonians" in Yoruba, 1830-1890.* Madison, Wis., 1965.

Kuczynski, Robert René. *Demographic Survey of the British Colonial Empire.* London, 1948.

Kup, A. P. *A History of Sierra Leone, 1400-1787.* Cambridge, 1961.

Kuper, Leo. *An African Bourgoisie.* New Haven, Conn., 1965.

Lardner, H. H. *The Agricultural and Commercial Problems in Sierra Leone, with An Illustration of a Prospective Railway Train from Freetown to Timbuctoo.* Sierra Leone, 1893.

———. *The Agricultural Question.* London, 1880.

———. *Correspondence with a View to the Development of the Export Fruit Trade of the Colony of Sierra Leone.* Lagos, 1899.

———. *Cotton Growing Problem in Sierra Leone.* Sierra Leone, 1904.

———. *Manual on Cultivation and Preparation for Export of Some of the Commercial Products Indigenous and Exotic in Sierra Leone and the*

Reasons Why Agriculture Should Be Encouraged in the Colony. London, 1890.

Lewis, Roy. *Sierra Leone.* London, 1954.

Lewis, Samuel. *A Few Suggestions of the Wants of Sierra Leone.* Freetown, 1885.

_____. *Paper . . . on Certain Questions Affecting the Interests of the Colony of Sierra Leone.* Freetown, 1885.

Linstead, E. P. *Morning at Mount Aureol.* London, 1948.

Little, Kenneth. *West African Urbanization: A Study of Voluntary Associations in Social Change.* Cambridge, 1965.

Luke, Harry Charles [previously Lukach]. *A bibliography of Sierra Leone, preceded by an essay on the origin, character and peoples of the colony and protectorate.* London, 1925.

Lynch, Hollis R. *Edward Wilmot Blyden, Pan-Negro Patriot, 1832-1912.* London, 1967.

McCulloch, M. *The Peoples of Sierra Leone.* Ethnographic Survey of Africa, Western Africa, pt. 2. London, 1964.

Marke, Charles. *Africa and the Africans.* Freetown, 1881.

Maxwell, Joseph Renner. *Advantages and Disadvantages of European Intercourse with the West Coast of Africa. A Lecture.* London, 1881.

_____. *The Negro Question, or Hints for the Physical Improvement of the Negro Race, with Special Reference to West Africa.* London, 1892.

May, J. Claudius. *A Brief Sketch of the Life of the Reverend Joseph May, Wesleyan Minister to the Colony of Sierra Leone.* Freetown, 1896.

_____. *Semi-Jubilee of the Wesleyan High School, Freetown, 1899.* Freetown, 1899?

[Melville, Elizabeth.] *A Residence at Sierra Leone by a Lady.* Edited by Hon. Mrs. Norton. London, 1849.

Memorial of the Jubilee of Her Majesty's Reign and the Centenary of Sierra Leone, 1887. London, 1887.

Merriman-Labor, A. B. C. *Britons Through Negro Spectacles, or A Negro on Britons.* London, 1909.

_____. *An Epitome of A Series of Lectures on the Negro Race.* Freetown, 1900.

_____. *A Funeral Oration Delivered over the Grave of the late Father John Merriman at the Kissy Road Cemetery in Freetown, Sierra Leone, on the Eve of Sunday, the 18th February 1900.* Freetown, 1900.

_____. *Handbook of Sierra Leone for 1901-1902.* Manchester, 1902.

_____. *Handbook of Sierra Leone for 1904-1905.* Manchester, [1903].

_____. *The Last Military Expedition in Sierra Leone.* Liverpool, 1899.

_____. *The Story of the African Slave Trade in a Nutshell.* Freetown, 1901.

Migeod, F. W. H. *A View of Sierra Leone.* New York, 1927.

Mockler-Ferryman, A. F. *British West Africa*. London, 1900.

Montagu, Algernon. *Ordinances of Sierra Leone*. 6 vols. London, 1857-1881.

Montague, F. A. *The Handbook of Sierra Leone*. London, 1959. (Revision of the 1925 edition by Thomas N. Goddard.)

National Congress of British West Africa. *Resolution of the Conference of Africans of British West Africa held at Accra, Gold Coast from 11th to 29th March, 1920* . . . . London, 1920.

Nicol, Abioseh. *Africa, A Subjective View*. London, 1964.

————. *On Not Being a West African*. Ibadan, Nigeria, 1954.

————. *The Truly Married Woman and Other Stories*. London, 1965.

Nicol, George Gurney. *An Essay on Sierra Leone*. Sierra Leone, [1881].

Page, Jesse. *Samuel Crowther: The Slave Boy Who Became Bishop of the Niger*. London, n.d.

Parkes, J. C. Ernest. *Elementary Handbook of Geography of the Colony of Sierra Leone and Its Hinterland*. Freetown, 1894.

Parrinder, Geoffrey. *West African Religion, A Study of the Beliefs and Practices of Akan, Ewe, Yoruba, Ibo and Kindred Peoples*. London, 1961.

Peterson, John. *Province of Freedom: A History of Sierra Leone 1787-1870*. London, 1969.

Poole, Thomas Eyre. *Life, Scenery and Customs in Sierra Leone and the Gambia*. 2 vols. London, 1850.

Porter, Arthur T. *Creoledom: A Study of the Development of Freetown Society*. Oxford, 1963.

Reade, Winwood. *Savage Africa, being the narratives of a tour in Equatorial, southwestern, and northwestern Africa; with notes on the habits of the Gorilla; on the existence of unicorns and tailed men; on the slave-trade; on the origin, character, and capabilities of the Negro; and on the future civilization of Western Africa*. London, 1863.

Roberts, J. T. *A Character Sketch of the Late Rev. Claudius May*. Liverpool, 1912.

Rolin, Henri. *Le traitment des indigènes dans les Colonies anglaise. L'insurrection de Sierra Leone en 1898*. Bruxells, 1903.

Ross, Ronald. *Memoirs, with a full account of the great Malaria problem and its solution*. London, 1923.

————. *The Prevention of Malaria*. London, 1910.

————, et al. *Report of the Malaria Expedition of the Liverpool School of Tropical Medicine and Medical Parasitology*. Liverpool, 1900.

Sampson, Magnus. *West African Leadership*. Bristol, 1951. (Includes speeches by J. E. Casely Hayford.)

Sawyerr, T. J. *Sierra Leone Native Church (Two Papers read at the Church Conference Freetown, 1888 held in Freetown, Sierra Leone, January 24th, 25th, 26th, 1888)*. Freetown, 1888.

Schlenker, Rev. C. F. *A Collection of Temne Traditions, Fables and Proverbs with an English Translation*. London, 1861.

Scotland, J. Allen. *Holiday Reminiscences: Being a Tour from Sierra Leone to Bonny and Back*. Sierra Leone, 1907.

Sibthorpe, A. B. C. *The Geography of the Surrounding Territories of Sierra Leone*. London, 1892.

_____. *History of Sierra Leone*. London, 1868.

_____. *The History of Sierra Leone*. Revised, Remodelled and Enlarged. 3d ed. London, 1906.

_____. *Sibthorpe's Africa First Unveiled to Europeans*. London, 1910.

_____. *Sibthorpe's Oration on the Centenary of the Abolition of the Slave Trade by the English Government*. London, 1907.

Sibthorpe's Age, Or His Celebrated Scholars of This Age. Appended to third edition of Sibthorpe's *Geography*. London, 1905.

Sierra Leone. Surveys and Lands Department. *Atlas of Sierra Leone*. Freetown, 1953.

Sierra Leone Agricultural Exhibition for 1895-96. Freetown, 1897.

Sierra Leone and Its Future, by a Native. Freetown, 1878.

Sierra Leone Company. *Report of the Court of Directors of the Sierra Leone Company to the General Court*. 7 vols. (title varies). London, 1791-1808.

Sierra Leone Year Book. Freetown, 1962—.

Sierra Leone Views. London, 1924. (Souvenir for the Sierra Leone Pavilion, the British Empire Exhibition.)

Smith, James C. *Impressions of Sierra Leone*. Freetown, 1897. ("Published by Sir S. Lewis by the request of the audience before whom it was read at a Conversazione held at his residence.")

Sufferings of Sierra Leone, or Gov. Rowe's Lampoon on the People, with Explanatory Correspondence, by a Native. Freetown, 1878.

Sumner, D. L. *Education in Sierra Leone*. Freetown, 1963.

Thompson, T. J. *Jubilee and Centenary Volume of Fourah Bay College*. Freetown, 1930.

_____. *People's Appeal for an Intermediate Court of Appeal*. London, 1911.

Tobuku-Metzger, A. E. *Historical Sketch of the Sierra Leone Grammar School, 1845-1935. Delivered in the School Hall on the 29th March 1935 on the occasion of the 90th Anniversary of the School*. Freetown, 1935.

United States. Library of Congress. General Reference and Bibliography Division. *Official Publications of Sierra Leone and Gambia*. Compiled by A. A. Walker. Washington, D.C., 1963.

Utting, F. A. J. *The Story of Sierra Leone*. London, 1950.

Wallace-Johnson, I. T. A. *Lecture Delivered . . . to the Officers and Members of the Preston Literary Club, Freetown, on Friday, May 6, 1938 at 4:30 p.m.* Freetown, 1938.

————. *Prison in the Muse*. 3d ed. Freetown, 1945.

Wallis, C. Braithwaite. *The Advance of Our West African Empire*. London, 1903.

The West-African Year Book, 1901-1902. London, 1902.

Wilson, Ellen Gibson. *A West African Cookbook*. New York, 1972.

ARTICLES AND ESSAYS

Ajayi, J. F. A. "The Place of African History in the Process of Nation-Building." In *Social Change. The Colonial Situation*, edited by I. Wallerstein, pp. 606-610. New York, 1966.

Awoyo, Johnson. "The Vocational Outlook of the Sierra Leone 'Creole.' " *Sierra Leone Studies*, old ser., no. 22 (September 1939), pp. 52-57.

Banton, Michael. "The Dancing Compin." In *West Africa* November 7, 1953.

————. "Social Alignment and Identity in a West African City." In *Urbanization and Migration in West Africa*, edited by Hilda Kuper, pp. 131-147. Berkeley, 1965.

Baritz, Loren. "The Idea of the West." *American Historical Review* 66 (April 1961): 618-640.

Berry, J. "The Origins of Krio Vocabulary." *Sierra Leone Studies*, n.s., no. 12 (December 1959), pp. 298-307.

Blyden, E. W. "Report on the Expedition to Falaba, January to March, 1872." *Proceedings of the Royal Geographical Society* 17 (1872-73): 117-131.

Buckle, V. E. J. "The Language of the Sierra Leone 'Creo.' " *Sierra Leone Studies*, old ser., no. 22 (September 1939), pp. 20-24.

Buxton, T. F. V. "The Creole in West Africa." *Journal of the African Society* 12, no. 48 (July 1913): 385-394.

Chamberlain, Alexander F. "Race Character and Local Color in Proverbs." *Journal of American Folk-Lore* 17, no. 64 (1904): 28-31.

Christophers, S. R. "The Prevention of Malaria in Tropical Africa." *Thompson Yates Laboratories Report* 3, pt. 2 (1901).

Count, E. W. "The Evolution of the Race Idea in Modern Western Culture during the Period of the Pre-Darwinian Nineteenth Century." *Transactions of the New York Academy of Sciences*, 2d ser., 8 (February 1946): 139-165.

Crowder, Michael. "An African Aristocracy." *Geographical Magazine* 31, no. 4 (1958): 183-190.

Curtin, Philip D. " 'The White Man's Grave': Image and Reality, 1780-1850." *The Journal of British Studies* 1 (1961): 94-110.

————, and Vansina, Jan. "Sources of the Nineteenth Century Atlantic Slave Trade." *Journal of African History* 5, no. 2 (1964): 185-208.

Dawson, John. "Race and Inter-Group Relations in Sierra Leone." *Race* 6, no. 2 (1964): 83-99, no. 3 (1965): 217-231.

Decker, Thomas. "An 'Air Raid' on Lectularia (A Dream Parable of the Long Ago)." *Sierra Leone Studies,* old ser., no. 22 (September 1939), pp. 45-48.

Denzer, LaRay, and Crowder, Michael. "Bai Bureh and the Sierra Leone Hut Tax War of 1898." In *Black Protest,* edited by Robert I. Rotberg and Ali Mazrui. London, 1970.

Easmon, M. C. F. "Sierra Leone Doctors." *Sierra Leone Studies,* n.s., no. 6 (June 1956), pp. 81-96.

Fitch-Jones, B. W. "Hill Station." *Sierra Leone Studies,* old ser., no. 18 (November 1932), pp. 2-25.

_____. "A Victim of the '98 Rising." *Sierra Leone Studies,* old ser., no. 16 (August 1930).

Fox Bourne, H. R. "The Sierra Leone Troubles." *Fortnightly Review,* n.s., 64 (August 1898): 216-230.

Fyfe, C. H. "A. B. C. Sibthorpe: A Neglected Historian." *Sierra Leone Studies,* n.s., no. 10 (June 1958), pp. 99-109.

_____. "European and Creole Influences in the Interior of Sierra Leone before 1896." *Sierra Leone Studies,* n.s., no. 6 (June 1956), pp. 113-123.

_____. "Four Sierra Leone Recaptives." *Journal of African History* 2, no. 1 (1961): 77-86.

_____. "The Life and Times of John Ezzidio." *Sierra Leone Studies,* n.s., no. 4 (June 1955), pp. 213-223.

_____. "Thomas Peters: History and Legend." *Sierra Leone Studies,* n.s., no. 1 (December 1953), pp. 4-13.

Ghazali, A. K. "Sierra Leone Muslims and Sacrificial Rituals." *Sierra Leone Bulletin of Religion,* 2, no. 1 (June 1960): 27-32.

Hair, P. E. H. "An Analysis of the Register of Fourah Bay College, 1827-1950." *Sierra Leone Studies,* n.s., no. 7 (December 1956), pp. 155-160.

_____. "Freetown Christianity and Africa." *Sierra Leone Bulletin of Religion* 6, no. 1 (December 1964): 13-21.

Halliburton, G. "The Nova Scotia Settlers of 1792." *Sierra Leone Studies,* n.s., no. 9 (December 1957), pp. 16-25.

Hamilton, William. "Sierra Leone and the Liberated Africans." *The Colonial Magazine and Commercial Maritime Journal* 6 (September 1841): 327-334, 463-469, 7 (January 1842): 29-43, 214-225, 286-296, 404-412, 8 (June 1842): 37-44, 220-223.

Hargreaves, J. D. "The Establishment of the Sierra Leone Protectorate." *Cambridge Historical Journal* 12 (1956): 56-80.

_____. "Sir Samuel Lewis and the Legislative Council." *Sierra Leone Studies,* n.s., no. 1 (December 1953), pp. 40-52.

Hayford, Adelaide Casely. "Memoirs." *West African Review*. Liverpool, 1953-1954.

_____. "Mista Courifer." In *West African Narrative*, edited by Paul Edwards. Edinburgh, 1963.

Johnson, H. H. "British West Africa and the Trade of the Interior." *Proceedings of the Royal Colonial Institute* 20 (1888-9).

Jones, E. D. "Krio in Sierra Leone Journalism." *Sierra Leone Language Review*, no. 3 (1964), pp. 24-31.

_____. "Mid-Nineteenth Century Evidences of a Sierra Leone Patois." *Sierra Leone Language Review*, no. 1 (1962), pp. 19-26.

_____. "The Potentialities of Krio as a Literary Language." *Sierra Leone Studies*, n.s., no. 9 (December 1957), pp. 40-48.

_____. "Some Aspects of the Sierra Leone Patois or Krio." *Sierra Leone Studies*, n.s., no. 6 (June 1956), pp. 97-109.

_____. "Turning Back the Pages (No. 1)." *The Bulletin of the Association for African Literature in English*, no. 2 (1965), pp. 19-26.

Johnson, G. Wesley, Jr. "The Sengalese Urban Elite, 1900-1945." In *Africa and the West*, edited by Philip D. Curtin. Madison, Wis., 1972.

Johnson, James, "The Relation of Mission Work to Native Customs." *Pan Anglican Papers, Being Problems for Consideration at the Pan-Anglican Congress, 1908. . . .* vol. 2. London, 1908.

Jones-Quartey, K. A. B. "Anglo-African Journals and Journalists in the 19th and 20th Centuries." *Transactions of the Ghana Historical Society* 4, no. 1 (1959): 47-56.

_____. "Sierra Leone and Ghana: 19th Century Pioneers in West African Journalism." *Sierra Leone Studies*, n.s., no. 12 (December 1959), pp. 230-249.

_____. "Sierra Leone's Role in the Development of Ghana 1820-1930." *Sierra Leone Studies*, n.s., no. 10 (June 1958), pp. 73-84.

July, Robert W. "Africanus Horton and the Idea of Independence in West Africa." *Sierra Leone Studies*, n.s., no. 18 (January 1966), pp. 2-17.

_____. "Nineteenth-Century Negritude: Edward Wilmot Blyden." *Journal of African History* 5, no. 1 (1964): 73-86.

Khuri, F. I. "Kinship, Emigration, and Trade Partnership Among the Lebanese of West Africa." *Africa* 35, no. 4 (October 1965): 385-395.

Kilson, Martin. "The National Congress of British West Africa, 1918-1935." In *Protest and Power in Black Africa*, edited by Robert I. Rotberg and Ali A. Mazrui. New York, 1970.

_____. "The Rise of Nationalist Organization in British West Africa." In *Africa Seen by American Negroes*. Paris, 1959.

Kirk-Greene, Anthony. "David George: The Nova Scotian Experience." *Sierra Leone Studies*, n.s., no. 14 (December 1960), pp. 93-120.

Little, Kenneth. "The Significance of the West African Creole for Africanist and Afro-American Studies." *African Affairs* 49, no. 197 (October 1950): 308-319.

_____. "Social Change and Social Class in the Sierra Leone Protectorate." *American Journal of Sociology* 54, no. 1 (July 1948): 10-21.

Kuper, Leo. "African Nationalism in South Africa, 1910-1964." In *The Oxford History of South Africa*, edited by Monica Wilson and L. Thompson. Vol. 2. Oxford, 1971.

Luke, T. C. "Some Notes on the Creoles and Their Land." *Sierra Leone Studies*, old ser., no. 21 (January 1939), pp. 53-66.

Lynch, Hollis R. "Edward W. Blyden: Pioneer West African Nationalist." *Journal of African History* 6, no. 3 (1965): 373-388.

_____. "The Native Pastorate Controversy and Cultural Ethnocentrism in Sierra Leone, 1871-1874." *Journal of African History* 5, no. 3 (1964): 395-413.

"The Malaria Expedition to Sierra Leone." *The British Medical Journal*, September 9, 16, 30, October 14, 1899.

Mannah-Kpaka, J. K. (Paramount Chief). "Memoirs of the 1898 Rising." *Sierra Leone Studies*, n.s., no. 1 (December 1953), pp. 28-39.

Marteroy, P. H. "Freetown 1899-1938." *Sierra Leone Studies*, old ser., no. 21 (1939), pp. 81-87.

Morrill, Warren T. "Socio-Cultural Adaptation in a West African Lebanese Community." *Anthropological Quarterly* 35 (1962): 146-155.

"National Congress of British West Africa: Delegation and Its Critics"; "Reply of the Delegates." *West Africa*, January 1921-June 1921.

Nicol, Abioseh. "Great Sons of Africa: Dr. Edward Blyden." *Africana, the Magazine of the West African Society* 1, no. 2 (April 1949).

_____. "Love's Own Tears." In *West African Narrative*, edited by Paul Edwards. Edinburgh, 1963.

_____. "West Indians in West Africa." *Sierra Leone Studies*, n.s., no. 13 (June 1960), pp. 14-23.

Pflanze, Ott, and Curtin, Philip D. "Varieties of Nationalism in Europe and Africa." *The Review of Politics* 28, no. 2 (April 1966): 124-153.

Porter, Arthur T. "Religious Affiliation in Freetown, Sierra Leone." *Africa* 23, no. 1 (January 1953): 3-14.

_____. "The Social Background of Political Decision Makers in Sierra Leone." *Sierra Leone Studies*, n.s., no. 13 (June 1960), pp. 1-13.

Probyn, Leslie. "Alcohol and the African—The Experiment in Sierra Leone." *The Nineteenth Century and After* 67, no. 400 (June 1910): 1008-1025.

Proudfoot, L., and Wilson, H. S. "Muslim Attitudes to Education in Sierra Leone." *Muslim World* 50, no. 2 (1960): 86-98.

Sawyerr, Harry. "Ancestor Worship—The Mechanics." *Sierra Leone Bulletin of Religion* 6, no. 2 (December 1964): 25-33.

———. "Sacrificial Rituals in Sierra Leone." *Sierra Leone Bulletin of Religion* 1, no. 1 (June 1959): 1-9.

———. "Traditional Sacrificial Rituals and Christian Worship." *Sierra Leone Bulletin of Religion* 2, no. 1 (June 1960): 18-27.

Scotland, D. W. "Notes on Bai Bureh, of 1898 Fame." *Sierra Leone Studies*, n.s., no. 5 (December 1955): 11-19.

Scott, H. S. "The Development of the Education of the African in Relation to Western Contact." In *The Year Book of Education 1938*. London, 1938.

"Segregation in Theory and Practice in West Africa." *West Africa*, July 9, 1921.

Sibthorpe, A. B. C. "History of Sierra Leone, Volume II." *The Artisan*, 1884-1885.

———. "Sibthorpe's Essay on Foofoo." *The Artisan*, 24 December 1888.

Spitzer, Leo. "Creole Attitudes Toward Krio: An Historical Survey." *Sierra Leone Language Review*, no. 5 (1966), pp. 39-49.

———. "The Mosquito and Segregation in Sierra Leone." *Canadian Journal of African Studies* 2, no. 1 (Spring 1968): 49-61.

———. "The Sierra Leone Creoles, 1870-1900." In *Africa and the West*, edited by Philip D. Curtin. Madison, Wis., 1972.

———, and Denzer, LaRay. "I. T. A. Wallace-Johnson and the West African Youth League." *International Journal of African Historical Studies* 6, no. 3 (1973): 413-452, no. 4 (1973): 565-601.

"Tales and Riddles from Freetown." *The Journal of American Folk-Lore* 43, no. 169 (July-October 1930): 317-321.

Williams, J. M. "Some Common Words in the Sierra Leone Patois and Their Origin." *Sierra Leone Studies*, old ser., no. 22 (September 1939), pp. 61-63.

Wilson, H. S. "The Changing Image of the Sierra Leone Colony in the Works of E. W. Blyden." *Sierra Leone Studies*, n.s., no. 11 (December 1958), pp. 136-148.

———, and Proudfoot, S. L. "Changing Social Functions at a Creole Feast." *African Affairs* 58, no. 231 (1958): 153-160.

Winder, R. Bayly. "The Lebanese in West Africa." *Comparative Studies in Society and History* 4, no. 3 (April 1962): 296-333.

NEWSPAPERS

For an excellent essay discussing Sierra Leone newspapers and their locations, see C. H. Fyfe, "The Sierra Leone Press in the Nineteenth Century," *Sierra Leone Studies*, n.s., no. 8 (June 1957), pp. 226-236.

The African Standard. 1938-1945.

The Sierra Leone Watchman. 1843-1846?

The New Era. 1855-1859 (with a few months break in 1858).

The African and Sierra Leone Weekly Advertiser. 1855-1861.

CMS Record. 1856-1890.

The Free Press and Sierra Leone Advertiser. 1861-1865?

The Sierra Leone Weekly Times and West African Record. 1862-1863.

The African Times [London]. 1862-1902.

The Sierra Leone Observer and Commercial Advocate. 1864-1866?

The Day Spring and Sierra Leone Reporter. 1865-1873?

The African Interpreter and Advocate. 1866-1869.

The West African Herald. 1868-1872 (in Freetown; continued later at Cape Coast).

The Negro. 1872-1873.

The Independent. 1873-1878?

The Watchman and West African Record. 1875-1886?

The West African Reporter. 1876-1877, 1879-1884.

The Freetown Express and Christian Observer. 1882-1884.

The Methodist Herald and West African Educational Times. 1882-1888.

The Sierra Leone Church Times. 1884-1886.

The Agency and Mercantile, Shipping, Agricultural, Advertising and General Reporter. 1884-1887.

The Artisan. 1884-1888.

The Sierra Leone Weekly News. 1884-1951.

Sawyerr's Bookselling, Printing and Stationery Trade Circular and General Advertising Medium. 1885-1886.

The Sierra Leone Ram. 1886.

The Sierra Leone Farm and Trade Report. 1886-1887.

The Commonwealth. 1888.

The Sierra Leone Times. 1890-1912.

The Trader. 1891.

Sierra Leone Church Guardian. 1905-1906.

Sierra Leone Guardian and Foreign Mails. 1906?-1932.

Saturday Magazine. 1907.

Colony and Provincial Reporter. 1910-1913.

Colonial and Provincial Reporter. 1913-1920.

The Aurora. 1918-1925?

The Sierra Leone Echo. 1920?-1921?

West African Mail and Trade Gazette. 1920-1932 (incorporated with the Sierra Leone Daily Mail, January 1933).

Daily Guardian. 1933-1938, 1938-1958.

West Africa. 1917—.

Unpublished Sources

Baker, E. D. "A History of Education in Sierra Leone, British West Africa." Master's thesis, University of Michigan, 1949.

Blyden, E. W., III. "Sierra Leone: The Pattern of Constitutional Change." Ph.D. dissertation, Harvard University, 1959.

Butt-Thompson, F. W. "Folk-Lore of Africa, No. 1. Stories That Tell Similar Themes Found in the Bible." Typescript in two exercise books. Sierra Leone Museum, Freetown.

———. "Handwritten Notes and Clippings in Army Book 129." Sierra Leone Museum, Freetown. (Contains some Creole songs and translations, a story, and many clippings from the *Sierra Leone Weekly News*.)

———. "West African Songs, 1917." Original manuscript in exercise book. Sierra Leone Museum, Freetown.

Carter, Arthur. "Changes in the Curriculum in Secondary Schools in Sierra Leone, 1860-1960." Thesis for the Diploma in Education, University of Durham through Fourah Bay College, 1963.

Cole, Aaron. "The Creole Language. A Pocket Grammar and Dictionary." Typed London: School of Oriental and African Studies, London University, 1955.

Coleson, Edward F. "Educational Change in Sierra Leone." Ph.D. dissertation, University of Michigan, 1956.

Crowther, S. A. "Letters of Archdeacon Crowther. Manuscript with an Index by Paul Hair." Sierra Leone Museum, Freetown. (The letters range from 1892-1899.)

Decker, Thomas. "*Julius Caesar* by William Shakespeare translated into Krio." Mimeographed privately, for the author, n.d.

———. " 'Udat DiKiap Fit.' A Krio Adaptation of *As You Like It* by William Shakespeare." Mimeographed privately, for the author, n.d.

Denzer, LaRay E. "The National Congress of British West Africa—Gold Coast Section." Master's thesis, Legon University (Ghana), 1965.

Dosumu-Johnson, T. "A History of Sierra Leone, with Special Emphasis on Education." Dissertation for Columbia University Teachers' College, 1935.

Edwin, J. Nelson. "A Critical Survey of the Kroo Community and the Effects of Its Social Organisation in the Education of Its Children." Thesis for the Diploma in Education, University of Dunelm, 1960.

Fergusson, H. N. "The Effect of Krio on the Learning of English in the Junior Section of Freetown Secondary Schools." Thesis for the Diploma in Education, University of Durham through Fourah Bay College, 1965.

Jones, E. D. "The Teaching of English in Sierra Leone Colony Schools." Thesis for the Diploma in Education, University of Durham through Fourah Bay College, n.d.

Lewis, Samuel. "Paper . . . on certain questions affecting the interests of the Colony of Sierra Leone." Paper read to the Sierra Leone Association, August 6, 1885, Freetown.

Lynch-Shyllon, H. E. M. "The Effect of the Ward System on the Schools in the Colony of Sierra Leone." Thesis for the Diploma in Education, University of Durham through Fourah Bay College, 1953.

Max-Peters, T. B. "A Critical Examination of the Creoles of Sierra Leone and the Effects of Their Religion, Traditions and Customs on the Education of Their Children." Thesis for the Diploma in Education, University of Durham through Fourah Bay College, 1962.

Migeod, Frederick William H. "Index to African Books." Notebook containing manuscript bibliographical notes on West Africa, compiled 1906-1924. School of Oriental and African Studies, London University.

Nicolls, Dulcie R. "The Effects of Western Education on the Social Attitudes of the Creoles in Sierra Leone." Thesis for the Diploma in Education, University of Durham through Fourah Bay College, 1960.

Ogunsulire, Omotayo. "The History of Fourah Bay College and Its Influence in West Africa from the Foundation to the Elliot Commission, 1943." Thesis for the Diploma in Education, University of Durham through Fourah Bay College, 1956.

Peterson, John Eric. "Freetown: A Study of the Dynamics of Liberated African Society, 1807-1870." Ph.D. dissertation, Northwestern University, 1963.

Porter, Arthur T. "The Development of the Creole Society of Freetown, Sierra Leone. A Study on Social Stratification and the Processes of Social Mobility." Ph.D. dissertation, Boston University, 1960.

Richardson, E. M., and Collins, G. R. "Economic and Social Survey of the Rural Areas of the Colony of Sierra Leone; A Report to the Colonial Social Science Research Council." Mimeographed. London: Colonial Office, 1952.

Sawyerr, H., and Jones, E. "The Story of Fourah Bay College." Radio script. Sierra Leone Broadcasting System, January 27, 1960.

Schott, John R. "Edward Wilmot Blyden: First Pan Africanist?" Paper presented at the Ninth Annual African Studies Association Meeting, Bloomington, Indiana, 1967.

Sesay, Sheik Imam. "The Development of Education among the Muslims of Sierra Leone." Thesis for the Diploma in Education, University of Durham through Fourah Bay College, 1959.

Taylor, P. J. "A Study of Some of the Reasons for the Poor Standard of English among Pupils in Sierra Leone and Efforts That Could Be Made for Improvement." Thesis for the Diploma in Education, University of Durham through Fourah Bay College, 1964/65.

Taylor Pearce, J. E. M. "The Sierra Leone Grammar School (C.M.S.)." Thesis for the Diploma in Education, University of Durham through Fourah Bay College, 1954.

Thompson, R. J. B. "Western Education as a Formative Factor in the Social Attitudes of the Creoles in Sierra Leone." Thesis for the Diploma in Education, University of Durham through Fourah Bay College, 1962.

Turner, Lorenzo D. "An Anthology of Krio Folklore and Literature, with Notes and Interlinear Translation in English." Mimeographed. Chicago: Roosevelt University, 1963.

————. "Krio Texts with Grammatical Notes and Translations in English." Mimeographed. Chicago: Roosevelt University, 1965.

Photographs

Royal Commonwealth Society, London. "Four Albums, Originally the Property of James Carmichael Smith, Postmaster-General of Sierra Leone, 1900-1911," contains:

1. Fifty-eight postcards c. 1903-1909 (mainly from Sierra Leone, but including some from the Congo and the Canaries).
2. Forty-five photographs of Sierra Leone c. 1910-1911; Governor Sir. L. Probyn with his A.D.C.; reception at Government House; departure of the governor; military parade; general scenes, groups, etc.
3. Thirty-eight photographs of the visit of the Duke of Connaught to Sierra Leone, December 15, 1910.
4. Twenty-five photographs of Sierra Leone citizens, including Bundu costumes and rites and groups of staff and pupils at Fourah Bay College.

Index

COMPOSED BY FOCUS/TYPOGRAPHERS, ST. LOUIS, MISSOURI
MANUFACTURED BY MALLOY LITHOGRAPHING, INC., ANN ARBOR, MICHIGAN
TEXT IS SET IN JOURNAL ROMAN, DISPLAY LINES IN TIMES ROMAN

Library of Congress Cataloging in Publication Data
Spitzer, Leo, 1939-
The Creoles of Sierra Leone.
Bibliography: p. 231-248
1. Creoles (Sierra Leone) I. Title.
DT516.42.S66   301.29'66'404   74-5908
ISBN 0-299-06590-1

74

75-76

126

130 Everyday frame of Rebert

132

137 lack of urgent explanation

138 £8

172

179

181 not an another

182

216